Uncertain Poetries

MICHAEL HELLER is a poet, essayist and critic. Among his many books are *Conviction's Net of Branches*, *In The Builded Place*, *Wordflow* and *Living Root: A Memoir* and *Exigent Futures: New and Selected Poems*. He wrote the libretto for the recently performed opera, *Benjamin*, based on the life of Walter Benjamin. His awards include the NEH Poet/Scholar grant, the Di Castagnola Prize and New York Foundation for the Arts Fellowships. He was born in 1937 in New York City where he now lives.

Uncertain Poetries

Selected Essays on Poets, Poetry and Poetics

MICHAEL HELLER

New York University

SALT

CAMBRIDGE

PUBLISHED BY SALT PUBLISHING
PO Box 937, Great Wilbraham PDO, Cambridge CB1 5JX United Kingdom

© Michael Heller, 2005

The right of Michael Heller to be identified as the
author of this work has been asserted by him in accordance
with Section 77 of the Copyright, Designs and Patents Act 1988.

First published 2004

Printed and bound in the United Kingdom by Lightning Source

Typeset in Swift 9.5 / 13

ISBN 1 84471 057 21 paperback

SP

1 3 5 7 9 8 6 4 2

For Burt, Henry and Norman, and for Peter,
for their friendship, for their poetry and their thought.

Contents

Acknowledgements

Many of the essays in this collection have been previously published or given as presentations as indicated below. I would like to thank the editors and organizations which gave me both the space and instigations to write these pieces.

"The Uncertainty of the Poet" presented at the Wolfe Institute of Brooklyn College. Published in *American Poetry Review*.

"Deep Song: Some Provocations" published in *Ironwood* magazine.

"The Narrative of Ezra Gorgon Pound or History Gothicized" was originally presented as a talk at the What Thou Lovest Well, Ezra Pound Centennial Conference at San Jose State College.

"Translating Form: Pound, Rilke and the Contemporary Poem" appeared in *Ironwood* magazine and was republished in *Conversant Essays: Contemporary Poets on Poetics* (Wayne State University Press, 1990).

"Rethinking Rilke" published in *Poetry Flash*.

"The True Epithalamion" published in *Sagetrieb* magazine.

"Notes on Stevens" was originally presented as a lecture at Poets House in New York City.

"The Objectified Psyche: Marianne Moore and Lorine Niedecker" presented at Naropa Institute and published in *Lorine Niedecker: Woman and Poet* (National Poetry Foundation).

"Imagining Durable Works: Lorine Niedecker's 'Wintergreen Ridge'" was presented at the Lorine Niedecker Centennial Conference in Milwaukee, Wisconsin in October, 2003.

"Typology of the Parabolist" was originally published in *Meaningful Differences: The Poetry and Prose of David Ignatow* edited by Virginia R. Terris (Alabama University Press, 1994).

Portions of "William Bronk and Form's Vertiginous Trace" appeared in *Sagetrieb* and *Talisman*.

Portions of "Armand Schwerner: The Semiotician of Self Work" appeared in *The American Book Review* and in *Talisman*.

"Our Mallarme" published in *American Poetry Review.*

"The Poetics of Unspeakability" part of this essay appeared as two separate review essays in *The American Book Review*.

"Diasporic Poetics" appeared in *Jewish American Poetry* published by Brandeis University Press in 2000.

"Journey to the Interior of the Symbol" was published in *Pequod* magazine.

"Poetry Without Credentials" was published in *The Ohio Review*.

"Encountering Oppen" was published in *The Ohio Review*.

"Avant-Garde Propellants of the Machine Made of Words" presented at the MLA in San Francisco, 1987, and published in *Sagetrieb*.

"Aspects of Poetics" was published in *Samizdat*. A version of this essay appeared on *www.cultural society.org*.

"Notes on Lyric Poetry or At The Muses Tomb" published in the *Chicago Review*.

"Even now poetic men (e.g. Emerson, Lipiner) still seek the limits of knowledge, indeed preferably of skepticism, in order to break free of the spell of logic. They want *uncertainty*, because then the magician, intimations, and the great sentiments become possible again."

– from *On the Poet* (1875), by FRIEDRICH NIETZSCHE

Preface

Poetry is always about to happen and also about to disappear, to be drowned out by conventional thought, to marginalize itself or to be marginalized by its writers, readers and critics. Lawrence Lipking speaks to this contradiction in *The Life of the Poet*, reminding us that "the poet, especially, must speak with a double voice. A destroyer and a preserver, he cannot be less than the caretaker of language, but cannot be less than original and free. He serves the remains of speech by making them new."

Any writing about contemporary poetry, then, must also speak with a "double voice," honoring an articulation which is original and free, one not yet part of *the* tradition but in which tradition can be seen at work. Tradition is a mysterious organism, and our image of it, as I note in "Avant Garde Propellants of the Machine Made of Words," may involve as much forgetting as remembering. For me, part of the job of commenting on contemporary poetry has been to recover and highlight some of that mysteriousness. The Italian poet Eugenio Montale called his own criticism rhabdomancy, the waving of verbal wands over objects to divine their secrets. I would hope these pieces produce a similar effect for readers, conjuring into a useful visibility the power of certain poets and their poetry and the range of ideas about poetry that constitute the substance of this collection.

~

A number of themes and currents run through the essays. First, there is no question that the tenor of contemporary civilization is marked by its uncertainty, its hesitant mood on matters both cultural and political.

Poetry, ever sensitive to the nuances of its surroundings, must limn or bode forth the environmental conditions out of which it arises. That poets, those presumed antennae of the race, might be picking up the signals and putting them somehow into the work seems only too obvious.

Thus the essays in this book, dealing with the work of such major figures as Lorca, Rilke, Pound, Stevens, Mallarmé, and Duncan and of more contemporary poets and poetry in the modernist and post-modernist lineage of Pound and Williams, touch on the complex and uncertain nature of twentieth and now twenty-first century poetry and poetics. The work of these poets is explored, not to offer definitive readings but primarily to see how they embody our contemporary skepticism concerning language, representation, and reality and yet manage, sometimes in the same breath, in the same line or stanza, to articulate both affirmation and doubt. Questions of form and meaning are discussed in the essays covering individual poets and their poems as well as in essays which deal with contemporary poetic movements and considerations of the act of writing itself.

The essays on De Chirico's painting *The Uncertainty of the Poet*, on Frederico Garcia Lorca's conception of "deep song," and on the relationship of the poetry of Rilke and Pound to the sculptors they were involved with, attempt to show how uncertainty and the relation of a poet to "otherness" or modernist dissociation and alienation are operant across the poetic spectrum. The essays on Pound and Rilke, and on contemporary experimental poetry, explore some of the problems that Pound's legacy and post-structuralist theory have created for the poet.

Almost all of the essays attempt to articulate the strategies which difficulty, ambivalence and uncertainty have forced upon poets and poetics. I try to show, for example, that the uneasy status of all forms of knowledge can make a poet like Robert Duncan yoke a mythic and cosmological past to his own contemporary history. For nearly identical reasons, the poets associated with the Objectivist, such as Lorine Niedecker, Marianne Moore, William Bronk and others, as Hugh Kenner has suggested, reject myth and instead write poetry which tests perception as though the poet *were* a phenomenologist not only of experience but of language itself.

Poetry, as Louis Zukofsky writes, "is precise information on existence." Many of the poets included here have, as with their Imagist and modernist forebears, the urge to treat perception as a kind of honor code, attempting to be precise in their renderings of an objective world.

In "The Objectified Psyche," I discuss the continuities and resistances to this mostly male-dominated tradition of Imagist and Objectivist thought as it relates to the distinctive work of Marianne Moore and Lorine Niedecker.

An equally powerful urge in contemporary poetry is to be profoundly skeptical of perception, to be aware that it too has a subjective and, to use jargon for a moment, constructivist, aspect. The essays on Bronk and Schwerner try to speak to this skepticism. Clearly, perception for a poet like William Bronk is quite problematic. His metaphysical etudes, seemingly rooted in the natural world, are at the same time deceptively structured poetic syllogisms and declarative arguments that ultimately undermine their own premises. In Armand Schwerner's *The Tablets*, the most ancient anxieties of being and language inherited through myth, complicate the whole project of spirituality and of the epic genre. Schwerner filtrates and updates these anxieties through the comic operations and thought processes of the Scholar Translator, a complex, often absurd figure whose hopes and fears closely resemble our own.

"The Poetics of Unspeakability," reflects on the Holocaust's effect on literature, on the difficulty of recuperating poetry in the face of an event that has put the entire question of 'civilization' into the category of the uncertain. Adorno's injunction concerning poetry after the Holocaust, challenged and rejected by contemporary poets, nevertheless throws a shadow over the writing of poetry, making poets aware that beside the mountains of books published since the Second World War lies an even larger pit into which the massacred innocents of Europe and the rest of the world have fallen, are continuing to fall. "Diasporic Poetics" and "Encountering Oppen" are essentially essays on how influences, personal, poetic and cultural, have shaped my own work. "Poetry Without Credentials" comes out of my experience teaching poetry to a wide range of students, an attempt to speak to the anxieties of younger poets starting out and yet, ultimately, as such things end up transforming themselves, into a response to my own concerns as I face the page and a sense of a life lived with poetry.

Essays in the last section of this collection such as "Avant-Garde Propellants of the Machine Made of Words" and "Aspects of Poetics" attempt to articulate more directly to the present activity of contemporary poetry some of the concerns discussed in the earlier writings in the book. In 1987, when, at the MLA conference in San Francisco, I delivered as a lecture a version of "Avant-Garde Propellants of the Machine Made of Words," the poetry scene was a fairly embattled place, and the words of that essay reflect the war of polemics occurring then. Still, I had hoped to start a discussion, to create what I termed "countercontinu-ities," which suggested that there might be a more useful way of think-ing about what poets do with the new tools and availabilites at hand. In that spirit, I tender the essay here again. The final essay in this collec-tion, "Notes on Lyric Poetry or At the Muse's Tomb" is something of a meditation in both prose and poetry on the possibility of the lyric mode.

Finally, the writings collected here are by no means a survey of any sort. They are best looked at as reflections of my pre-disposition or taste in poetry and, *sub rosa*, as an intermittent discussion of the values I find inherent in poetry. With respect to these values, I hope they will be seen by a loyal opposition of other poets not only as arguments but as liminal points of discussion, indirect asides toward some potential opening for rethinking our current modes or ideas about the reading and writing of poetry.

As well, since they are selected from nearly twenty-five years of work, these essays ought to be read as something of an intellectual biography of a working poet. In this last regard, readers should remember that an individual poet's "canon" is quite different from almost any version of an official one, that what is important for a working poet are those writ-ers with whom he or she is in constant conversation. In a sense then, these essays constitute my side of a dialogue with poets, some of whom are dead, poets that one sees, with all due modesty, as contemporaries with contemporary things in their work and on their minds.

(2004)

Part I

The Uncertainty of the Poet

I am here investigating the floating filigree of doubt and fear, that feeling of being on the edge, which often accompanies poetic composition. The governing fiction of the creative act, occurring within the unique dynamics of an encounter with oneself, one's culture and traditions, arrives as a kind of summation or annunciation, a 'truer' moment among our moments writ large across being and culture. We know that the gesture of the pen or the keystroke initiates the beginnings of a poem or novel or essay, a making. But what of that unmaking which the same act engenders, more subtle and hidden, more disguised in the anxiousness or irritability of creation, the unannounced lever of a word or the leap into a strange linguistic rhythm which functions almost as a resistance to the total sense of one's being? This double-sidedness of the literary act is what I wish to explore here.

Writing, the act of writing poetry specifically, may present itself not so much as a choice as a labyrinth. As Joseph Riddel puts it in his discussion of Charles Olson in *Textual Strategies*, "A writer must use the elements of poetry to reenact a moment of 'original research' that cuts through the 'history of accumulated texts'" (214). Poetic language in this sense contains many avenues, many narrow paths and *cul de sacs*. With each word chosen by a writer, what will be written or said next becomes more fixed, more determined, perhaps more arbitrarily controlled by usage or tradition or impulse. What the literary artist experiences is a recognition that he or she has been drawn down a corridor made of words, pulled or birthed into and surrounded by language in all its manifestations. Our entrapment, our sentencing to language terminates, as the poet Paul Celan punned, only in the parole of death.

There is then, in writing, the belongingness of each human experi-

[3]

ence not only to the world or to the self but also to language. And thus, in this view, the singular or unique quality of a poem or novel means only that, in comparing it to other works, turnings different from our own have occurred, that in fact it was only through the poem that we have been shown them. Which brings us again to language's labyrinth or maze, to its corners and blind alleys. Contemporary literary theory reminds us that we look at language's labyrinth in two almost fundamentally simple and opposed ways, that is, as being made up of either forms or signs. If for centuries, under the general aspect of the word as sign, language was haunted by the idea of presence, that a word belonged to, that it could restore to consciousness, an object in the world, it is now equally haunted by non-presence, by the Saussaurean ruled line which separates signified and signifier and ghosts language not with a world but with other texts. That a word so haunted will be governed not by its relation to the objects it might name but by a design, authorial, cultural, musical.

From the point of view of forms, our labyrinth contains patterns, pre-structurations, language games, self-contained linguistic envelopes. I am referring here to a view resonant with the work of Saussure, Jakobson and some of the language-inclined logical positivists. This view, I believe, is close to the structuralist and post-structuralist positions concerning language.

From the point of view of signs, language, although it is patterned and has form, is yet endlessly combinatory, not because it is self-referential and manipulable, but because signs are constantly trying to pattern the flux of what exists beyond language. The sign, the name, the symbol, the referent, the signified, comprise a family of linguistic usages which can only exist by being predicated on there being something which lies outside language, and yet which language refers to, that induces form and structure. One could call this the Romantic or traditional view of language, or, as Gerard Genette has recently termed it, the idea of language under the aspect of "mimology" which aims to hide (deceitfully?) the irremedial gap between sign and thing.

At the moment in which we engage the word, where we take it upon ourselves to utter or write it, these two views of language must present themselves as nearly incompatible and yet as unavoidably interdependent. Such are the boundary conditions, ones that are now atomic and granular, in the psyche of any writer. Uncertainty lives here first of all, between the game and the sign, between our linguistic selves and a world, the source of the poet's uneasiness.

~

I was mulling over these two somewhat extreme views of language when I first encountered, in the Tate Galleries of London, in a travelling exhibit on early twentieth century Italian neo-classic art, Georgio de Chirico's 1913 painting, "The Uncertainty of the Poet."

I must admit that it was the painting's title which first struck me because it seemed, in the moment, to echo the thoughts and confusions I was having. It was not only the permissive and transgressive title, but something itself in the work which seemed to empower me to speak, at least to myself, about poetry. That is, my comments here should be taken not as art criticism but rather as a moment in literary autobiography, in a personal "poetics" invoked by the presence of the painting.

Now this painting, one of de Chirico's so-called "enigma landscapes" contains all the familar stylistic marks of that painter's work. Here dream and geometry seem to meet in the depopulated, fabulized cityscape reduced to angles, curves and menacing shadows. In the distant background, at the painted horizon, a train with its trailing plume of smoke scurries for the edge of the canvas as though the modern world or—in my imaginings at least—modernity itself were trying to flee the canvas, the scene or siting of art in de Chirico's world.

What constitutes this particular scene of art? As we can see in the de Chirico, the place for art is a wide public area. A space, as with a writer's blank page, which has elicited a demand for art, is in fact an empowering potential, one waiting to be filled by an imaginative act, by a sculpture or monument. The space is a solicitation.

De Chirico answers this solicitation the way a poet might respond to the blank page. In the foreground of this space where art might take place, brought to prominence on a raised area, sit the two central objects of the painting. One is a sculpture, a crude representation of the torso of the Venus de Milo, headless, armless, legless, a good bit squatter and thicker than the original. The other object, also lying on this raised stage, is the torn off branch of a banana tree clustered with bananas. The jagged end of the branch is pressed against the statue's marble thigh. One or two bananas have fallen to this stage and lie apart in the sun casting their own stark shadows. There is no banana tree: some human agency, a person or the painter's imagination, has brought the branch to this place.

So here is art and even signs of life in the work itself, but no one to view this, for the plaza is completely empty. Normally, such a space is filled by crowds, by orators, by strolling citizens, occasionally by solitary figures, lovers perhaps who decide on an evening rendevous and are found walking toward each other across the empty vastness as into the face of a destiny. In de Chirico's world, the vacancy of the plaza, the abandonment by people and by many obvious forms of modernity is a key sign of what has befallen art or at least its spirit in his time. Even the childlike irregularities of the lines of perspective add to the feeling of pathos and desertion.

It would be natural to assume that we are to be witnesses to certain oppositions at work, to infer that de Chirico has staged a symbolic struggle. The absence of people in the square and the foregrounding of the pedestal suggest an *agon* within the realm of art between the classical or mythological *isness* of the torso, for instance, and the banality of bananas. To feel perhaps that a 'timeless' art object has been set against the mundane 'natural' fruit, to infer what is transitory or even comic. As well, one can imagine something even more oppositional, a debate between high art and low art given in spacio-symbolic terms, one which brings with it the foreshadowings of the absurd, of the pre-echoes of the surrealist and *dada* movements that will later programmatically invoke juxtapositions such as that of a Venus and a banana.

And yet, one also feels that this juxtaposition is somewhat unreal. Aren't both symbols — the second-hand grotesquery which de Chirico has made of the Venus and the already ironical self-reflexive banana— over-mediated items in the art-repetoire? Possibly, no one is in the plaza because this struggle is boring, is old history, initiated in religious and allegorical paintings and done to death in desacralized nineteenth century still lifes, finally to lie buried under the return of the object world in the luminous work of the Impressionists. Absent religious aura from an object world and the well-painted banana always wins.

Clearly, de Chirico knows this: in the painter's gesture of having banana and Venus touch, the once-oppositional stance of high and low is consciously neutralized, their antagonistic energies dispersed.

For me, the drama of this painting lies elsewhere, in the painting's finish. One notices—in what, temporally, must be one of the final bits of work by the painter on the painting, that almost everything on this canvas—the torso, the bananas, the objects and the backgrounds, are worked with a faint lurid green. This green discolors the marble and browns the yellows of the bananas until the whole picture radiates with a slight vibratory motion of overripeness. The sickly green, unifying the entire painting, weakens the vision we might have had of objects in conflict, of transmigratory entities bearing away different aspects of the spirit. Instead, we are presented with an arrestment, a spectacle, faintly nauseating, of objects bearing only the category of their own decay. This stasis, accompanied by the absence of human presences, is stifling and oppressive.

I mention nausea; I could also mention its accompanying dread. For here we must remember the great importance that nausea and dread have come to play in the socio-aesthetics of the twentieth century. I am thinking not only of Sartre and the existentialists, of course, but also how one could follow out the emigration of these terms from Kierkegaard through Heidegger, their later modulations as boredom and anomie.

Now the special intelligence of a work which focuses on nausea, on boredom or dis-ease rather than on anger or rage or desire, lies first of all in the apparent fact that these latter emotional states or passions are concerned with the gratifications of the ego. Anger and rage and desire come with a kind of built-in bipolarity, with goals and objects, with reminiscences of a graspable world. They suggest that if something or other were once obtained, achieved or avoided, the emotion which lay behind the effort would now be rendered useless or comical. Nausea and dread, on the other hand, although one wants their surcease, have no such apparent goals in this sense. They seem, biologically at least, more intractable and primary, more banished from will and willing as feeling-states than our day-to-day passions.

De Chirico brings to the fore this nausea or dread by using the lurid green, the bile which washes over the entire canvas and holds every object in the painting's field in that state. He has captured in paint a certain historical moment of stasis in the state of art and (through the permissions of the painting's title and my own sense of the predicament of writing) the state of poetic language. The empty stretches of the plaza (as in his other paintings) are the cups and receptacles of the time of art's passing. The obvious conflicts or prophetic struggles within art, the elevation or degradation of objects, are reduced to a kind of inertia. In fact, what appears to be most "real" in this painting is not conflict but a pathos generated by the fallen condition of art as de Chirico senses it. The painter, and by implication the poet, no longer faces a variety of modes to choose from, high or low, artifice or nature. Instead, there is only disquiet, nausea, uncertainty in the deepest sense, in the self-cancellations of oppositional definitions of what art is to be. Why then (once more re-echoing Holderlin) to be a poet—or painter—at all?

There is at least one step more. It is clear that de Chirico's painting reminds us of the endlessly recursiveness of art history. Of the dead-ended view of thinking of art as being on a treadmill. Yet what seems equally important is the realization that de Chirico has brilliantly played back our own entropy to us, that through the cross-cancelling of the cliched objects marshalled for the painting, objects we might take as signifying even in their ironic aspect, something else has emerged beyond the pictorial representation of stasis.

Again it is the green. For in using the sickly color which tints these objects, he has actually prevented us from looking at this painting as if it were merely the depiction of the terminination of a struggle or as a didactic message.

Instead, we are made to contemplate the art work, its faintly bilious decay and rot, not as something intellectual, but through the agency of our own dis-ease. In this way, de Chirico succeeds, even against the subject matter of the painting, in giving life to the composition beyond the confines of the canvas (a dream implicit in the poet's hope as well for the poem's life beyond the page). It's as though we were asked to view the elements of the painting—to make a contemplation—while subject to the smells and reeks of an upset stomach, *our own*, or of a hospital ward or garbage dump.

In effect, the painting brings us back to a kind of 'before art,' to an artistic ground zero. For isn't it the case that in the movement to confront and relate to our uneasiness, in the manuever which is something like an organism's attempts to deal with pain, we escape from the confines of the subject of art? Rather than being mired in the fascination of the painting or finding ourselves lost in its beauty or in the intricacies of its forms and arguments, we are delivered to the outside, suddenly reminded again by our dis-ease that our lives are adjacent to art but not enclosed within it. Our dis-ease, in effect, liberates us. Baudelaire, who knew well the boredom and dis-ease I'm writing about, who addressed it directly to the hypocrite reader, puts this idea very well in his poem, "The Consecration." As though he were echoing Meister Eckhart, he writes: "I know that pain is the one nobility/ upon which Hell itself cannot be encroached."

Such psychological pressure, perhaps after lengthy meditation on the matter of painting in a time of the breakup of art, may have had considerable if not oppressive force on de Chirico. Shortly after completing "The Uncertainty of the Poet," he abandoned altogether the modern idiom he had till then cultivated. He then embarked on what must look to us like a rather retrograde career as a painter, working thereafter in a heavy, highly imitative classicism, making near-copies of Old Masters in museums, a mode well-suited to the Fascist "realism" which Mussolini inspired or demanded from the painters of Italy. In retrospect, this mode of painting looks like a means by which to forswear coming to terms with the visual present about him. Surely, the later paintings were no longer expressive either of an articulation of the present nor of an open vision of the future.

∼

Wallace Stevens in *The Necessary Angel* remarks that "Modern reality is a reality of decreation, in which our revelations are not the revelations of belief, but the precious portents of our own powers." He writes as well that both the modern painting and the modern poem are a "horde of destructions."

De Chirico's painting appears to obey Stevens's thought in a curious and powerful way, for the force of the painting is that of repulsion, a decreation of the categories of art, and a move back toward an incarnate "reality," the world and the body in it. Not by some transport or fascinating simulacrum but by the offices of art disabling such transports, forcing us back onto another ground. The French poet Yves Bonnefoy tells us that the function of a poem ought to be to make us lift our eyes from the page, that a serious work must have the strength to rescue us from Art so that we can reflect on life.

Someone might protest the nature of this discussion: painting is about painting, poems about poems. To which I would reply that, in the first place, de Chirico's title, as a framing device, insists upon a mediation between the genres of painting and poetry, and that any dialogue between the two requires that the act of reflection break the plane of one genre in order to deliver us to the other. Indeed, we are cleverly entrapped by de Chirico's uncanny genius, by the endlessly disabusing effects of the totality of the work, one of which, the title, drives the 'effect' of paint toward a consideration of language (poetry). In this space, language and paint, which are no longer about themselves alone, are made equally communicable, even if we are unsure what is being said to us.

I must relate this communicability as something personal to myself, for there was in my contemplation of the painting, as I mentioned at the outset, an act of resonance, an almost mystical moment of synesthesia when the painting and the feeling of entrapment in the labyrinth of language came to me with the force of one unified significance. And it was then, in the dynamics of the effects arising from de Chirico's entropic playbacks, in my personal take, so to speak, that I could envision uncertainty's claim and attempt to demonstrate how it is active in the poet.

I am here proposing this analogy: in its effects on us, the labyrinth of language, with its forms or signs or its forms *and* signs, can be likened to de Chirico's painting. That is, to be in the labyrinth of language (contemplated as a composition, a 'state of affairs' in the Wittgensteinian sense), to be within this convoluted maze leads us only to dis-ease. There, places of closure or refuge, recourses to fundamentals or groundings, are denied to the poet. They are denied, first of all, because the two views of language, form or sign, are incompatible within the same linguistic space; indeed one is the Venus and one the banana of language practice. And yet, as the writer well knows, one is always caught wavering between the form and the sign, between one's love of a word's play and one's desire to grasp the reality it would name. No matter how one chooses, certainty is denied. For the literary effect of a word is inevitably shadowed by the mundane literalism with which it denotes something not present on the page and not present in the mind of a reader. Every usage borders on the vertiginous, and therefore, as Maurice Blanchot writes, "there comes a moment when the literary man who writes out of loyalty to words writes out of loyalty to dread."

Even if one is at the other extreme, bent only towards form, toward the structural properties of language, thus willing to forsake all else about a word but its music or arrangement, there too, the language labyrinth or composition, undergirded by past usages, reminds us that any self-awareness of a language pattern tends to instantly de-authenticate that pattern. Every bit of textuality (as the French would say) is already written, not under the imprimatur of one's authorship but by history, tradition, the *zeitgeist*.

In effect, our attempts to retreat into sincerity or to advance into formalism (where art becomes the only category) are suddenly impoverished by our memory, our irony and our sense of the artificiality of the categories. What then is left?

I don't know if anything *is* left, unless it be the uncertainty from which a new state of affairs always emerges. In other words, uncertainty has now become the only promise which the activity of writing can guarantee. In this regard, it might well be the first duty of a writer to resist violently the culture's language games, including a duty to resist the fashionable romance of resistances which is often part of the ongoing mythologizing of one's times. Suddenly, vigilantly, the writer is required to employ a kind of knowing yet willed refusal, one which is still full with the knowledge of art and of language.

In such a knowing refusal, all language, including the discursive or scientific, again becomes completely available. The condition of language privileges no specific usage; this we know from history, from memory, from experience. A poet rejects one discourse in order to pick up another because the ongoing sense or feel of reality prefigured in what is rejected is as stulifying as those painted symbols in the de Chirico.

One thinks here of founding historical examples such as Lucretius and Blake. Lucretius, the poet-philosopher of ancient Rome, we remember, in his great poem *De Rerum Natura*, in attempting to rewrite the language of scientific inquiry, actively had to resist the theistic encodings of a world governed by Gods and divinities. To do this, he had to find something which would undermine the metaphoric, animistically inflected pantheon of gods and the supernatural. Lucretius fights "untruth" not with literature but with its antithesis, an almost rational descriptive language. In Blake, by contrast, in a time when a mechanistic scientific world-view predominates in 18th century England, the poet's call is reversed, away from a 'scientific' language and towards an embrace of allegorical invention or new mythologizing because these are the oppositional tools to be used against the heavy rationality being produced in the culture. Lucretius and Blake remind us of the subversive aggressivity of poetry, that the linguistic environment of a poet's specific times, perceived as an entrapping edge or boundary, determines the working tools.

～

What constitutes poetic uncertainty, poetic lostness? One component, as we have discussed above, is the instability of literary language. This instability applies as well to the languages of our "inner" life, to the rehearsals and operations of memory. Dream, fantasy, reality, these distinctions are blurred in that peculiar symbolic language of the mind formulated first and most clearly by Freud. In the realm of the psyche, words, which were once the self-testimonies of objects, no longer present an inventory of the world; instead, the sign-function of the word gives up insisting on the masquerade by which it called itself reality. The sign now proffers itself as intermediary between writer and reader, a communion wafer of taste and substance. Rather than raise a mutually definable and 'scientifically' accurate world, the sign engages us in a commentary on our pleasure or pain.

As in the de Chirico where objects threaten to deliquesce their thing-ness into the liquidity of emotional states, into pathos and despair, words, from the viewpoint of uncertainty, achieve an odd rightness of voice. They speak to us, in Bonnefoy's words, as "the discourse that desire is always constructing," that is, as the witnesses of love, sex, the taste of food, humiliations or a cut finger, outrage at perceived or real injustices.

The poem, whether we are readers or writers, provides phantas-magorical testimony or witnessing of experience, as though the stirring of the language machine were evidence of something unconditioned which at a prior time had entered the quiescence of one's distraction or boredom. We have been lifted above the steady states of our existence. So, in effect, for the purposes of art, the catalog of reality means only that the words by which we name things, in the contexts of other names, pulls secretly and without any clear scientific warrant, on the loose strands of our psyches. Memory (and this was Proust's and Bergson's great discovery or invention) shows that every concretion of language and every name, such as that of the Madeleine, the sweet cookie whose taste creates *Le Temps Perdu*, once uttered, points to or even explodes with a burden of immense meanings. Perhaps all that such a word can do is to remind us that, in order to experience lostness or uncertainty, one has to remember when, whether for an instant or an eternity, something was 'true.'

&

Let me quote from the poet George Oppen:

> The type of mind necessary to the artist—or simply the mind of interest—is touched   always by experience, by particulars; cannot remain within dogma, no dogma but this which is not dogma but another and over-whelming force which we speak of or speak of nothing
>
> something like that, maybe in order not to speak of any kind of *correct-ness* other than awe. (*SL*, 231)

If I understand Oppen correctly, the poet is caught between a philosophical sense of his or her craft and a religious sense of the mysteriousness of the world. To name means not to appropriate but to invoke, to establish a relationship. Clearly, the discourse of poetry can barely approximate the discourses of the sciences and philosophy and ought not to be confused with them. For these latter philosophical or systematic ways of speaking or writing make as their project the movement toward certainties. The experimental method, the formulation of general theory, the search for the "meaning" of behavior, all have as their goal predictability and classification. Against the quest for certainties, for locking up reality in one particular world view, the poet is caught in the secret knowledge of language, that it speaks not certainties but explores uncertainty, that it is endless and so foreswears the gestures of premature closure or easy elegance.

The poet needs, it would seem, to cultivate, at a minimum, a hypersensitivity to the "mythologies" of poetic craft, including those narcotics we call beauty, harmony, symmetry. In this sense, the poet can not afford to be merely a literary figure. His field of activity is the entire language production of the available culture. He must be acquainted with the discursive currents which operate in that culture, which valorize certain modes and denigrate others, which bring to prominence certain kinds of thinking or activities and significantly forget or neglect others. He must see these practices for what they are, not overarching truths (even though they may hold 'truths') but forms of rhetoric or ideology.

Indeed, a more complete understanding of rhetoric seems now to be essential to *poesis*, that is, to seeing most forms of thought as seductions. For, as I see it, rhetoric's functions are at least twofold. In a totalizing or even totalitarian mode, rhetoric tries to build a world, to hold it together as though it were a syllogism. But in a different mode, in the field of dialectics, in Socratic irony, in Bahktinian dialogics, rhetoric functions to undermine previous conventionality. This is rhetoric which, like de Chirico's vile greens, tries to drive us away from the entrapments of linguistic logic and toward the simultaneous possibility and impossibility of a world.

Poetry, if it aligns itself with this second function of rhetoric, is essentially bent on deconstructing its own pre-suppositions in order to be open to the uncertainty it had first come to. "The Uncertainty of the Poet," even as it conveys to us our palpable dis-ease, reminds us that all

completions and all moments of rest or stasis, are only new opportunities for beginnings. The next poem is always the aim of the prior poem,
and this is how poetry develops, not by offering us truth upon truth, but
by reminding us how truth is always passing into a lie.

(1995)

Deep Song: Some Provocations

When I came to live in Andalusian Spain in the mid-sixties (finding myself by sheer accident in a small town to which members of Garcia Lorca's family had returned after their long exile from post-civil war Spain), I learned that one of the small coins, a five peseta piece, was nicknamed the *duro*. The *duro* (the word rooted in the Latin *durus*) is composed of a hard nickel alloy. A *duro* held on edge can cut a groove in any other coin; no other coin so employed can make a mark on the *duro*.

In each culture, in each language family, poetic *duros* exist. They are the irreducible songs, the almost sub atomic particles that form an invisible order on which a literature is built, on which the psychology, the complexity and variety of literary forms seem to rest. In Spain what are called deep songs (*canto hondo*) are the *duros* of Andalusian literature, and it was Garcia Lorca's concern, as made evident in his essay "Deep Song," to both rediscover and preserve the power and potential of *canto hondo* for his own art and the larger sense of art in Spain.

Deep song, Lorca insisted, is both lost and recoverable, indeed, presently obtainable; its recovery has less to do with filling out an historical record than with renewal of artistic form. In this sense, Lorca's essay is a potential provocation to the contemporary writer, in particular the contemporary American writer for whom the injunction "make it new" often means make something both anti-traditional and anti-historical. Such a provocation seems both timely and creative, for Lorca's sense of deep song, in his search for both the new and the authentic, suggests a path through the shrubbery of literary modernism and through the formalization and ossifications of our ideas about art and life.

I take both the meaning and the term "deep song" from Lorca's essay on the subject, the Spanish word for deep song, *canto hondo*, having no genuine equivalent in English or in American-English, though the simple word 'song' on one level may approximate. (Nor is deep song synonymous with—indeed, may be antithetical to—the term "deep image" as used by such poets as Robert Bly, Robert Kelly or Jerome Rothenberg.) To speak of song in poetry—and this applies most directly to deep song—is to mean something unadorned, musical, phraselike, seemingly standing in little need of exegetical machinery.

Lorca tells us that deep song refers to something primordial, originary, buried beneath the apparent surface of literature and, possibly, of thought or what might be called pre-thought. It does not, however, in Lorca's usage, suggest sublimation nor the sub-conscious nor its hidden or surreal manifestations. Looked at from Lorca's perspective, deep song is both seed and root of literary art, and is, possibly, its most determining factor. It is the art behind art, the connection to or liberator of a certain sense of truth, a barely post-Adamic speech-act, the hidden and continuous subject of the artist's quest. Thus, to study deep song joins one, as Lorca put it, "to the marvelous chain of spiritual solidarity that is the chief end of any work of art" (*DS*, 28).

And yet, the study or search for deep song can never be merely historical, can never be a quest for some literary cause of causes. Lorca, and the poets, musicians and folklorists he cites, noted that *canto hondo* was itself a transplant, a graft offshooting from Arabic and Indian influences, yet partaking of the local, of the 'inimitable character' of a place. Deep song occurs 'in time' and is, as well, *of* its enviroment. The search for deep song then was not so much a search for first things as for the most concentrated of essences, "the treasure hunt, in the sea of thought, for inviolate emotion" (*DS*, 29).

Inviolate emotion. Irreducibility. Lorca's terminology hints that these, the most profound aspects of deep song, are nearly undiscussable, but that this unsayable aspect, the lack of ornament, either linguistically, psychologically or culturally, the very silence embodied in deep song's existence, are important. By lack of ornament, I mean that deep song occurs (even within so called primitive contexts) as though its creator were keenly aware of the seductive nature of language and of culture, aware that the societal world, named, ordered and organized, is least able to offer insight or solace at the level of experience out of which deep song arises. Thus, though shaped by culture, deep song is neither sentimental nor nostalgic toward it. Rather, it is aloof to the consolations of place, ethnicity, etc. (and by that, paradoxically suggesting that it is the one element existing in a culture which is transcultural, transmittable, translatable). According to Lorca, deep song's roots are "truly deep, deeper than all the wells and seas that surround the world, much deeper than the present heart that creates it or the voice that sings it . . . (it) crosses the graveyard of the years . . . it comes from the first sob and the first kiss" (*DS*, 30).

Such awareness also applies at the level of nature or the natural world. Though deep song, necessarily, has its roots in a pre-urban, pre-industrialized world, nowhere can it be said to be informed by either nature worship or pastoral aesthetics.

For Lorca, deep song is the repository of a culture's pain and mystery. The lines he offers as examples, for instance: "The moon has a halo,/my love has died" (*DS*, 31), are at a great remove from our usual ways of relating, through language, to the world, to other or to what we deem impossible and ineffable, particularly where rational or conventional means of communication are of no avail. Depending on one's notions of the rational, deep song will seem either terribly crude or immensely prescient. Let me explain further. Another example Lorca gives is:

> Only to the earth
> do I tell my troubles,
> for there is no one in the world
> whom I can trust.
>
> Every morning I go
> to ask the rosemary
> if love's disease can be cured,
> for I am dying.

(DS, 34)

The poet here has sung himself or herself to some space beyond inter-pretation, beyond even the binding tie of a metaphor. Notice that in these two examples the poet addresses that which is mute, which cannot actually answer. Note also that the moon, the earth, the rose-mary are not stand-ins for some supernatural agency, nor are they 'reli-gious' symbols to which it is appropriate to ask for help or ease. (And while it is possible that these things which are addressed do offer conso-lations of another kind, through their physical beauty or potentialities, they are definitely neither symbolic nor mediational in the usual sense.) We could say that in such poems, everything remains grounded, remains what it is: death is death, the moon is the moon, there is no transcendant order which will resolve the distance between them and the hopes and fears and pain of the speaker. The speaker is merely in the world with them, hence aware of existence through awareness of the pain and beauty of existence. The connection, nevertheless, seems one of language, a last straw of linguistic linkage, a cry which comes when reason fails, when nearest to the incomprehensible, the cry affirms pain and existence. Deep song affirms pain almost automatically in its cry, its nearly animal suffering and reflex quality. Yet it simultaneously affirms human self-knowledge by inditing in that cry the relational and inter-subjective nature of language. Such activity goes to the very heart of man the language user, to the Heideggerian notion of man as one who must witness. And yet deep song, close up, is a nearly gratuitous act accomplishing nothing, for it is at best an entity constructed of symbols, one which only serves to instruct us concerning the ultimate failure of symbolic entities. "Deep song sings" says Lorca, "like a nightingale with-out eyes" (*DS*, 32).

Deep song then is as much an understanding (or better, refusal of understanding) as it is literary form. Still, it is, at the same time, some-thing dynamic, a spontaneous apperception of or creation of a pattern or 'meaning', a feeling-full response which is independent of utilitarian (although that may be available) value to the thing perceived. Deep song intuits a world, intuits both its expressibility and inexpressibility, for the very suggestiveness of deep song is inescapably connected to its irre-ducibility.

An American example of poetry tending toward deep song might be found in George Oppen's poem "Psalm" where he speaks of "The small nouns/Crying faith/in this in which the wild deer/Startle, and stare out" (*NCP*, 99). The tenor of Oppen's poem is somewhat different from Lorca's examples, taking in, as it does, our contemporary doubts about poetic meaning, yet it involves a consciousness concerning language ("the small nouns crying faith") which Lorca's citations are similarly concerned with. For this "faith" that is cried out is as non-utilitarian, as non-prescriptive as the rosemary addressed in Lorca's example. What is also similar is the non-symbolizing linkage, the linkage which rather than demand a transcending bondage between subject and object, acknowledges relational existence and nothing more. In such a linkage there is nothing sacred nor profane, nothing which can be utilized or established as 'higher' or 'lower'. (A similar implication lies behind that much overstudied line "so much depends upon" of Williams's "The Red Wheelbarrow".)

Deep song, viewed this way, operates to replace mythology with truth, fantasy with reality. It is an Ockham's razor of a poetics that, once admitted (or admitted to), undercuts and deflates the pretentions of our conceptualized and conceptualizing life. Such a 'razor' slices, like the *duro* through the weaker alloys, the false counters and projections of society and the self. In the case of the latter—in a curious reversal of our usual notions of the person—deep song becomes astonishingly revealing of the personality and interiority of the poet, for it exposes, as the actual shape of character—beneath the overlays of socialization and conventional modes of ego formation—the meeting or collision of mind/body with the most telling kind of experience. In this collision, the poet is exposed in the nearly gratuitous act of naming, caught at a powerful moment of significant indeterminacy—where the poet turns to aesthetic (hence deeply mysterious) choices as opposed to culturally determined ones. Deep song seems to perpetually keep the secret of this mystery, its energy hovering on the edge of referentiality and non-referentiality in ways that are yet to be fully comprehended by our literary studies.

Such energy, it would appear, arises from the most basic ground of existence, from the very flutter of matter and energy, as though partaking of the flux and impermanence of the world. And it is this flux which, in its ungraspability and insecurity, is often perceived as threat and is disguised or mitigated by our other more ordinary forms of discourse. Deep song, by contrast, seems to sound this flux, to re-install its troubling potentialities—the ultimacy of change and death—in our minds.

Deep song, if I read Lorca right, is the precise and ultimate unity of play and death, for deep song, like Lorca's *duende*, can only be manifest when an awareness of death is present. Nowhere is such a possibility more suggestive than in the essay "Play and Theory of the *Duende*" (*DS*, 42–53). If the essay on deep song identifies the well-spring and sought-for qualities of Lorca's art, the *duende* essay, Lorca's 'theorizing' so to speak, is its invocation, methodology and recognition. This latter essay cuts against much of what has been written concerning Lorca's *duende*, especially against those commentators who have chosen to see in duende something occultic or artistically privileged. For Lorca, *duende* is something far healthier, something both ancient and immediate and involving a sense of tradition as not solely the artist's business to create.

The *duende*, Lorca tells us "is a power . . . not a work" (*DS*, 43). It is immediately recognizable, identified "accurately and instinctively (by the most common people) whenever it appears . . . It is a struggle, not a thought. . . . It is not a question of ability but of true, living style . . ." (*DS*, 43).

Lorca contrasts the *duende* with the muse or angel who "comes from without" (*DS*, 44). The muse (i.e. as in musing) is fanciful, ornamental, an inspiration to disguise or decorate, to evade rather than be at play with reality. The *duende*, on the other hand, is interior, is awakened "in the remotest mansions of the blood". The duende cannot be summoned or tricked into appearance, for *duende* is synonymous with a full compre- hensive view of life, with what is both given and gratuitous. Thus "the *duende* does not come at all unless he sees that death is possible" (*DS*, 49,50).

And it is this sense of death—almost Rilkean in its moment—which is life-enhancing and transformative. "The magical property of a poem," Lorca tells us, "is to remain possessed by *duende* that can baptize in dark water all who look at it, for with *duende* it is easier to love and under- stand" (*DS*, 50). Hence *duende* is not interested particularly in skillful artifice; it "demands not forms but the marrow of forms . . . It draws near places where forms fuse together into a yearning superior to their visible expression" (*DS*, 46).

Looking again at the examples of deep song given above, one notes that a "yearning" is precisely the inherence they register, yet that no term in the poem of deep song, be it moon and death or lost love and rosemary, is adequately equilibrated, that, indeed, the yearning such poems strive to acknowledge or resolve is superior to the forms. For what the poet of deep song is expressing is the incommensurable, the moment where the conceptual or rational aspect of language fails to do justice to experience. Here language becomes a kind of flailing or weak yoking, an admission of vulnerability and inability to control the event. And the poet, instead of expressing an imagined wholeness, is broken apart: inner state and desired object are only linked by pain, by a matter of nerves burning on the air which distances state and object. Deep song is almost always about the inability or failure of possession.

Such articulations, as Camus once observed, are the creating of conscious-deaths, deaths which intimate, as they 'imitate', the actual death we cannot know. Yet this awareness of death initiates the play aspect of all activity—for actual death gives life a meaning by the finality of its own meaning-taking-away for him/her who would mean, for the poet or the seeker. It colors all activity with the shade of not meaning for one's self, since at death (as in deep song) one can not possess one's meaning. (It is just such an awareness and our attempts to overcome it which lie behind our notions of posterity and tradition, and the desire or fear to be thought well of or badly of after death.)

This half-shaded understanding of dying bears with it a number of implications: instead of practical concerns, the possiblity of transpersonal connection is raised, of, if not living for oneself, of living for others as residual memory trace, of passing something on, in a glint of creative openess borne not by ourselves, but by the work done. Pyramids, funerary monuments, poems, especially those poems in which dead poets accompany the living in the quest for truth, such are the testaments of this understanding, of the spiritual solidarity Lorca speaks of. Deep song, as the poet's cry of conscious death, becomes the occasional, the primordial instance of this paradoxical situation. And it is on the foundation of this paradox that Lorca builds an ethic, for deep song makes it "easier to love and understand"; deep song at its most powerful level is a counsel to accept one's most difficult and painful emotions—love and grief—emotions which can neither be avoided nor 'solved', only tolerated and lived through. In this, deep song could be said to work against our aggressive will to power, our demonic need to possess and justify, our tendency to self-righteousness as it permeates culture.

If culture and its transmissibility are rooted in language, then deep song is not only literature's atomic structure, it is also the primal active ground of culture, for it brings all aspects of culture under these signs of play and death where they shimmer like an equation out of quantum mechanics half within reality and half within unreality. Perhaps, without this vibration, language and its creative reformations—even its hardening into concept and consciousness—could not occur, would have no basis in the fluctual nature of how things are. Again, one would want to define cultural decadence as that condition where the evasions of deep song's pointing are so elevated and amplified that the sound of deep song is drowned out.

And yet like the indeterminate physical entities of energy and matter which are everywhere, deep song is an ever-present i.e. a contemporary possiblity, one which begins—in the context of our overmediated world—with the poet's ancient resistance to the suspect order mankind has overlaid on experience and on 'reality'. It begins in the poet's pain or pleasure *as primary intelligence* and only, if then, ends in the cleverness of words.

With deep song we walk what Heidegger claimed for language: the "boundary of the boundless", the border of hope and fear, the acknowledgment that poetry is rooted (if we can here use such a word as rooted) in uncertainty—that any trope of language leads always to a beautiful and terrifying indeterminacy. This is close to what Heidegger elsewhere, in speaking of Nietzsche, means in saying that "the frightful is what is affirmed, indeed, affirmed in its unalterable affiliation with the beautiful".

For texts 'mean' in ways insufficently stressed: they disclose, if nothing else, that we desire certainty—certainty of meaning, so to speak. And yet the poet's paradox is that as he or she intends to mean, to trace the irruption of a meaning within experience, such a trace must ironically in the same moment destroy previously held meaning. Deep song does not bring us to something we can call reality; rather, it brings us into profound contact with this desire and intention. It aligns us, whether as reader or writer, to that mature sense of loneliness and isolation out of which so much of what we mean by being human arises—love, compassion and irony.

The gist of deep song, then, is also a tonic to critical smugness, i.e. to the idea that interpretation can be fixed or dispensed with, or to the hubris of those who chatter endlessly about the autonomy of language. We know full well that chatter can be dropped, but that we cannot so easily drop our living or our death.

In deep song, death is perceived as both occurrence and recurrence, part of the cyclical which doles out the ambiguity of return and colors all our desires for permanence and security. We are fixed, and happy or dispirited, locked in our worlds, have it "sewn up" as we are wont to proclaim. And then we are invaded by our contraries—our own or the world's—by the message that deep song alone communicates: this life is utterly and finally relational. For deep song would disclose that point where we link ourselves via language and art to the world, where we inscribe, as the philosopher Gadamer formulates it in *Truth and Method*, the universal linguality of behavior relative to the world. It is not that we create or re-create that world or its truths but that we communicate a truth about ourselves. And so vulnerable is the representation of this communication that it is nearly a form of love. Pound, late in his life, after attempting and failing to impose a vision of culture on his world, brings what I see as deep song's measure to the very fore of his work. As he notes in *Canto 116*:

> And I am not a demigod,
> I cannot make it cohere

If love be not in the house,
there is nothing.

(TC, 796)

It is in such measuring that separateness and unity are honored. Deep song, as a practice, would concern itself less with the production of poems than with relating thoroughly and properly to our experience. One would almost call this a religious attitude except that in its force and depth, deep song penetrates through theologies and hierarchies. In deep song, poet and world, the entire scope of existence and non-existence too are at once sacred and profane. Thus the attitude which may be said to engender deep song is precisely that of Coleridge's aim for art, to present "distinction without division".

(1983)

'Translating' Form: Pound, Rilke and the Contemporary Poem

Ezra Pound quoting Gaudier-Brzeska: "works of art attract by a resembling unlikeness." Or say more simply and generally: this leaf *not* that leaf. Enough in the mind to call it leaf or to hear wind and imagine a stirring. What is of interest here are the possibilities—likeliness of unlikeness—of a relation between dissimilars, between stone or material alive on the air and words or a song of words alive on the page and in the hearing.

The dumb show of an art, even a verbal art is its end in silence. If the poem excites the hearing, it is only to bring hearing to a resolute close. If the stone prompts an eye to move across its surfaces, to 'take it in', there comes a point, a fullness of seeing in which eye and intellect rest, where response ends in awe. Consider what has been seen or overheard: surfaces and angles of stone, words and expressions, images, terms, chinks and chunks of the discrete. Look at some object or person beside you, immediately the rest of the surroundings diminish. By what magical act will you set object with object, word with word, surface with surface in some organization which succeeds in expressing a wholeness without diminishing any of its parts in the process. Art's silence and wholeness.

And yet, how such silence still manages to speak, how such wholeness and completeness can invoke the incomplete. Consider how one artist's work seems to speak. not so much to its creator but to another artist's work, as though a dialogue were carried on between quite dissimilar works, dissimilar forms. Consider this as a kind of translation; that is, consider two forms, even in two entirely different idioms, attempting to express what commonality there is between them. And this commonality, since it exists as much between works as in works and is thus never defined entirely within any one of them, going bv such names as tradition, spirit, *zeitgeist*.

I am concerned here with two well-known instances of such translation: the work of Ezra Pound and its involvement with Gaudier-Brzeska's and that of Rilke with Rodin's.

I want not simply to recapitulate the well-told stories of how the poets in question were influenced by the sculptors (Both Hugh Kenner s *The Pound Era* and Donald Davie's *The Poet as Sculptor* are exhaustive studies of Pound's connection to sculpture and the other arts.) Rather, I am concerned with how the notion ot attraction and of 'translating' from one art to another throw light on the problem of form, and what such interaction suggests by way of lesson and exemplum for the contemporary poet.

A little backtracking from Kenner's book. Let us re-imagine Ezra Pound in his twenties, wandering London before the Great War, an American casting his eye on the overblown, optimistic art of the Empire or on that other art (Beardsley and the Rosettis, for example), in such revulsion against its milieu that, by a theatrical decadence, it had become a Tartarian mirror of Victorian respectability.

Now Pound, one of the last to be educated in the classics, was concerned to know "by thirty years of age" as he put it, "what is accounted poetry everywhere ... to know the dynamic kernel from the shell." By this time, his head was full of snippets ("gists and piths" he was later to call them) of an admittedly idiosyncratic "best" of some half dozen languages. Pound, as we know, meant to employ these snippets, to rescue and reanimate them from the deader than dead exegesis of scholars.

It was here that Pound encountered Gaudier's work and the ideas behind it as formalized in Gaudier's *Vortex*. It was that work and writing which helped set modern poetry on its present course.

Pound was coming at the act of writing from two similar and self-reinforcing standpoints. First, poetry could be seen as an act of literary translation; that is, one could draw a parallel between a literary artifact in one language with its own set of parameters, stresses, inflections, etc. and its conversion into an equivalently charged piece of English. This translation, Pound sensed, was not dissimilar to what happened when a poet tried to render what is seen or thought or overheard into the vigorous, emotionally charged language of the poem. Secondly, Pound was reinventing what he called in "The New Method in Scholarship" the notion of the "luminous detail." The "luminous detail" was an alternative way of rendering the meaning of a time, place or epoch. Instead of the usual fact-heavy accumulations of standard history, Pound proposed that a time or place could be rendered or at least implied by a single heightened fact, a single inimitable gesture such as a work of art. Seen thus, a tomb scroll opened up all of Egypt, a passage of Homer radiated the psychological make-up of its age. As we know, further support for these notions would come very shortly in Hulme's Imagism and Fenollosa's study of the Chinese ideogram. Yet the one thing all these notions lacked, and which may have caused Pound to wonder what one does with all these gists and piths, was an organizing principle, a methodology by which to transform a collection of "dynamic yet isolated kernels" into a work of art. At this point, Pound's encounter with Gaudier becomes significant.

The meeting of Pound and Gaudier was in no sense a confrontation: rather, it was as though one parallel track had run into another. Gaudier's work suggested a solution to Pound's need for a principle of poetic construction, a principle which in its working out is a major aspect of the sometimes anguished history of poetry in our time. Consider, for example, how these sentences from Gaudier's *Vortex* may have spoken to Pound: "Sculptural feeling is the appreciation of masses in relation. Sculptural ability is the defining of these masses by planes." (GB 20) Substitute gists or images for masses, translate the visual-spatial "planes" into their poetic equivalents such as lines or spacing or image-constructs, and one begins to appreciate how Gaudier and Pound nearly resonate with each other's theorizing. Again and again, we see this echoing. Gaudier, for example, in a letter to Pound reaffirming the principles of *Vortex*, writes: "I shall derive my emotions solely from the ARRANGEMENT OF SURFACES. I shall present my emotions by the arrangement of my surfaces, the planes and lines by which they are defined." And Pound (in "Mauberly" later, but looking back to the London period) recalls: "Turned from the eau-forte/Par Jacquemont/to the strait head of Messalina/An art in profile . . . This urge to convey the relation of eyelid and cheekbone/by verbal manifestation" (P 198). We note that in each of these artists' conception there is the sense of something discrete (call it mass or pith) with an expressive life of its own which it is the artist's business to group into a whole that renders the total artistic meaning.

Pound's purpose in the *Cantos* was to write "a poem containing

history." Not another linear textbook of events, but Pound's individu-
ated vision of what History meant to one man in the here and now: how
it is that, in his magnificent phrase, "all ages are contemporaneous." In
this vision, the *Cantos* itself, the 'planes and masses' are discrete pieces
of history's verbal manifestations: Confucian wisdom, troubadour song,
quotations from Jefferson and Adams, politics, economics, on and on—
not as anthology of thought or interesting memorabilia, but as plane
against plane, mass against mass, time against time—here by direct
presentation, there by enjambment or by a phrase mocked in the poet's
translation. And always with the eye taught by Gaudier to make beauty
in the details, fulfilling something Pound had also overheard in
Brancusi's studio, that "every one of the thousand angles of approach to
a statue ought to be interesting, it ought to have a life (Brancusi might
perhaps permit me to say 'divine' life) of its own." And like Gaudier's
work, the mystery of the *Cantos*, its expressive life, is 'between' its
elements as much as within them, so that it too has a kind of totemic
power.

~

Gaudier-Brzeska (from *Vortex*): "The fair Greek saw himself only. *He*
petrified his own semblance" (*GB* 21). Both Gaudier and Pound (Pound,
probably because of Gaudier) saw Greek sculpture as a narcissistic decay
of that interest in form which marked the power of Egyptian art. Yet,
put the way Gaudier had said it, "The fair Greek saw himself only," one
can imagine Rilke's wishful concurrence. For the art to which the
German Romantics looked was above all Greek art and in Gaudier's
condemnation one finds both the reason and the problems of Romantic
art. For in the Romantics, this looking on was not formal in the sense
that the artist wished to acquire the technical means of the Greeks, as
say Pound wishes in studying the troubadours. Rather, it was an
inspired looking, a hopeful looking wherein the Romantic imagination
saw the ideal closure of subject in form. Whether either view—that of
Gaudier's which saw decadence, or that of the Romantic which saw
embodied idealization—is true to the Greeks is another question. What
does seem true is that Gaudier's perspective can be set in opposition to
the Romantic, especially the classical romantic tradition as exemplified
by Rodin for whom Rilke worked, and whom Rilke felt himself
influenced by. Also, we can pose an opposition in Pound's way as a poet,
his emphasis on the objective notion of the art, and Rilke's, in some

respects the quintessential subjective poet.

Such an opposition, between objective and subjective, lies at the very center of the problem of form and of those tensions which animate the contemporary poem. The poet, leaping into the modern and post-modern phase of his or her art, may ignore one of these opposing poles only it would seem at great artistic peril. With Pound and Rilke, we can see this opposition as problematic—bearing with it a complexity which forces us to rethink the objective/subjective dichotomies. Again, a bit of historical backtracking.

Rilke (as translated by M. D. Herter Norton):

ARCHAIC TORSO OF APOLLO

We did not know his legendary head,
in which the eyeballs ripened. But
his torso still glows like a candelabrum
In which his gaze, only turned low,

holds and gleams. Else could not the curve
of the breast blind you, nor in the slight turn
of the loins could a smile be running
to that middle, which carried procreation.

Else would this stone be standing maimed and short
under the shoulder's translucent plunge
nor flimmering like the fell of beasts of prey

nor breaking out of all its contours
like a star: for there is no place
that does not see you. You must change your life.

(*TRMR* 181)

Is it not an accident—blessed accident—that some division, some separate solitary path leads one of us to the form alive in the air, and another to the form shaped in speech or in print? And yet, do not these utterances, by their different means, do they not converge in the perceiver? Is he not lifted, crushed, anguished, overjoyed in the appre-hension? Is it not, as Rilke insists, that life must change "breaking out of all contours like a star" before either the song or the stone?

Yet come another way into this: A song of the stone? Before the stone, before the world, honoring, praising? Is it not, in this poem, a way of speaking which intertwines with the stone, gathering in a movement toward further possibility, toward a deepened sense of life. Rilke, before the torso: "You must change your life." Because, of the stone: "there is no place that does not see you." The marble 'gazes' back, prompting the utterance, prompting in the observer the desire to alter by act of eye-consciousness, to take 'within' one, the movements of the stone, which Rilke thought would modify the soul. Humankind's stone and humankind's song caught in a particular nexus.

Rilke often suggested that the purpose of his art (see, for example, the letters he wrote during the composition of the *Duino Elegies*) was to keep "life open towards death"; not the sense of death as extinction, but "imagined as an altogether surpassing intensity." I wonder if we do not all recognize the truth and intention of these words of Rilke's, that far from being a call to morbidity, they ask that we open ourselves to the world, to, in a sense, 'give over' to the thing seen. I wonder if we do not all experience this at one time or another, before nature or a work of art or a deeply loved person; do we not, as the artist will say, "die into the form of the other."

I am speaking here metaphorically of course, not so much to bind us to an image as to admit the lack of adequate knowledge and terminology. Consider the thing across the room, the print on the page, the voice on air—these are somehow complete, closed in on themselves, yet they all gesture outward. Now the gesture may not be the artist's first consideration. He may be concerned with arrestment, with "solution," with some re-arrangement of the visible or the oral which will ease a tension which really began in his addressing himself to the materials at hand, or to an as yet unspoken or unvisualized image. From the tension and its resolution there emerges the outward gesture.

Now what amazed and enraptured Rilke and the German Romantic movement about classical sculpture was the sheer perfection of its solution (even fragments conveyed its wholeness: "else would this stone be standing maimed and short"), its seeming closedness, along with the power of its outward gesture. It did not ask you to complete *it*, but to complete *yourself*, i.e. to discover what it means to face that death-into-another-form of surpassing intensity.

Rilke's poem is a virtual textbook of the struggle within the Romantic imagination. For while this urge for completion, for changing one's life, is universal, it has its peculiar historical *moment* in the Romantics. We know that while the Greeks lived in a world of gods and men and perfected themselves in the glare of the deities, the Romantics, who loved Greek art above all other art, had no deities they were accountable to but had instead to confront a mechanical world indifferent to man. Romantic man had first to create his own purpose, his own *raison* of existence. The poem is a paradigm of this situation. First, we have the gaze upon the statue, the taking in of its qualities and suggestions; then, suddenly, the leap inward to another space, another dimension with the last two lines:

> . . . for there is no place
> that does not see you. You must change your life.

The descriptive passages up to that point do not logically entail the conclusion. One can imagine the poem ending with the words "like a star," a praising of the statue. But the Torso, by its seeming wholeness *punishes* the Romantic observer, confronts him with his own sense of uncertain being. It is this wholeness (as Gaudier remarked of the Greek) which the observer would be quite happy to see in himself.

⁓

Let us speak again of form. Before all the forms, the poems and the marble, there is a sense of awe, of "surpassing intensity." There is that miracle, that "resembling unlikeness" which attracts, which alters consciousness, which prompts us as spectators or artists to "die into form."

In sculpture, the visual forms twist and play among each other, deferring then fulfilling certain expectations. So too, in poetry, the logical, the linear progression of a thought, a line, or a musical idea is deformed in the interest of making the poem. The problem in both is the subtilization of the deformation so that "unlikeness" is not banality nor exaggeration (though sometimes exaggeration is sought for satiric purposes).

On the other hand, certain problems of the poet and the sculptor appear apposite. If the problem of the sculptor is to enliven inert mass, to force solid and form into outward gesture, the poet's problem is that his words continually point beyond the poem's use of them. An untouched stone has a kind of indifferent, enigmatic beauty; the enigmatic beauty of even the simplest words is their referential depths quite beside the poet's use: indifference again, but this time to the poet's will. (One thinks of the poet using words like 'love' or 'peace' with their millions of individualized meanings; how does he *mean* one over the many?). All this deformation in the service of a form.

Rilke, Pound, Gaudier-Brzeska, all three at one time or another were interested in the Egyptian cult of the dead, the preparation in this life for the next. Gaudier-Brzeska saw the Egyptian sense of form as a way of man reaching into divinity, connecting with the gods: Rilke's life and work were an open metaphor towards death. Pound, somewhat differently, saw his task as the creation of a "Paradise terrestrial"—to bring the gods to earth. It would not be misleading to see these as reaching symbolically for the same thing.

The capstone of the form, of the arch is, as the Egyptians thought, to carry one from this life into the next. Pound, his being consumed by a surpassingly personal vision of history, sought, as he says in the later *Cantos*, "to make it cohere" to complete the vision. Though his organizing principle, derived from Gaudier, was presentation and juxtaposition, the ultimate purpose was to complete the form, "to make Cosmos" as he defined it. If, like the Hieratic Head of Pound done by Gaudier, or like a cubist painting, it truncates the world of history and tradition (the only world in which the poem can truly live), it is still like those works in the service of a new imaginative wholeness.

If, on the other hand, we consider Rilke looking at the Apollo and reminded of a wholeness which had fled and could only be restored, and then only *possibly*, by a transcendent leap of faith, we can see this too as a principle of organization. For it is the rested totality of the Apollo, the work of art perfected to the point where no distinction can be made between content and form, which is what it means to have made Cosmos. Because only gods make perfect objects. And it did become a lesson and a principle of Rilke's, as he confessed in that famous letter of November 13, 1925 to his Polish translator, that the perfect objects of the world, first its works of art, then the world of Nature itself, drew one towards one's own wholeness: "Transitoriness is everywhere plunging into a profound Being. And therefore all the forces of the here and now are not merely to be used in a time-limited way, but so far as we can, instated within these superior significances in which we share . . . Yes, for our task is to stamp this provisional, perishing earth into ourselves so deeply, so painfully and passionately, that its being may rise again 'invisibly' in us" (*DE* 128).

The capstone; the form. This life, this term of years, this 'life' as an entity, the capstone of death which is the final closure. Pound, toward the end of his life facing the world, struck, if somewhat mellower, the note heard earlier in the young Rilke before the Apollo. As Rilke saw in the Apollo's unity and wholeness a call and challenge to being, so Pound: "the verb is 'see', not 'walk on'/i.e. it coheres all right/even if my notes do not cohere" which is at once a joyous and terrible admission.

And Rilke, at the writing of the *Ninth Elegy*, has begun to echo Pound: "So show him some simple thing, remoulded by age after age, till it lies in our hands and eyes as a part of ourselves. *Tell him things*" (*DE* 77). Yet these are resonances, not resolutions. Our problematic (to use contemporary jargon) concerning form contains further implications.

~

It should be noted that Pound who disliked Rodin's work, did not think much of Rilke's either. It may have been in part due to Rilke's seemingly easy acceptance of the verse conventions of his day. Pound makes mention of this in his *Guide to Kultur*: "As in English there is a god awful slump . . . so in German . . . And you do NOT get out of such slumps by a Tennyson or a Rilke. . . . Without a rigorous technique NO renaissance" (*GTK* 204). The dislike may have stemmed as well from Pound's antipathy to subjectivity, to psychology and speculation. And yet one feels in reading the early Cantos that it is precisely this lack of subjectivity which is their failure, that some study of the self co-lateral with the study of history is necessary to say something authentic about either. (It is just such an infusion of subjectivity by the way which makes the later *Pisan Cantos* great literature.)

We find ourselves in many ways dissatisfied with much of the art produced today. One reason is that artists seem to have too heartily embraced either the path of early Pound or the private inwardness of early Rilke. Pound's initial notions of a renaissance involved perhaps too much of an attenuation of subjectivity in the service of technique. Today, in poetry, perhaps as a result of Pound's attitudes, we often see a mechanical acceleration of technique in conquest of technique, an historically conscious wave of trend upon trend, until the meaning of a work of art, like Rilke's subjective uncertainty, no longer seems to lie within the work itself. In relation to the techniques of past works of art, the worth of new work is judged not by form-content values but by its novelty. The once necessary overthrow has now become an empty convention, so that much of art, far from trying 'to get the modern in', moves toward diminishment rather than enlargement. It is as though Gaudier-Brzeska's manifesto had been rather neatly edited to remove all the implications that the living vortex was given birth in the wedding of expression and technique.

At the other end of the spectrum is the art of unstructured expression—a kind of neo-dadaism which operates on the idea that there is still a convention of rigid (one might say 'bourgeois') formalism such as obtained in the 1910's and 20's which must be fought against. It is this work which strikes one as romantic in the bad sense of the word, because it offers only chaos to shock one, when it has always been order —new order, in, of and critical of its age—which is the most radical form the artist can offer. It is this radical form which has the outward gesture that commands us to change our lives.

∾

Form. Rilke, we recall, had written of "the love that consists in this, that two solitudes protect and border and salute each other." He was, of course, speaking of how two individuals might relate maturely together, how the very essence of love was the awareness of solitude, of great space across which lay the other. Some of Rilke's critics, most recently Robert Hass, in his introduction to Stephen Mitchell's translations, have suggested that Rilke's words are a deflection from the intensity of relationships, that this was in keeping with Rilke's "drawing back" whenever he came too close to forming an attachment. The critics continue that this was so for Rilke because, as Hass puts it, his "final confrontation was always with himself." To this one wants to say, possibly. There is, I think, another way of looking at these remarks of Rilke's: they are less concerned with the risks of engagement or how to rationalize keeping one's distance than with profound recognition. The border of solitudes Rilke speaks of is not the space of not knowing but the space of *not being*. Love here involves the awareness of difference rather than sameness; it only superficially resembles the mystical union of two in one, the fictional stuff of romance that has, in our time, been transformed into the dominance of one and the surrender of the other. (Imagine, if you will, the violence of the phrase "I know you.") Rilke, by contrast, seeks to find, against the cultural programming of his time (and ours), what constitutes love and the nature of its interanimation.

For Rilke, love is more dancelike, characterized by uncertainty of possession. This dance is many things, pleasure, poise, give and take, pain and humor—many things—but never actual possession of one partner by the other.

For Rilke then, love is not a violation of boundaries but an awareness of them. Love can violate the boundary only at the cost of violating itself, of transforming that which one loves into something else. In this it is remarkably like hate, for hate too acknowledges possession from a similar point of view; to violate its object is to attempt to transform it into that which is no longer hateful. Thus, with both love and hate, the object is entire. It can be broken or manipulated or made subservient only at the cost of love or hate. The object, once broken or tamed to another's sphere of power and interest, is no longer the object once loved. Thus Rilke, writing about Socrates, portrays a harried Eros "always a little out of breath, sleepless, troubled day and night about the two between whom he trod, to and fro, hither and yon. ceaselessly accosted by both." For Eros must mediate, Eros must deal with two individuals who live and change and who sometimes perceive (or mistake) their union as the melting of two into one.

And when then does Eros rest? In Rilkean terms, Eros rests only when one of the lovers assumes a form in the eyes or gaze of the other. To imagine the other as a form is not to imagine a static block of stone, but to imagine the other as something already perfected—not 'ideal'— merely perfect and complete, the very thing which you began by loving and, as with Apollo's broken torso, that insists you change your life. When we properly relate to form, we do not try to change it, but allow the form to animate us, to stir us perhaps into change. This is the Rilkean soul-work, indeed a "final confrontation with the self" as Hass puts it, because in its respect for the solitude of others, its affective point is our own egoistic clingings, our desire to lock up and control the object of love. This would be the transformative or, in Rilke's sense, the proper form of love. Eros rests when we acknowledge the presence of the other to be a form for us, to "salute" and tell us (from itself) about ourselves. This recognition would no longer involve form as being merely an instrument of knowledge but as having affect, involving its utter mysteriousness, its gratuitious, concept-breaking characteristics, its inability to be fully comprehended even as it is desired.

Love here is then form, and both love and form are related to our premonitions of death. For change, authentic change which risks everything, not because it is a gambler but because no change is meaningful unless the entire order of oneself is involved, implies this complete remaking of one's form. The *du*, the you of Rilke's last line in the Apollo poem, is a self-address, a command to the self as it exists. And in the transaction with the statue, Rilke has understood the deeper meaning of form.

This deeper meaning can be expressed quite simply: form calls to form. That is, in order to call or be called to, one must see oneself as a form. We could mean by form such terms as "self-conception" or "reference point," or even how we see ourselves. The main thing here is that without such a point there can be no real transformation, just a kind of thrashing about. What Rilke seems to suggest is that to have such a reference point, to be *this* and not *that* is to acknowledge incompleteness. The inmost heart of Rilke's poetry, the *Elegies*, amounts to nothing less than an attempt to abolish, if only in their moment, the this/that distinction, to "stamp this provisional, perishing earth into ourselves so deeply . . . that its being rises again." In this formulation, the statue, or the poem for that matter, does not address the human but what I would call the form of the human, the human addressed as he or she sees his or her own psychic constitution. In this sense, the "call" is not so much something recognizable but that which evokes or suggests conditions to change. There is nothing *gemutlicht* in this transaction, nothing coy or cosy or slyly knowing. The "call" respects the receiver, and to that extent it is uncomfortable. (The precision I'm aiming for here is significant.) For the human (as opposed to the form or self-conception of the human) is dynamic, is capable of enacting change upon its own form. We could say that this is what we mean by working on one's self. The form is the "one's self" and what works on it is what is only loosely nameable as human, something which can not be contained by a conceptualization but is rather a dynamic potentiality *and actuality*. The total human is ungrounded; it is, if we think of the Buddhist conceptions of mind and space. unoriginated, without attributes, without character. This is the 'entity' which makes form possible, for form is an aspect of it, a dimension or attribute which can appear out of it. Form is love in this understanding because it is a communication. In the Buddhist terminology, it is Nirmanakaya, the form of instruction or teaching, the instance of being in the world.

Rilke, in his essay on Rodin, points to this understanding. In speaking of Rodin's attempt to capture the meaning of Balzac in sculpture, Rilke describes Rodin's elaborate preparations and discoveries, the many models and attempts the form of the statue undergoes. Of the final version, Rilke comments, "That was Creation itself, assuming the figure of Balzac that it might appear in visible form" (*WSR* 127). If we are to understand that by Creation we mean all that is humanly possible and discernible, then Balzac's figure is but one form of the human, the modality by which the immense power of creativity is communicated.

In the passage immediately following this discussion, Rilke hints at something equally suggestive. Here he discusses Rodin's methods for maintaining unity not only in a single figure but among groups of figures: "flat marble bands have been left here and there between the figures and between their individual parts, like cross-pieces, uniting one form with another in the background. Nor is this accidental. These blocks prevent *useless vistas which would carry the eye beyond the object into empty space* ... " (my italics). The point of form, the "illusion" of form, is its inviolate boundedness. Seeing 'wholeness', as Rilke saw in the Apollo, is the appropriate response to form; aleatory interpretations do not apply. What punishes—in creative fashion—is the unity, the wholeness.

⌒

Pound and form. Pound we might look upon, at least in all but the latter stages of his life, as a kind of Confucianist. The meaning of history for the Confucianist, Joseph Levenson has written, is not in a fulfillment of the end stages of culture but a kind of "sage-antiquity"; to put it another way, the Chinese classical past provides man's good examples. In Pound, the impulse is to see the art-culture-antiquity nexus as exemplary. Another aspect of the Confucian sense of history is that its emphasis is not on process but on incident. This, too, strikes me as characterizing Pound's poetics up to a point. And indeed, what is remarkable about Poundian poetry is the typology of the formal break that Pound makes with the poetry of his time in order to enact a poetry of historical incident. Pound's method, as Laszlo Gefin points out in *Ideogram*, is paratactic; Pound layers event against event, as the sculptor—Gaudier-Breszka in particular—lays mass against mass. The reader/see-er constructs or infers the whole. In other words, the function of the *Cantos* is to restore via ideogramatic technique a catalog of significant history. Again, this history is not processional or developmental but exemplary.

What is most interesting (and most peculiar) is that if we examine the notions of form as formulated by Pound and Rilke, the inescapable conclusion is that Pound is much more traditional in his concept of form, is, if one can use the word without invoking a concert of groans, mimetic. Pound articulates this quite clearly in *Gaudier-Breszka* where he says "Every concept, every emotion presents itself to the vivid consciousness in some primary form" (*GB* 81). Pound's intentions it would seem — often powerfully exceeded in his work—are to find a kind of rightness or propriety of form, an almost Platonic sense of ideation hinted at in the phrase "primary form." Rilke, as with Holderlin and German

Romanticism in general (though, again, one must not easily equate these), is enthralled not so much by the technical perfection of Greek form as by its assurance. The Apollo is not something to be imitated, but, in the face of the general European cultural collapse, becomes a focus for the poet/artist of immense longing, of the desire to express, against the very erosions of certainty, a wholeness and integrity.

Were we to carry this analysis a bit farther we might see (again, curiosity of curiosities) that Rilke's work, though coming earlier than Pound's is a kind of critique, not of Pound's form, but of his content. For in Rilke we encounter a modernity which has already understood the failure of the art and institutions which Pound has drawn upon. Yes, Rilke, so-called "traditional" in form (the charge Pound levels against him), anticipates the problem of formlessness (of culture, of thought, of art) in a far more original manner than Pound, the formal avant-gardist. It was this anticipation which moved Robert Musil to recognize in Rilke the poetic voice of the age. All his poetry, Musil was to write, was a matter "of the feeling as totality, on which the world rests like an island. . . . He was in a certain sense the most religious poet since Novalis, but I am not certain whether he had any religion at all. He saw differently. In a new, inner way."

My impression is that the "inner way" for Pound came only with the cage at Pisa. As with all authentic inner ways, it came unexpectedly and as a confrontation with his entire being. The true meaning of the civilization for which Pound had proselytized comes to him there in all its failure if not its horror. And though its final "sinking in" may have come with his own final period of silence, it is as powerful a source of inspiration, of inner seeking, as Rilke's facing of the Apollo.

∼

To conclude, I would like to hazard a crude formulation and suggest a few of its implications. If Rilke seems, in this piece, the wiser poet, it is because he lived out the content of his poetry. Pound, by contrast, until his later phases, lives out his formal inventiveness, possibly at the expense of content—we remember how much of Pound's poetics are reaction to prevailing conditions of the art.

Our contemporary interest in form often seems to involve a willingness to revel in new discoveries, even new concepts of thought and language, as they occur through the manipulation of the medium of language. The content, as it were, is not a source or inspiration toward action and knowledge but a throwaway, a mark of the power of the work underhand, of its formal inventiveness, to be creative, inventive, spontaneous, in other words, to show forth those contemporary "values" which themselves are already mystifications. In this, the inventiveness nearly mimics the pre-World War Two poetry of Pound. Yet Pound's sense of history, as I have tried to show, his desire to prescribe and judge, is theoretical, unlived and even sentimental.

Now a parallel process is also identifiable in early Rilke; in particular, one thinks of the charms and sentimentalisms of his period work. It is poetry as surely sentimental about its bourgeois origins as is Pound's sentimental version of history. As with Pound in the Pisan cage, Rilke had to outgrow this taking for granted of the unspoken assumptions of his time. It was only when Rilke went beyond, only when, as Musil noted, Rilke's poetry no longer had anything to do "either with philosophy or skepticism or with anything else except experience" that Rilke could speak to his time. Such "experience" is not, one must insist, the manipulation of dead or received counters, nor is it psychologizing; least of all is it a capitulation to the anti-intellectualist cult of feeling, the banking of experiences for their own sake regardless of personal or social cost. This, if nothing else, Rilke (and Europe) have to teach us. For Rilke does not give us so much a picture of *his* experiences as of the experience of relatedness, a way of bringing into the open the new connections and the fictions of connectedness between individuals and their world.

Finally, I would suggest that this sense of Rilke's "experience" is coterminous with poetic responsibility (and license for that matter), and that what the new formalisms endanger is not the status of the old poetries but the poet's connection to meaning and language, and that this in turn leads to both evasion and illusion. Equally illusory, of course, is the self-centered inwardness found in so much confessional and surrealistic work of our time.

The poet as always is left only with his being human and perhaps with the possibility that his poetry, like the figure of Eros described above, is harried, "always a little out of breath ... troubled about the two," world and human, between whom he or she must continually mediate.

(1984)

The Narrative of Ezra Gorgon Pound
or History Gothicized

From the *Encyclopedia Brittanica* concerning the Gorgon: *More reasonable is the explanation of anthropologists that Medusa, whose virtue is really in her head, was originally a ritual mask. It is also possible that the staring or pursuing faces in nightmares have a good deal to do with her.*

It is the first decade, give or take a few years, of the twentieth century, and a young American with powerful poetic ambitions, Ezra Pound, arrives in London with an itch for some form of travel and adventure. Indeed, his friends back in the States have noticed and even been alarmed by this urge, and he has had to send letters home such as one to William Carlos Williams explaining his "unconstrained" and "arrant vagabondism" (*Letters*, 5, 6). Such a spirit of *wanderjahr* in this American is rather curious, for nearly all of the physically known world has been mapped, and what is referred to as an "inner" world, posited and even formalized in the work of Freud and Jung, interests him only in so far as it suggests *techne*, as it sheds light on the procedures of the artistic imagination, and not as *topos*. Later, he will look upon Freud's work with nothing but scorn.

So where to travel, where to journey? The other great world, opened and developed in the nineteenth century, is that of the temporal. Here there has been a lot of on site-research and speculation concerning such places as Troy, Egypt, the Orient, many primitive cultures, also an incredible thickening of European history as new tools of historical research generate new texts and textual approaches. Yet few have tried the game of cross-connections, of travelling, as it were, from one time to another as though island hopping in the Caribbean. Our young man, seeing his chance, will visit, not unknown parts of the world, but Time's many landfalls and continental shelves. Still, how to journey, for any one of these historical sites with their welter of material evidence could take up a lifetime of sifting and reconstruction. To get around this problem, our American, making use of the poetic techniques he has learned, invents a method, one which he calls at various times "the luminous detail in scholarship," "imagism," "vorticism," "gists and piths." The "luminous detail," the central datum of a particular time or culture, is to be derived from a consideration of a singularly unique element of that culture, from a particular work of art or from the life of an exemplary individual or even from the monetary system and its relation to the artist's use of line in a painting. The study of the past will be lyrical rather than empirical. For if cultures and sites in time can be likened to islands, this method will bring to light their mountain tops. For these peaks, as our traveller envisions them, are not only the sufficient but also the necessary indices of these locations. What lies below the alpine, what is obscured in misty vales and lowlands where masses toil, is of far less interest. Our poet-robed hero writes very early on yet already suggestive of his method: "To me the short so-called dramatic lyric—at any rate the sort of thing I do—is the poetic part of a drama the rest of which (to me the prose part) is left to the reader's imagination . . . (*Letters*, 3, 4)" History or time, then, will be seen as a particular kind of continuum, not a number of self-enclosing stories but a series of complex yet summative lyric moments or excitations.

Curiously, these lyric excitations, their peculiar sweep of monument or natural setting or personality, will resemble each other—at times physically, nearly always psychologically. There will be a certain pattern to the lives and actions of the exemplary figures; there will be severely cut stone and phallic overtones to the forms of the images by which landscape and architecture are presented, to the themes dwelt upon. Later, of course, when the work is complete, scholars and critics will attempt to look at this work as a "new" kind of epic. They will relate it to Homer's *Iliad* or Dante's *Commedia*; they will look for overall structure, coherence, seed methodology, clues.

Yet in their labors, few critics will have looked at *The Cantos* as a version of the American Gothic, something it resembles as much as any epic work with which it has been compared. Among American gothic tales, I am thinking in particular of Edgar Allan Poe's *The Narrative of A. Gordon Pym* with which *The Cantos* shares many typological features such as an invented blurring or indeterminacy of authorship, thematic repetitions, made-up scholarship, truncated scriptural citations, an evil and vicious Other which haunts the text, even the insertion into the prose of ideogrammatic symbols.

Our traveller, Pound, in another of his letters, remarks that "Poe is a good enough poet . . ." but "He is a damn bad model and is certainly not to be set up as a model to any one who writes in English . . . (*Letters*, 50)" In yet another letter, he confides, "Personally I think an ambition to write as well as Poe a low one" (*Letters*, 55).

Now I know that in some quarters the fierceness of Pound's rejection of Poe is in itself a sign of the undue influence of Poe on Pound. My purpose here is not to trace influence, however. What I hope is that by bringing the work of these two American writers into relation, by bringing out certain parallels in their work, new readings of *The Cantos* will be suggested and that, consequently, a whole new round of critical texts will be generated.

What I am getting at is that one can look at Pound's *The Cantos* as a species of nineteenth century American gothic Romance, very much like *Pym*, symbolist and private in nature, and thus representative of that kind of literature Richard Chase points to as dealing with abstract quests and metaphysical questions and arising as a result of the absence of a clearly defined and stable society of manners.

Of course, to treat *The Cantos* this way is only to follow Pound's prompting in *The ABCs of Reading* where he likens the critical act to the comparative or descriptive-scientific act, specifically drawing on Frobenius and Agassiz. You may recall in the *ABCs* the story of the student in the classroom and the fish. Here, I am looking at Pound's work and Poe's, asking the question: are they both fish?

My purpose is not to offer yet another shorthand attempt at debunking the idea of an objective coherence in *The Cantos* but to argue instead that coherence—if that is the word—involves something like a Rorschach response on Pound's part to certain select material from history and myth, material held together by the internal psychodynamics of its author (and perhaps never completely recoverable for that reason). Like a gothic romance, the poem can be seen as a series of *frissons* which not only affect the reader, but, far more deeply, assuage the torments of its author. In this view, Pound is not so much the man of ideas or vision but someone who binds up his anxiety with a certain kind of storytelling.

Let us consider the slippery matter of authorship in both Poe and Pound, its appearance and disguise. Poe's narrative begins with a

Chinese puzzle box of an "Introductory Note" authored by Pym concerned that he may be misunderstood, fearful that his memory will be given to "unavoidable exaggerations". He will share authorship with the writer, Mr. Poe, and "trust the shrewdness and common-sense of the public. (*Poe*, 200)" Indeed, Mr. Poe has been most helpful to Mr. Pym, publishing the earlier portions of the narrative "*under the garb of fiction*" (author's ital.) (*Poe*, 201). The effect of the note on the reader is to cast uncertainty on the 'real' events and on the 'fictional' events of the tale.

Consider in this light, the notion of authorship in Pound's "poem containing history." Christine Froula, in *To Write Paradise: Style and Error in Pound's Cantos*, a book which my presentation is both indebted to and critical of, gives much evidence of a trope similar to Poe's in the relations of Pound to both history and his poem. Froula's argument is marvelously ingenious, drawing on contemporary deconstructionist and reader-response theory as well as on her own sense of literary misreading. According to Froula, Pound is caught on the horns of a dilemma. Until modernism, the epic and its ability to come to closure is based on belief, an "Aquinas road-map" as Pound called it, which he did not and could not possess (*TWP*, 51).

As Poe, in *Pym*, shams narrative for fictive purposes and fiction for narrative purposes, so Pound, according to Froula, must make his work look like History and Epic while being anti-historical and anti-epical. We might note in passing how this was accomplished with *Pym*. When Poe's manuscript was initially rejected as being too fantastic and unreal, Poe revised the work by copying out and incorporating in *Pym* huge chunks of previously published travel narrative to give the work an air of believability and realism.

Now Froula sees Pound in the epical tradition in which error, the root meaning of which is "to wander," is the constitutive modality of the epic and also of *The Cantos*. But, whereas in the prior epics, closure was achieved when the epic hero came into the light and saw the confirmatory belief, the time of Pound has no such belief system. History must be conceived by Pound apart from the certainty of closure and story, but formal epical machinery and parameters (heroes, underworld, wanderings) will sneak epic—non-epic tension back into the enterprise.

Froula bases this thesis in part on the way Pound dealt with errors in *The Cantos*. According to her, Pound has a complex relation with the errors and mistakes which occurred in the generation of the work, whether they were caused by his own inaccuracies in reading or by others in the course of the work's production and printing. Froula cites correspondence in which Pound, made aware of his or of the typesetter's errors, prefers to let the error stand, prefers his version of events over the "facts." For Froula, the willingness of Pound to let mistakes stand is a sign that, in Pound, a mistake is the site of the invasion into the poem of real-time contingency which ironically undermines the neat fables of History. Textual error must be allowed to stand; it must look like truth but also like error, or, better, inhabit the no-man's land between the two; thus signifying how official History gets written as a compilation of lesser misreadings and errors (quotidian and asymmetrical) which are then totalized to give us History with a capital H. Pound (in a significant passage from *Guide to Kultur* cited by Froula) puts it this way: "It does not matter a twopenny damn whether you load up your memory with the chronological sequence of what has happened, or the names of protagonists, or authors of books, or generals or leading political spouters . . ." (*Kultur*, 51,52). What is necessary for Pound, claims Froula, is "to create the aura of historical process in *The Cantos*, even at the expense of the facts surrounding the poem's literal process. (*TWP*, 160)" Pound not only lets errors stand, including those of the typesetter as well as the historian, but recasts and revises legend and fact to suit his purposes while at the same time maintaining the illusion or aura Froula speaks of as "allowing the incursions of lower-case history into upper-case History" (*TWP*, 153). Froula tells us that *The Cantos* "failure to resolve into story paradoxically is its story" (*TWP*, 154).

Let us examine this "failure" from another perspective, that of Pound, approaching the project of *The Cantos* in the guise of "Mauberley." The poem, as we know, is Pound's "farewell to London," but, more importantly, it is also a leave-taking from certain kinds of poem-making, specifically the mannered poetry of Pound's early phase. "Mauberley" is a program for Poundian "making it new," but it is also an interesting psychological portrait of failure and displacement. The poem continually directs us to the by now highly excitable nerve-ends of Pound's narrator, and his search for "surcease": "I was/ and I no more exist;/ Here drifted/an hedonist" (*Persona*, 203). The poem announces the poet's voyage-drift through times, the peripatetics of which might be, Aquinas-map discarded, the principle of repetition which Pound, on the level of culture identifies as the "repeat in history." But the word "hedonist," even taken ironically, proposes a kind of psychological epicurianism marshalled under that rubric. Hedonism, in the sense Pound uses it, becomes a key concept, as does drifting. The two terms, in a sense, have been made functional.

The narrator of the poem asks "time to be rid of his bewilderment" as he drifts along until he finds "his sieve . . . (*Persona*, 199)" A "sieve" is a filter, in Pound's case screening out all but the luminous detail, the "selected perceptions" mentioned in the poem. Now, in the Ur-Cantos of the same period as "Mauberley," Pound is also developing the idea of persona and mask as devices for carrying immediacy into the mythic and historical sections of the poem. But a mask is also a kind of sieve. For the guise, the persona, the masks with their eye-slits are not only ways of presenting oneself to the world or even of shielding one's personality from the world, they are also ways of filtering the world, delimiting the world to the objects and sensations one is pursuing.

The mask, then, not only disguises but frames and reduces the perceptual field, cuts off wide-angled prospects and even standardizes the response of those who see, instead of a person, a mask. The hedonist here is on the drift, or on the prowl through times and texts, awaiting opportunities, but he suffers a kind of tunnel vision.

Hugh Kenner, in an early essay on Pound in *Motive and Methods in the Cantos*, writes: "Pound's way . . . is to await with a vigilance of his own the exact events that will enter his purpose without modification. (4)" There is a circular, obsessive ring in Kenner's description of Pound, one I find accurate, for it suggests that Pound's aim is first of all to satisfy his expectations (his particular form of hedonism?).

The "aura"of history as described by Froula (if one thinks of Kenner's version of Pound's method) may have less to do with historical contingency than with a very refined solipsism. Pound plays revisionist and re-writer, accepts error, not because history pressures him to do so, but because he must obsessively transform the multiplex phenomena of history into its "repeats". History is by this process 'gothicized.'

Now the 'gothic' character of a work shows in two ways. First, the work will have a repetitious rhythm of rises and falls, of dread and hope, of danger and salvation. Secondly, this rhythm must occur within a kind of "make-believe", in a fictive world isolated and free from a reader's actual uncertainties of being. This is why the ideal situation for reading Poe or any other gothic tale is the bedroom, dark but for the reading light, safe from all interruption. Do Pound's "dramatic lyrics" which leave behind "the prose" of daily life, his "luminous details" and cultural ideograms, provide such a rhythm and such a world? The case is worth examining.

As Richard Seiburth points out in his essay "In Pound We Trust: The

Economy of Poetry/The Poetry of Economics," another work to which I am indebted, the repetitiveness of *The Cantos* is one of its most apparent characteristics. "*The Cantos*," Seiburth maintains, "are not a fiction but a dispensation of likenesses, a disposition of facts given by History, an arrangement of verities. (Seiburth, 168)" Pound's "repeats in history" are not concerned with the production of meaning but with that strange *sub rosa* project of Modernism pointed out by Ellmann and Fiedelson in their preface to *The Modern Tradition*. Modernism, in their view, "sets out to achieve, under the guise of the immediacy of experience, a control over the resources and dangers of the present through a rediscovery of a relevant past." Pound's plunge into history takes in not one past but many pasts, converting them all into similar rules or lessons or "likenesses", as Seiburth puts it. Pound's repeats, in other words, can be seen as an obsessional form of history-making, the kind where, as Walter Benjamin has written, "Neuroses manufacture mass-produced articles in the psychic economy . . . The idea of the eternal recurrence transforms historical events into mass-produced articles."

Here we see another parallel between Pound's methods and Poe's. One of the most striking sections of Poe's *Pym* concerns the cargo in which Pym hides as a stowaway. This 'labyrinth of lumber" (216) and ballast with its oily smelling casks and other disjecta, its poisonous atmosphere, shields and secretes Pym from others while, above, on deck a murderous mutiny is taking place. Poe, in the middle of the adventure, interpolates a mini-essay on the dangers of improperly stored cargoes, on the inertial shifts of ballast and stores that can topple and sink the vessels in which they ride. The cargo is overt symbol for the contents of the 'civilized' mind, a mind in which things are cognizable and familiar but imperfectly ordered or 'stored' and hence subject to the ruinous seas and winds of natural and historical calamities.

Pound too has his cargo; *The Cantos* do not merely sweep out and gather up the past but, like a stevedore's crane (again "with alacrity and vigilance"), pick up the right crates and boxes and attempt to put them in the appropriate holds. This is not chronicle or history making in the ordinary sense if what we mean by history making is the act of an historian seeking a method which will assimilate or account for historical event. As Froula demonstrates, when one of Pound's crates don't fit in the hold, he will saw off a corner or tinker with the wrappings a little. Pound's impulses for storing the contents of his historicizing should be seen for what they are, highly selective, overtly didactic, Confucian, rule- and maxim-ladened, meant to show, not the course of events but how to live in the present. They should not be automatically equated with history or formal historicizing.

Pound is writing the drama of his historical finds. Since the finds are scattered throughout various histories, since they do not follow out of the evolution of any single train of cause and effect, Pound must organize them paratactically rather than causally. Unlike his Chinese historians, Pound will not leave "blanks" for what he does not know, at least not until the late sections of the poem. Most of *The Cantos* has room only for presentation and definition; there is no room, Pound himself has said this over and over, for speculation, for doubting or unknowing. Like the gothic narrative, which is crowded, seamless, incident-packed, *The Cantos* abjure rests or creative silences. Rather, as Michael Andre Bernstein tells us in *The Tale of the Tribe*, "Pound tends to repeat his favorite *exempla* throughout the poem." Furthermore, Bernstein reminds us later in his discussion, "Pound frequently intends, as I have said, to create the fiction of a 'work that is not a fiction,' . . . Such a strategy is designed to deflect our habit of treating any poem as a purely subjective aesthetic vision . . ." Yet, this strategy creates other problems related to authority and authorship; as Bernstein suggestively continues, "the problem of selection (or rather, the problem of *who* is determining the selection) still remains. The difficulty is that while Pound has not established any authoritative voice *within* the poem whose principles of selection and judgment we are ready to accept, he has also refused to let us see the text's diverse enunciations as originating in a single, omniscient author standing outside the narrative."

A gothic, even totalitarian, 'history' might be written under the conditions Bernstein, in discussing *The Cantos*, describes above. A key element of such history would be, first of all, the selecting out of historical details only what the historian-propagandist can use for effect, eliminating the space of contemplation and ignoring historical material which might contradict or lead to speculation. We are imagining here, to borrow an idea from Hayden White, how Pound's poem (or any other which incorporates historical material into a work) "disciplines" history, that is, how it shapes, edits and configures historical information. And, as White suggests, we are then in a position to ask what is *ruled out* of history's history by disciplining it in this way or that way?

The motives of disciplined histories (there are *no other* kind) are often all too clear, especially so in our recent past. They are in the service of an idealized version of event or culture, one often congruent with the dominant socio-political machinery of the State. In, for example, the historical propaganda films of the Nazis, as Saul Friedlander in *Reflections of Nazism* shows, editing and selecting processes produce cultural images which are disciplined or reduced to a small monolithic range of symbolic or ideogrammic images. These images never contain photographs of the German industrial segment with its marvels of synthetic fuels, armaments, etc., because such pictures had no place in the history *cum* mythology of beautiful Aryans living in cottages in the Black forest, the source of Nazi kitsch. Friedlander finds other examples in contemporary media and art, in particular with that art dealing with the Holocaust.

Pound's 'history' exhibits certain similar tendencies. Its purview of economics, for instance, as Seiburth has pointed out, is rooted in agrarian or natural economies. These pre-industrial economies allow Pound to "subsume labor and production under natural process." He quotes Pound: "work does not create wealth, it contributes to the formation of it" (Seiburth, 166). This type of economic analysis is in keeping with Pound's theories of usury and of poetry where usury, like metaphor, produces more than its transfer-effect of money and products, generating excess profits just as the metaphor generates excess meaning. Pound's economics, with their simplified modalities of production, are, like his poetics, anti-metaphoric. In their fusion in *The Cantos*, they emulate the gothic model by continually end-stopping philosophical or moral speculation in order to drive on to the next *frisson*. *The Cantos'* cargo of images is, in this sense, perfectly stored, well-insulated from history or historical process, and thus, as the psychologists might say, imperfectly 'reality-tested'.

This is interesting in the light of Froula's claim that the protagonist of the *Cantos* is not the Greek hero but the "authority of experience" (*TWP*, 158). Such a claim strikes me as suspicious, particularly if we ask what "experience" is being "ordered" in *The Cantos*. Is it not rather the case that "experience" is what is being excluded, and that what is being offered in its place is historical information removed from the burden of being experienced, posed rather as an authority of an order? Once the poem's parameters are grasped, once we recognize how well-stored its contents are, experience, except in the late sections, barely enters. For Pound has made up his mind about history, and his vigilance enables him to grasp reinforcing and ramifying "likenesses" as he goes.

There is no history, as we usually know history, in *The Cantos*, (the point well-developed by Michael Andre Bernstein) nor is there, in a sense, any historical error. Rather, Pound continues the lineage of the poem which regards language as outside or above history. In this modal-ity, as Seiburth suggests, "language serves not to create meaning but to carry or convey or 'get across' antecedent facts or meanings or values." Pound subscribes, Seiburth continues, "to the totalitarian plenum which institutes an absolute continuum among the signs of the natural, political and economic world, thus guaranteeing both the order of representation and the representation of order" (Seiburth, 159). This "continuum" is action and goal-driven. It is purposive rather than descriptive; it proclaims Statist values over those of the individual. As Pound writes, "Humanity is malleable mud and the arts set the mold it is later cast into." Kung in "Canto XIII" performs the operative trope, raising his cane against the meditating Yuan Jang and ordering "You old fool, come out of it/ Get up and do something useful" (*The Cantos*, 59). The command is prototypical, not only of Pound's historical heros, Kung, Mussolini, Malatesta, etc. but also of Pound himself. What is of course absent is the trace of exchange, of historical middle ground between the incarnated subject (the poet) and whomever he is signify-ing to. The mediation of the language is purely presentational, fore-shortened into effect. As Gadamer might well say, the poem lacks the fusion of objective and subjective horizons. This, I would claim, marks it off as a 19th century rather than 20th century work.

We might usefully compare Pound's troping of history with the poet-ics of poets such as George Oppen or Robert Duncan for whom historical contingency is continually registed in the voice, suggesting that history can never be entirely read as 'the past', nor as the present either, and so, in order to be meaningful for the present, must be passed through an active vocalizing subject. In Oppen or Duncan, the strata of history as a series of weights on the being of the poet, no longer remain discrete but are cumulative and so prevent anything as straightforward as Confucist re-inscription of historical maxims. At the sama time, conscious revi-sionism or admittance of known error are luxuries these poets must deny themselves; in Duncan's case, because the event or its linguistic signature is the gateway for entrance into a living past which is all process continually working itself out in times and individuals; in Oppen's, because today's word is burdened with the totality of historical knowledge. Their 'vigilance' is of an entirely different order from that of Pound's.

I want to conclude my discussion with a brief look at what we can say about Pound's methodology in terms of present-day practice of poetry. My spring-board is a recent essay by Charles Bernstein in *Sulphur* entitled

"Pounding Fascism" in which Bernstein attempts to save Pound the technician from Pound the fascist. Let me say at once, that I suspect the motive behind this essay has less to do with Pound than with Bernstein's revising of literary history in an attempt to valorize, it would seem, language-centered writing as it leans on or is beholden to Poundian poetics.

Bernstein begins with the claim that Pound's fascism, "far from hindering the canonization of his poetry by American literary culture, has been a major factor in its acceptance" (C. Bernstein, 99). Now I know of few mainstream or establishment studies of Pound that support this view—the very places it ought to be encountered if Bernstein is correct; in fact, the 'technical' side of Pound is what is praised in even as conservative a critic as Blackmur who, *en passant*, insists that even as we admire Pound's craft, we ought to drop the notion of Pound as a thinker or literary critic.

Bernstein goes on to say, and this is the crucial issue, that he does not "equate Pound's politics with Pound's poetry. *The Cantos*, and other of Pound's work, are in many ways basically at odds with the tenets of Pound's fascist ideals" (C. Bernstein, 99). They are at odds, according to Bernstein, because "the 'hyperspace' of Pound's modernist collage is not a predetermined Truth of a pan-cultural elitism but a product of a compositionally decentered multiculturalism . . . a polyvocal textuality . . . the result of his search for deeper truths than could be revealed by more monadically-organized poems operating with a single voice and a single perspective" (C. Bernstein, 100).

Now it is most probably the case that if Pound were a maker of 'monadically-organized' poems, if he had written in the style of D'Annunzio for example, few in the American literary establishment would have insisted on his canonization. On the other hand, if one perceives *The Cantos* as something like a gothic, its 'multiculturalism" is an illusion, its "polyvocal textuality" a chorus of foreign-sounding voices all mouthing the same rules and verities. If you accept this point of view, then Bernstein's analysis leaves one major question still begging, the one I have tried to develop in this paper: whether Poundian techniques, in particular the cultural plundering, revising and activity of selection induced by the search for history's repeats, the absence of a clearly defined authorial voice, tend to undermine fascist tendencies or aid in furthering them.

At this point, my own answer to the question must be necessarily quite tentative, but my argument goes something like this: Recent studies of the aesthetics of fascism (such as Friedlander's mentioned above) acknowledge not only the fascist need for rigidity, its fears of social and cultural disorder, but also demonstrate how fascism creates imagery and phantasms and other machinery for the generation of fear and anxiety in order to maintain itself. These are what Elias Canetti, in speaking about fascism, calls "the adjacency of construction and destruction".

The mechanisms of fascism not only respond to the indeterminate but use it, feeding it back into the social system, creating anxiety and paranoia in order to maintain and accomplish political purposes. Friedlander describes this as "the fusion of kitsch and death" where through aesthetic devices, anxiety and authority are everywhere and nowhere, a blend of domestic, mythic and archaic materials which produce a disembodied *gotterdammerung* of calculated effects.

I would suggest that *The Cantos*, seen as a gothic, approximate, on the linguistic level, this technology of fascism. Pound, as he selects from history and rewrites where necessary, may in fact be operating his own Orwellian Ministry of Truth (or as Plato would probably call it, The Ministry of Poetry).

For what most effectively maintains a totalitarian state of mind is not unassailable logic but unassailable 'thought'. And thought is first of all unassailable when 'authorship' is put in doubt, when history seems like a series of repeats, and texts are no longer the products of writers but historical inevitabilities. The sense of historical inevitablity, as both Froula and Michael Andre Bernstein point out, is precisely what Pound sets out to achieve through his maskings and erasures of authorship. And it is this troublesome legacy which has been raised to an unexamined and somewhat mystical status in much contemporary theory of writing and reading.

As in the gothic, Pound's poem has elided the very rule of 'sincerity' he set for himself. For sincerity demands in a sense accountability, and accountability demands an author or voice. *The Cantos* like *Pym*, obscures authorship, not because of its polyvocal texture, but because the gothic form must trade, not on believability but on a vicarious believability, the emotional conviction that this dangerous stuff called history is safely happening to you. The gothic thrall, the fictive aura of terror inspired by Poe's stories, is close to the dramaturgy of Pound's poem with its parade of decisive heroes performing their deeds. I would add that these kinds of emotional tonalities may not be far from that which the Leader creates when he tells the crowd how powerful it is and its members believe it.

The textual multivocality of *The Cantos*—some of extraordinary beauty —is, in this regard, like all the snakes of the Medusa, rooted in a sometimes nightmarish head. Pound may well have been the twentieth century's most didactically motivated poet as well as its most beautiful and inventive. And yet the ironies. At the conclusion of Poe's story, Pym's adventures and experiences end up counting for nothing; his boat is about to be sucked into a looming white mist which enshrouds a gigantic human form. Nothing avails, and we are left with dread and dread's powers over us. And so it almost is with Pound. True, Pound eschews the organ stops of melodrama, but the repeats of history, the monologues of rightnesses, may induce another kind of fear and weariness. Pound's gothic of history with its foreshortened development induces both the psychological excitement and dread necessary to sustain movement, emotional, intellectual and political, without recourse to explanation.

(1986)

Rethinking Rilke

A friend writes: "If you can find a positive way in Rilke, please let me know what it is—I see him leading to orphic silence, luxurious melancholy and a kind of stellar voice that few are capable of." I take up my friend's word, "positive," and bobble it before me in amusement. How much we want our ironies (Rilke claimed no civilization could be built on irony!), and how little we want them to cost us. In the last twenty years, we've built our ironies around discourse and "language," on their duplicity and on their power to impose, and that, I presume, is what makes for something "positive." During this time, we've thought little or at best, indelicately, about the word as emanating from a carnal being though perhaps with the appearance of Bakhtin's work and with Elaine Scarry's *The Body of Pain* a balance is being restored. In this new atmosphere, Rilke's work ought to be reconsidered, and I can think of no better place to begin than in this collection, *Letters on Cezanne*. The volume consists of letters and extracts of letters written from Paris mainly in the fall of 1907 to Rilke's wife, the painter, Clara Westhoff.

Rilke, it is true—to respond to my friend's comments—in the quest for Western art's sense of presence, its quest for "being," walked the last linguistic mile, so to speak. He imagined, against any situation in which a verbal act, let alone the poem, took place, a world of silences, of muted existence. It is this orphism, with its seemingly abstracted pain, its metaphysical hunger, that we tend to dismiss in Rilke's enterprise. Further, Rilke's admixture of *extremis* and care-fulness, the exactitude with which these marked his poetic trail, appeals neither to dionysians nor apollonians. Finally, that he is not easy, not "humorous," not frameable by theory, leads as well, to the charge that he is not positive.

Still, as I have written elsewhere, Rilke represents a fruitful direction, one which since Pound we have been reluctant to take up. Thus, my reading here is an attempt to understand Rilke not as a historical figure but as a potentiating force for contemporary poetry.

$\sim$

In late May of 1907, after a ten-months' absence, Rilke returned to Paris in a curious and feverishly receptive state of mind, a state which continued into the fall. In October, the annual Salon d'Automne exhibition opened with two rooms dedicated to the paintings of Cezanne, who had died only the year before. Rilke's letters to his wife of this period show not only the agitations of his mind but testify also to an atmosphere of psychological vulnerability where, as he put, seeing and working were "almost one and the same." Before his eyes, the world seemed to be reforming itself as a kind of benison: "All the things of the past rearrange themselves, line up in rows, as if someone were standing there giving out orders; and whatever is present is utterly and urgently present, as if prostrate on its knees and praying for you" (*LOC* 3). These words are not fanciful, especially if we consider that they issue from one of Europe's great workers in homelessness, a poet whose reputation in large measure was built on rootlessness and alienated consciousness. What they suggest is an unusual psychological climate in Rilke, an alteration of his characteristic dis-ease with surroundings.

For Rilke, artistic creation was less a matter of learning than of unlearning, of foreswearing intellectual or psychological certainty by making some sort of radical leap. "Surely," he writes a month after his return to Paris, "all art is the result of one's having been in danger, of having gone through an experience all the way to the end, to where no one can go any further . . ." "Therein," he continues, "lies the enormous aid the work of art brings to the life of the one who must make it,—: that it is his epitome; the knot in the rosary at which his life recites a prayer" (*LOC* 4). The religious tone is instructive. Homelessness, Rilke's artistic *donnée*, is set aside, and the world is perceived as animated and, more importantly for Rilke, uncharacteristically welcoming and beneficent. Suddenly, the work of art is not so much an alienated jewel in the world's crown but a tutelary device, a way for entering and participating.

For Rilke, the encounter with Cezanne's paintings in the months immediately after his arrival, marked, what he called, "a turning point." In part, the drama of the Cezanne encounter, a muted subtext throughout the letters, is the difficulty of "assimilating" Cezanne's work which, as it turns out, becomes the most useful demand ever placed upon the poet.

Rilke through the course of his life sensed himself a kind of laborer in beginnings, in unending preparations for work still to come. This attitude was an essential part of his openness and receptivity; it colored his life and work with a certain tentativeness. And yet, it also brought with it a thirst for great precision. Heinrich Petzet, in his introduction to the *Letters on Cezanne*, writes about Rilke's concern for "the smallest units of language" by which entire areas of experience could be illuminated. Rilke scoured the moment—the very point at which something caught his attention—for every detail and nuance, for every psychological, historical or aesthetic implication. One finds, despite its metaphysical vastness, little dreaminess or vagueness to Rilke's work. Its much criticized "incompleteness" may be, all things considered, less the product of the work than testimony that the human psyche itself, which the poetry so completely investigates, operates by virtue of an active incompleteness. This incompleteness (an inadequate word) is, in Rilke, the very basis for exchange and dialogue, for change and growth. And, in a very powerful sense, Cezanne does not give to Rilke something which might complete the poet. The painter's life and work are instead a kind of pressure: to contemplate the radical nature of Cezanne's work, to view the paintings, is to put oneself "in danger." This is the supreme value one artist has for another.

Rilke's work, the poems and prose, the entire corpus of his letters, are best seen as way-stations toward some unfinished and unfinishable project. The all-pervasive sense of incompleteness is a tidal swell on which the texts float, which at times bouys them up, at times pulls them under. For Rilke, the poem records at best only a momentary feeling of completeness, a simultaneous if fleeting instant when the work of art and the life are mutually realized. For that moment, a kind of totality is achieved, but it always seems to point forward to an ideal goal or condition. The poem never acquires the status of a thing, nor does it degenerate into an ornament and thereby become a bourgeois object in the usual sense. For Rilke, the artist's function is to catch this moment of being/non-being. One of his best-known poems of the period, "The Panther," is nearly a textbook example of this moment. In it, the poet and the object of the poem seem so completely interanimated that "An image enters/ and pierces the long restrained limbs/ and stops being within the heart" (*TRMR* 158). The aim of the poem can hardly be to paint a picture of the panther. Rather, the ambiguity of the passage, especially the way "being" can be read as both verb and noun, recreates the dissolution of the border between the poet and the object of his attention. Rilke calls such a work a "thing-poem," but the poem deconstructs even as it constructs. The poetics here are indirectly related to those of the imagist and objectivist poetry of American and English poets who came later.

Rilke believed himself able at last *to see* Cezanne's paintings because, as he put it, "I had just reached it [the turning point] in my own work or had at least come close to it somehow, after having been ready for a long time, for the one thing which so much depends upon" (*LOC* 164). What caught Rilke up was that he could sense in Cezanne things he most earnestly desired to do himself. There was first, as Petzet's introduction relates, a desire to resolve an "inner war" against representation, against the all too sentimental and easy stylization of the visible which had become the artistic coin of the day. What Rilke admired in the painter was the difficulties he had set for himself. "Cezanne," Rilke noted, "had to start over again, from the bottom" (*LOC* 43).

Still, Rilke could not envision poetic form without closure. For Rilke, the act of closure has a formal structure: it is that which signals the death of an older form as the very ground of new creation. (One finds a similar parallel concerning closure in Bakhtin's notions of "the limits of utterance," limits which are deeply connected to semantic interaction, communal awareness and the dictates of genre.) Rilke could not conceive of any break in artistic tradition which did not somehow value that which it had broken from. Tradition, writ large, was not to be abolished but conserved, particularly at the very moment when its latest instancing was about to be surpassed. Thus, form and closure are nearly always spoken of in Rilke, through the metaphor of death. And yet the poem, like the death of an actual person or thing, always leaves a residue of memories and of its marks upon the earth. The new form is best viewed as a kind of resurrection, a rebirth of the old but secreted within the new.

Rilke, as one of the important letters show, mused on the fact that Cezanne's favorite poem was Baudelaire's "La Charogne" ("Carrion"), where dead flesh is made beautiful, not in the conventional sense, but in Baudelaire's ability to raise carrion out of the conventional formats and value structures which had left its beauty unarticulated. If, in Cezanne, painting allows that which was formerly unseen to be seen, "La Charogne" allows that which was formerly inarticulate to be heard.

The completion of the poem is the moment of truth because it is the point where the poet surrenders mind, ego, world-view, to the necessities of the perception. At this point, he is no longer a maker but an element in the equation of the poem. The perception, the poem-work, like the countryside around Cezanne's house or the face before the painter, is an otherness which imposes its demand. Closure recognizes the other as other by carrying the art work to it but never fully arriving there. Someone writes a poem about the moon but the moon is still in the sky when the act of poetic "defamiliarization" ends, and she will have to take up the moon again. Thus, for Rilke, learning from Cezanne, poetic "defamiliarization" was not in itself sufficient to create great art. What would be necessary—instead of novelty erasing novelty—would be "the wrestling with, rather than abolishing, of memory."

Modern and contemporary poetry's concern for "the new" has perhaps obscured the revolutionary nature of the challenge Cezanne posed to Rilke. In these letters, the "wrestling" between memory and the present is no simple thing, for it does not take place at the level of convention or morality but at the much deeper level of the nature of psycho-physical reality. And yet, because of that depth, it cannot help but irradiate the social and cultural realms as well. Let me try to explain this challenge by referring to one of the most evocative works ever written about the painter, Merleau-Ponty's magnificent essay, "Cezanne's Doubt" (*MP* 9–25). Merleau-Ponty writes that "Cezanne makes a basic distinction not between 'the senses' and 'the understanding' but rather between the spontaneous organization of the things we perceive and the *human* organization of Ideas and Sciences." (my emphasis) Cezanne, as Merleau-Ponty views him, prompts in the viewer a way of perceiving and being that are initially alien to him. The paintings thrust the viewer, as they did Rilke, into the *terra incognita* of artistic creation where biases, ideologies and methodologies lose their hold. Echoing Rilke's comment about having to "start over," Merleau-Ponty tells us that "Cezanne's difficulties are those of the first word." They are difficulties, however, precisely because they must come to terms with memory, particularly that aspect of memory exemplified by tradition.

For Rilke—and this is the heart of the transmittal from Cezanne— "reality" is a habit of the mind, a "tradition" deeper than all the other traditions, neither true nor false, but an anchor by which one holds fast against the new or the troubling. A break with the "real" can never be merely a matter of technique or even philosophical stance, since the stance itself is already a form of conceptualization. Technique and stance by themselves are but aspects of the rigor mortis we name reality. What Cezanne could teach Rilke, in Merleau-Ponty's words, was the example of one who "abandons himself to the chaos of sensations," not that sensations themselves are more 'real' but that by the central act of abandonment one also drives a wedge into one's own propensities for methodologies and the seeking after pre-determined effects. In this regard, the Cezanne letters articulate a kind of Dantean passage from confusion to knowledge.

For Rilke, Cezanne was a way of crossing Limbo, a way of preparing himself for the late work of the *Sonnets to Orpheus* and of completing the *Elegies* already begun in this period. Cezanne's work is, among other things, a personal quarrel with the Enlightenment tendencies of crafts-manship, with the Old Masters who, he wrote, "replaced reality by imag-ination and by the abstraction which accompanies it." It was necessary to return to the real, but not as to an object which would then be put back into the work where it would lose its potency (as a controlled act of representation, for example). The 'real' would have to exist *en face* before the artist and the artwork, where, as Rilke noted of Cezanne's blues, they would no longer have any "secondary significance." Craftsmanship here is redirected away from producing effects or knowingly manipu-lating the viewer or reader of the poem and towards making possible and articulating discoveries.

Still, as Rilke remarks, "memory must be wrestled with," not merely abolished. What Cezanne gives to Rilke is a way to use the past. Rilke's letters speak of our usual relationship to the past as one of comfort, of sentimentality and nostalgia; our identity, our sense of the world is all part and parcel with the 'real.' His metaphors and personifications of the past all carry with them the warmth of familiarity. Struggling with his own bourgeois heritage, Rilke, in the Cezanne letters, attempts to see into the past with the same clarity he would bring to the present. The problems are co-terminous. The past is a "palace" rich in decor and memories. Yet, he remarks in a memorable passage, "even someone who had such palaces to utter would have to approach them innocently and in poverty, and not as someone who could be seduced by them." Elsewhere he writes that one must reject "the interpretative bias even of vague emotional memories, prejudices and predilections transmitted as part of one's heritage, taking instead whatever strength, admiration or desire emerges with them and applying it, nameless and new, to one's own tasks. One has to be poor unto the tenth generation" (*LOC* 73).

The hold the past has on Rilke is likened to an old "*grand mère*" whom one visits partly out of duty and partly out of genuine affection. The decisive moment for him, half-real and half imagined, comes as he wanders past some noble houses on his way to the Salon. A servant at one of them, about to close the gate, turns and gazes at Rilke "carefully and thoughtfully." Rilke meditates "at the same moment it seemed to me that it would have taken only a very slight shift in the pattern of things at some time in order for him to recognize me and step back and hold open the door." Within dwells the "*grand mère*" who would receive him, and there, walking about such a house with its beautiful furnishings, Rilke would "feel the presence of all the interrelated things: the gaze of portraits, the dials of musical clocks and the contents of mirrors in which the clear essence of twilight is preserved" (*LOC* 25–27).

The image is marvelous for both its richness and ability to signify the poet's relationship to the past, that "clear essence of twilight" which has had such a nostalgic hold on him. The grand' mère, "the old lady in violet and white," is described in enigmatic terms, very much as Pater described the Mona Lisa, in that she can barely be pictured in the mind's eye "from one time to the next because she is made up of so many things . . . " This old woman has great but unbending dignity, and he wonders what he could tell her of the exhibit he is going to see. One thing is clear: "Cezanne is no longer possible for the old lady" (*LOC* 27). The passage is full of claustrophobia and secreted ambivalences, for in it the poet is striving to break into open ground, to acknowledge, as Merleau-Ponty says of Cezanne, that "the meaning of what the artist is going to say *does not exist* anywhere" (*MP* 19).

Rilke found himself in deep affinity with Cezanne precisely on the above point. An art which could dispel the "essence of twilight" would be an art of perceptual faith, of bringing to the fore not conception but the act of attention. Thus Rilke was delighted when the painter Matilde Vollmoeller, accompanying him to the Cezanne exhibit, remarked that Cezanne was "like a dog, he sat there in front of it [the thing to be painted] and simply looked, without any nervousness or irrelevant speculations" (*LOC* 46).

Cezanne moved Rilke in a way the Impressionists could not. He saw in Impressionist work a struggle to convince the viewer of how much "they loved" what they painted. Their paintings, he wrote, "*judged* instead of *saying*." Cezanne had shown him how to move beyond such considerations, even "beyond love," to what the thing itself revealed.

Cezanne's work was the painterly form of the "thing-poem," and the ambiguities it gave rise to—the kind Rilke felt were essential to his own poetry—were psychological and ethical: to return the world to the possibility of a not-as-yet conditioned response. On this level, Cezanne and Rilke seem involved in rescuing the world from the mechanistic scientism of their day. To rescue an object in art does not mean to give it scientific or objective status, but to break it free of its role as part of some prescribed conceptual scheme. A like moment can be discerned in contemporary poetics, in, for example, that of the Objectivist poets, whose aim was never to make the poem scientifically "objective," but to free the poem from the claims of scientism and so re-animate it by refusing the reductions which science and philosophy would impose on our perceptions of the world. Such a search for freedom in the act of poetic composition necessarily began with the break from Imagism and its strategies, which were, by the time of Zukofsky, a literary version of scientistic principles.

Rilke sought to keep the question of existence open. The ambiguous flavor which steeps his work is in no way the result of some procedural indeterminacy. Rather, what he learned from Cezanne was that there was a way of attending to the world which can apply pressure and so expose to the looker the bias and ideology with which his or her gaze is infected. Rilke could then go beyond the simple-minded poetry of rendering or representation toward a poetry in which precision and uncertainty were inextricably united. It was this unity which for Rilke demonstrated that consciousness is never co-terminous with either world or language. Not only other's words but silences surrounded the poetic act; therefore, he sensed that being a poet only incidentally involved the production of texts. Much deeper was a "devotion" to perception which "without ever boasting of it, approaches everything, unaccompanied, inconspicuous, wordless." (*LOC* 68) Without this devotion, he noted, everything said or written was only "hearsay." In some regards, his work stands, not with, but against many of the 'experiments' of the twentieth-century modernists, and by implication, against many tendencies in the Anglo-American line of Pound and Lewis, and even Eliot. The great danger in reading Rilke is that the uncertainty will be taken as vagueness, sentimentality or existential ennui. The letters on Cezanne show us how ill-founded is that charge. But they are also about less understood matters: utterance and voice. Rilke sought a nearly impossible goal, but a noble and liberating one. As he put it after studying Cezanne: "One has to be able at every moment to place one's hand on the earth like the first human being."

(1992)

Part II

Notes on Stevens

My thesis is quite simple, that the lyrical voice of a poet [the Stevensesque poet] arises or is occasioned by the breakdown, for that poet, of the philosophical web or system or series of understandings in which that poet lives. That a poet is pushed toward the lyrical when he (or she) discovers that he is hemmed in by authority, by discourse or rhetoric, in short, by the 'philosophical' as it hardens into concept or rule or "truth." Further, that when we speak, even if only glibly, about a poet preserving "the mysteries," what I think we are pointing to is not some hidden obscurity or secret but that the poet has made a vow to unboundedness, to resisting any sort of limit, either one proposed by tradition or theory. Another way of saying this is that the poet's pledge is to the "mysteriousness" of that which remains to be articulated. To giving meaning and to respecting non-meaning as the ultimate events of language.

Now unboundedness, in the sense I claim here, is not an idea, but a recognition of the continual, generative power of the creative mind, what Armand Schwerner, in his brilliant study of Stevens, refers to as the poet's attention to "the movemented shuttlings of the world" which open up possibility rather than "add another limiting attitude to those which constrict the possible grandeur of the imagination." Poetry's uncertain or outsider status lies in its refusal of any "limiting attitude," hence every officialdom's continual ambivalence toward poetry, exemplified early and most clearly in Plato's quarrel with the rhapsodes, a subject I will touch on again in this talk.

Now for a poet, the imagination is first a matter of words, of language. An article of faith to the poet's calling, as when Stevens's insists that "in poetry, you must love the words, the ideas and the

[63]

images and rhythms with all your capacity to love anything at all"
(*OP* 188). He reminds us of language's creative power, in the *Adagio* where
he writes that "a new meaning is the equivalent of a new word" (*OP* 186).
That poetry has the same inherent dignity and thingness as any natural
object in the cosmos. He proclaims this dignity, not as supposition but
as fact, throughout the entire body of his work, as in these wonderful
late lines from "An Ordinary Evening In New Haven:"

> The poem is the cry of its occasion,
> Part of the res itself, not about it.
> The poet speaks the poem as it is,
>
> Not as it was: part of the reverberation
> Of a windy night as it is, when the marble statues
> Are like newspapers blown by the wind. He speaks
>
> By sight and insight as they are . . .
> . . . said words of the world are the life of the world

> (*S* 221)

For Stevens, then, the life of words and the life of the world are
compact, if not in unity, at least, as he puts it elsewhere, in "equilibrum." The poem is not 'about' a world but rather an instancing, "a res,"
of it. Thus, for Stevens, it is in the nature of this compact, that what
appeared to be merely the descriptive function of language (a function
closely allied to philosophy's instructive bent) is alchemically transformed in the imagination so that the poem itself, the lyric which has
broken the bounds of previous thought, is no longer philosophy's hand-
maiden but takes its place in the world, possibly as the object of philosophy itself.

"*Said words.*" Stevens thought stands almost diametrically in opposition to much post-structural theorizing about language and literature.
For him, the act of the poem is intensely personal; poetry, as discussed
in his aphorisms or as conveyed in the work itself, is mediated through
a litany of personally charged words like "self," "perception," "personality," the "character of the imagination." "The subjects of one's poems,"
he writes, "are the symbols of one's self or of one of one's selves"
(*OP* 191). And yet, he can also assert that "poetry is not a personal
matter" (*OP* 191), that it is always about the relationship between the
poet and the world. How escape from the charge of being solipsistic? Let
me digress a moment.

Allen Grossman, in his remarkable study, *Summa Lyrica*, insists that "lyric begins with the founding of linguistic man, with the "I," that "lyric . . . is the artistic form generated by the conditions and consequences of I-saying." This is an idea he takes from Emile Benveniste's well-known maxim: "Language is so organized that it permits each speaker to appropriate to himself an entire language by designating himself as *I*." Benveniste's thought here is especially intriguing, in a time when the "I" has been under attack in a number of guises ranging from the Foucauldian "death of the author" to the critical abuse (some of it surely justified) heaped on the so-called lyric voice, to the end of subjectivity and the recent preference in art (and its attendants in the academy) for surface rather than depth or interiority. Intriguing, because Benveniste suggests the positing of an "I" not as the ego-centered and ego-driven cypher of post-structuralist thought but rather as the figure of capaciousness, one who, because of language's ever-present availabilities, can see, via his or her own receptivity, through and around the imprisoning engines of totalitarian and utopian thought. It is this redefined "I"—neither ego nor "objective" eye— which is at the base of Stevens's poetics. Listen for instance, to these lines from "Description without Place," as they suggest to us that it is the enabling power of language which itself creates the "I" (or self:

> . . . the theory of description matters most.
> It is the theory of the word for those
>
> For whom the word is the making of the world,
> The buzzing world and lisping ferment.
>
> It is a world of words to the end of it,
> In which nothing solid is its solid self.
> As, men make themselves their speech: the hard hidalgo
> Lives in the mountainous character of his speech.

(CP 345)

Like Grossman's formulation, where the office of the poet is, of course, to be seated as "linguistic man (or woman)," to make "lyric . . . generated by the consequences and conditions of "I-saying," Steven's poet is the one "for whom the word is the making of the world," "the hard hidalgo," who makes one's self in the act of making one's speech.

For Stevens, to say that "a word is the making of the world" is to suggest that, already, our "I-saying" is entangled, beyond solipsism, with the real. In "The Supreme Fiction," the pre-existence of a world, of fact—he writes earlier in the poem, that "the clouds preceded us—becomes the condition of poetic making. Evolutionary forces, tradition, an almost Darwinian basis to poetry and the imagination, are the poet's belatednesses, his givens, before the act of the poem:

> There was a muddy centre before we breathed.
> There was a myth before the myth began,
> Venerable and articulate and complete.
>
> From this the poem springs: that we live in a place
> That is not our own, and, much more, not ourselves
> And hard it is in spite of blazoned days.
>
> We are the mimics. Clouds are pedagogues.
> The air is not a mirror but bare board,
> Coulisse bright-dark, tragic chiaroscuro
>
> And comic color of the rose, in which
> Abysmal instruments make sounds like pips
> Of the sweeping meanings that we add to them.

(S 161, 162)

Idealism, (philosophy's first fruit) as we have it from the Greeks, proposes a world of perfected forms, forms that with adequate training in the Academy of the Good will be revealed to us. Though it may not be immediately apparent, the poem, in its envisioning of life as both tragic and comic, is both a direct assault on and a plaint for a lost philosophic idealism. In its juxtaposition of "pips" of sound and "sweeping meanings," it almost seems to enact the Platonic parable of the cave where mankind sees only shadows, "pips" if you will, of what is Real and Good, the "sweeping meanings."

And yet, Stevens, resists the platonic turn; writes in *Adagio* that "the ideal is the actual becoming anemiac" (OP 190). Elsewhere, in *The Necessary Angel*, he tells us that the "the imagination loses vitality when it ceases to adhere to what is real." And so, the "I-sayer," the poet, if we are to believe Stevens, is caught on the reality of the imperfect and contingent, on the "tragic chiaroscuro" of a "place that is not our own." The world exists as material for the imagination to remind the poet of fluxual existence, where clouds are not so much "clouds" as pedagogues pointing almost always to the constant inadequacy of the Good. The very condition of our speaking, our "I-saying," is our birth (and our death) into external phenomena and our need to continue in our mimicry of it.

So yes, Stevens would have us infer that the contingent is always at war with the ideal, and, yes, Plato's banishment of the poets is not so much a moment in the history of ideas as it is, indeed, the constant parable of the relationship between the lyrical and the philosophical.

2.

In our time, the keeper of this parable, its oracle and progenitor, has been Stevens. For him, the poet's job is to deconstruct the philosophical and the conceptual, to bring us back to, as he calls it, "primary noon," that moment or place where the mind starts up afresh, where thought's shadow is momentarily abolished. Not in naivete but in full knowledge of how thought itself has overlaid the world. "Begin, ephebe [young man, learner]," he writes in "Notes Toward A Supreme Fiction,"

> by perceiving the idea of this invention . . . .
>
> You must become an ignorant man again
> and see the sun again with an ignorant eye
> and see it clearly in the idea of it.
>
> (S 157)

Here, in the two primary tercets of "Notes . . . ", Stevens has unified the disparate ambitions of poetic willing to not only turn toward the world with the ignorant eye of the child, to recover it in the old discredited idea of the lyrical imagination as "childlike" and innocent, but to see as well how much this turn of the eye is itself an "idea." Innocence is lost or displaced in Stevens's thinking not to a weary jaded maturity, but to the far more pervasive effect—perhaps it is the same thing—of its trans-formation from desire into concept.

Such a trope is perhaps the central one of many of Stevens's "horde of destructions," as he called them in his essay on poetry and painting, repeated as both idea and *poesis* in the poetry and prose. For what the lines achieve is a peculiar doubledness of innocence and knowledge; they remind us of poetry's inherent capaciousness and paradoxicality to contain a thought and its other, or, in Stevens's words, to find in the poem that "the true imagination," as he puts it in *The Necessary Angel*, "is the sum of our faculties" (61).

Now grandeur, or Steven's term "nobility," are themselves, if we think Platonically of such words, figures of unboundedness, denominatives that point our attention toward complex arrangements of language or world. Such words exist on, they may even be said to name, the border where meaning and non-meaning meet.

Awe or terror, as we know, most often induces silence. Stevens remarks in *The Necessary Angel* "that to confront fact in its total bleakness is for any poet a completely baffling experience." And yet, it is that very confrontation, the willingness of the poet to lean into it with all his power, which comprises poetry's sublime beauty. Here, for Stevens, is poetry's function writ large: "the need," he writes in *The Necessary Angel*, "which it [poetry] meets and which has to be met in some way in every age that is not decadent or barbarous, is precisely this contact with reality as it impinges upon us from outside, the sense that we can touch and feel a solid reality which does not wholly dissolve itself into the conceptions of our own minds" (*NA*, 96).

Here, as I will claim of Stevens's poetry, words like "grandeur" are precise and accurate. They respect, as with Stevens's poems, where language's power lies and where it doesn't, and what precisely constitutes language's deliverance. Take, for instance, this passage from "Credences of Summer:"

Postpone the anatomy of summer, as
The physical pine, the metaphysical pine.
Let's see the very thing and nothing else.
Let's see it with the hottest fire of sight.
Burn everything not part of it to ash.

Trace the gold sun about the whitened sky
Without evasion by a single metaphor.
Look at it in its essential barrenness
And say this, this is the centre that I seek.

(*S* 148)

Unboundedness, delivering the poet to the "centre" that he seeks, poses itself as a kind of *via negativa*, a use of words uttered in the spirit of difference i.e. getting or seeing beyond to a place which does not "wholly dissolve itself into the conceptions of our own minds." That is, beyond the "physical" or "metaphysical pine" of the conceptual mind, a visionary burning away until reality comes back as something beyond our conceptions, something solid—but not its "solid self," for that would be to mistake an exquisite fiction for a non-fiction.

The "evasion of metaphor" is a life and death issue for Stevens. "Metaphor," as he writes in the poem "The Motive For Metaphor" (*S* 123), one of his most ambivalent utterances on poetic making, is a "shrinking from/The weight of primary noon,/ The A B C of being . . . steel against

intimation—the sharp flash/ the vital, arrogant, fatal dominant X"
(*S* 123).

To the extent that poetry represents that language activity least
governed by *a prioris* or logical strictures or by ironclad fealty to its own
traditions, it represents the imagination's most capacious gate. In the
"fiction making" of belief, as he calls it in "Asides on the Oboe," the poet
is "the philosopher's man [who] alone still walks in dew." Here, the
poetic function precedes the philosophic because its freshness, the
poet's walking in dew, is a constant originary possibility unlike philosophy's dependence on systemization, precedent, logic or rule. Truths in
this instance are alchemical presences, "figures of the imagination," as
Stevens calls them. And so the texture of the coinage, "philosopher's
man," is suggestive first of all, then, of the poet as advance "man" or
even the philosopher's butler, if you will, who in his imaginative act is
philosophy's first cause. Which is why Stevens refers to him further on
in the poem as "the impossible possible philosopher's man, the man
who has had the time to think enough./ The central man, the human
globe, responsive/ as a mirror with a voice, the man of glass/ Who in a
million diamonds sums us up" (*S* 121).

Stevens's achievement has as its dynamic a yoking of thought and
world, a "precise equilibrum" between reality and the imagination. And
it may well be that he inaugurates (to use Jacques Derrida's term) a
mode of writing which already sees the fictive nature of the philosophical, which takes this fiction for granted, which loves the *jouissance* of
rubbing one philosophical idea against another, and is unrelentingly
skeptical of philosophy's urge toward certainties. He writes in *Adagio*
"The final belief is to believe in a fiction, which you know to be a fiction,
there being nothing else (my italics). The exquisite truth is to know that it
is a fiction and that you believe in it willingly" (*OP* 189).

It is in this "exquisite" truth/fiction that Stevens makes the relationship of language to the philosophical immediately critical and parodistic. His poem "Connoisseur of Chaos," for example, begins with its
initial mockery of the syllogism, "A. A violent order is disorder; and/B. A
great disorder is an order. These/Two things are one. (Pages of illustrations.)" (*S* 111). But the poem is also a critique, directed at the mind's
pressure toward totality, a rather more serious matter than mere sati-
rization. This is something one hears in the poem's crisp sonorities:
"opposite things partake of one,/At least that was the theory when
Bishops' books/resolved the word. We cannot go back to that" (*S* 111).

Admittedly, Stevens, in his dramatic and potentially inimical encounter with the agency of philosophy, often indulges in a kind of shaking hands with buffoonery. On this basis, Stevens is the playful Socratic figure of the poem, a comedic parser—and debunker—of our thought systems. So much of Stevens, the *con brio* of his diction, the bright, clean spaciousness of the lines, which make them look like the most highminded sky writing, this efflorescence, this overly strong sunlight, often hides the near ground and the close facticity of the poetry's deeper notes, the "intelligence of his despair," as he calls it in "Esthetique Du Mal."

But we need to go only one more moment with the image of mocking Socrates, to see that Stevens's poetry throughout is, as in the *Apology* and *Crito*, also a re-annunciation of the figures of fate and tragedy. The sail of the vessel marking death is almost always on the horizon of its words. That is, foreshadowings of meaninglessness or dying have entered Stevens's lyric/dialectic from the first, as in Peter Quince's *arpeggios* where "in the muted night," Susannah "turned" to her dying or as in the "nothing"-ness of "The Snow Man." One could, indeed, "give pages of illustrations." Again, one thinks of Stevens's "fatal dominant X." In other words, the phenomenology of Stevens's poetics, the good humored yet serious nature of the verbal play at the edge of thought, a dance on the rim of the logical abyss, is tinctured with mortality.

The eternity of philosophy, which must speak as though written by God, is continually undercut by poetry's awareness of temporality and the contingent. Fate, the truism goes, makes one 'philosophical,' but the deeper tonalities of Stevens, particularly in the late poetry, do not constitute the hold of a philosophy on his poetics. Rather these tones are already a more profound reach beyond the philosophical as I've defined it here into lyricism. For ultimately what strikes me as wedding all of Stevens's work into a unity is less a matter of stylistics or even its occasional romantic pre-occupations with death and non-meaning; rather, it is precisely the poem's engagement with the problematic which I have been addressing in this paper all along: that the poetry is occasioned by a breakdown, in the margins so to speak, of the means of philosophy. This is not the usual talk about the breakdowns of language, for Stevens's imagination has been, first to last, a transmigratory shuttle between the failed logic of the meditative mode and the uncaptureable reality of common nouns such as "sky" and "moon" and "shadow."

For Stevens, as he puts it in "The Figure of the Youth as Virile Poet" in *The Necessary Angel*, the poet "must get rid of the hieratic in everything that concerns him," that is, the tendency of the machinery of philosophy to establish and impose hierarchies and subordinations. "He must move constantly," Stevens continues "in the direction of the credible. He must create his unreal out of what is real" (58).

What is axiological, what is generative of further and more complex poetry in Stevens comes to us as the disguise and the undoing of the disguise of the philosophical. Thus, he writes of the poet in the poem "Men Made Out of Words" as one whose fate is cast in "propositions torn by dreams," by "incantations" which 'go public' by the way of language and so are necessarily—as poetry *cannot not be*—"eccentric." In "An Ordinary Evening in New Haven", he names this forever interruptive eccentricity: "Desire, set deep in the eye, behind all actual seeing." We keep "coming back and coming back to the real," the poem insists, to find in it all that is strangely liberating by the act of the poem: "the coming on of feasts and the habits of saints/ the pattern of the heavens and high, night air" (*S* 219). Again, I find in this poetic geometry, an admittance of incommensurable worlds, as in this last section of "An Ordinary Evening in New Haven":

> The least legible of sounds, the little reds
> Not often realized, the lighter words
> In the heavy drum of speech . . .
>
> Flickings from finikin to fine finikin
> And the general fidget from busts of Constantine
> To photographs of the late president, Mr. Blank,
>
> These are the edgings and inchings of final form,
> The swarming activities of the formulae
> Of statement, directly and indirectly getting at,
>
> Like an evening evoking the spectrum of violet,
> A philosopher practicing scales on his piano,
> A woman writing a note and tearing it up.
>
> It is not in the premise that reality
> Is solid. It may be a shade that traverses
> A dust, a force that traverses a shade.
>
> (*S* 228)

"Poetry," Stevens has been warning us so often and in so many ways, "must resist the intelligence almost successfully." We must pay attention to its finikins as opposed to its premises. The armatures of philosophy, the stepladders of tradition (like Wittgenstein's ladder of thought) have no other purpose, Stevens seems to say, than to enable us to climb above them, to break free. It is not surprising then, that we find in Stevens's late poem, "The Sail of Ulysses," these lines which, as they run down the page, are entangled in the characteristics of both the philosophical and the lyric:

> . . . We come
> to knowledge when we come to life.
> Yet always there is another life,
> A life beyond this present knowing,
> A life lighter than this present splendor,
> Brighter, perfected and distant away,
> Not to be reached but to be known,
> Not an attainment of the will
> But something illogically received,
> A divination, a letting down
>
> From loftiness, misgivings dazzlingly
> resolved in dazzling discovery.
> There is no map of Paradise.
>
> (*OP* 128)

Entangled, but finally released, for isn't the freedom sought here one that is "known" rather than "reached," "illogically received" rather than calculated, "dazzlingly resolved" in "misgivings"? Pound complained of having "no Aquinas map" but Stevens, with a kind of sweetness rarely found in Pound, only wants to throw the discursive or philosophical maps away. The only means to get out from under is poetry, glorious poetry, in the search for the mapless Paradise of mysteries.

I am reminded of Bakhtin and his notion of unfinishability, by way of his late essay exploring the nature of the 'dialogic', "The Problem of the Text." There, he reminds us that authorship is, in some way the violation of the planes of discourse, and that such a transformation "always makes a departure beyond the boundaries of linguistics" (*SG* 119). "The *given* and the *created* in a speech utterance," he reflects, "always create something that never existed before, something absolutely new and unrepeatable, and, moreover, it always has some relation to value (the true, the good, the beautiful and so forth)" (*SG*, 119–120), Stevens was acutely aware of this "departure;" for him, it occurred because, as he writes above "there is always another life," one that is beyond the "premises," one that is mapless and suffused with desire. Lyric, the occasion for "I-saying" is here a gate, a means, an identity of an author and unbounded thought, thought which, as Stevens's poetry continually demonstrates, cannot contain us. Stevens's poetry is a celebration of this life in language. As he exclaims in the great summary stanzas of "Esthetique Du Mal," a poem deeply investigative of life's joy and pain:

> Speech found the ear, for all the evil sound,
> But the dark italics it could not propound.
> And out of what one sees and hears and out
> Of what one feels, who could have thought to make
> So many selves, so many sensuous worlds,
> As if the air, the mid-day air were swarming
> With the metaphysical changes that occur,
> Merely in living as and where we live.

(S 141)

(1998)

The True Epithalamium

> Our poetic task remains to compose the true epithalamium where chastity and lewdness, love and lust, the philosopher king and the monstrous clown dance together in all their human reality—*The Truth and Life of Myth*
>
> (*TLM* 38)

According to the myth which informs much of the material of Duncan's "A Poem Beginning with a Line from Pindar" (*OF* 62–69), Psyche's beauty was so great, she was so admired by men, that Venus found her own altars deserted and so set Cupid (Eros) on a mission to punish the youthful beauty, a mission which ends in his own enchantment and, ultimately, his marriage to Psyche. The issue of the marriage is a daughter named Pleasure. The proper issue of a marriage, the myth suggests, certainly one between those figures of the heart's work and the animated soul, ought to be pleasure. And, the question Duncan's poem both proposes and resolves is how might such a marriage be accomplished; in this, the poem is a true epithalamium, a true nuptial poem.

In the myth, marriage is accomplished after much overcoming of hazard and barrier; in this sense, the marriage is a victory, worthy of a poet's celebratory ode. So Duncan's poem is an "ode", and in this, Duncan is consummately Pindaric. For Pindar's odes, as we know, are mainly celebrations of victory, their form, as Duncan tells us by interpolating into his own poem bits of critical commentary on Pindar—a kind of mosaic or montage, making use of both history and mythology oddly enjambed into the praise. Duncan draws the opening lines of his poem from Pindar's "1st Pythian Ode," an ode which ostensibly celebrates Hieron's winning of a chariot race, but as Richmond Lattimore, one of Pindar's translators, notes, the poem is equally in praise of Hieron's founding of a city and the setting up of his son, Deinomenes, as its king.

~

In order to "read" an epithalamium we must read it as a discourse on love's ways, as a vanquishing of that which keeps lovers apart, and so its meaning is given only as we bring to it all that may bear on or be in conjunction with our senses of love. The epithalamium (and here it is like an ode) moves us beyond its occasion, rises above the trivial declaration of an event in time, only as it confronts our notions of the nature of love. Thus to read Duncan's poem as epithalamium is to read it as a disquisition on love, as an investigation of love's modalities.

In taking up the myth of Psyche and Cupid, one implicitly takes up the figure of Venus; for in the story—and this is part of the background to Duncan's poem—Psyche and Venus suggest contrasting forms of love. Venus, in myth, is characterized as the goddess who turns the human heart. When men worship Venus, they worship in the hopes of satisfying their love of beauty, their longing to possess such beauty in love and lust. Venus, in this sense, represents, and even honors, a kind of possessiveness.

As the myth goes, Venus's jealousy stems from her losing some admirers, from being *less loved*. Venus, as I have suggested, does not return love unless it is to the image of the lover she has made—that is, unless it is to some projection of her own mind; instead, she puts on the magic girdle which inspires others to love her. In the backdrop to Duncan's poem, Venus, though she never appears, may very well be—in this configuration—the embodiment of a "sin," the one Duncan refers to in *The Truth and Life of Myth*: "Now, I understand sin as Man's refusal of Love Itself, his refusal to love in his desire to have love." (28) This seems to characterize both the narrowness of Venus's own "loving", and the unattainability of Venus herself. With Psyche, as both myth and poem tell it, the discourse of love, as we shall see, is markedly different.

Duncan, in *The Truth and Life of Myth*, referring to the composition of "A Poem Beginning with a Line by Pindar," describes as follows the players of his poem: "He (Cupid) was the primal Eros, and she (Psyche), the First Soul." (He recalls the genesis of the poem as occurring when he was reading or overhearing in his own mind the lines of Pindar's. "My mind" he says "lost the hold of Pindar's sense and was faced with certain puns, so that the words *light, foot, hears, you, brightness, begins* moved in a world beyond my reading, these were no longer words alone but also powers in a theogony, having resonances in Hesiodic and Orphic cosmogonies where the foot that moves in the dance of the poem appears as the pulse of measures in first things. Immediately, sight of Goya's great canvas (*Cupid and Psyche*) . . . came to me . . . " (25) Sense is lost, replaced by punning not only of words, but of times, myths, poems and painting. Possibly the proper marriage of all these disparate elements is a pun, as with the story of Psyche and Cupid, where human and god are wedded to produce pleasure (and what comes from punning before all else but pleasure?).

What are the grounds then on which punning may take place? That is, when can words or states of mind or entities be punned? Certainly not in our busy utilitarian communication, in our rationalized psychologies and histories. But in literature, in poetry, an opportunity presents itself. The French critic Maurice Blanchot, in *The Gaze of Orpheus*, reminds us that "literary language is made of uneasiness," that by a curious inversion which literature alone accomplishes, the name of something within a poem is the very absence of that something from the real world.

The word or name no longer refers to that something *in reality* but to a new presence which could only occur by virtue of that "something's" absence. Literary language, if we follow this argument, is nothing, nothing but pun, not only internally within a work, as in a joke, but also with reference to the reality to which it is linked through the common orthography of the word.

Thus Pindar's words, as Duncan reads them, sanction not only Pindar's sense but the very power of poetry to bring all reality into pun. And so Psyche, the beautiful woman of the myth can be, is already—and automatically—punned with Duncan's view of her as "the First Soul" and with the conceptualized term "psyche" of the psychologist. Let us examine this little point a bit: in the myth, Psyche is a woman; in Duncan's statement, a figure of the imagination; in the contemporary textbook, a general term for mind or 'soul.' In the myth, Psyche is beautiful, gratuitiously so; in Duncan, she appears more like a principle or force; in the textbook, psyche is neither a beauty nor a principle but an instrumentality. We could reason so indefinitely. And, if we pursue this line of thought relentlessly, we in no way mistake the textbook psyche nor Duncan's forceful principle as a 'derivative' of the mythic Psyche; rather we see or encounter vastly different entities, and it is only by virtue of their being punned that these entities can be made to reflect or interact with each other. I am not suggesting here that one "definition" is better than the other. How could that be? For when I mention the word "psyche," each power or attribute denied to the word in a specific usage, be it seen from the partial perspective of reality, myth or psychology, is present. You see, the not-quite marriage of meanings here is a kind of punned coupling.

The myth is amazingly clear on this point. Psyche and Cupid, before they are actually wedded, make love in the dark. Psyche cannot call out her lover's name, for she does not know it. Yet the punning described above holds true within the myth, for although, early in the story, Psyche and Eros have their own, hence different, names, both for themselves and for any others who know them, they have the same name within their not-quite-marriage, *that of "lover"*. All they are for each other is lovers. But when Psyche brings a light to the bedchamber to discover that her former tormentor, Cupid, shares her bed, the hot wax from the lamp burns Cupid's shoulder. He is awakened and, in anger, rejects Psyche, telling her "Love cannot dwell on suspicion." What has joined the two, that they know each other in the pun of "lover" is destroyed for the moment—and the importance *is* that it is momentary—by the discovery that they are not "lovers" but Psyche and Cupid. It is this scene which Goya paints, a scene, we might say, that is only half the story, the opening scene of Duncan's poem.

If Psyche and Cupid, once revealed to each other and so no longer punned "lovers," are driven apart, how are they to be reconciled? For they are no longer in the dark, and the rhyme of their future wedding must be not as "lovers" punned but as Psyche and Cupid, whole individuals who must face, and in a sense, know each other. This is the burden of a true epithalamium, for in such a work, two individuals in all their fullness will be joined, will dance together. I say "dance" because the word has significant usage in Duncan's poem (a children's dance is conjured in the poem itself). In the dance, figures only momentarily fuse; to dance is to come together and to come apart, to join with another and yet to retain the capacity for separateness and singular identity. And here, the dance can be likened to the pun since both unite separate entities. The authentic nuptial poem must allow all of a human's actual being its dance, it must pun dissimilars without sacrifice of individuality—not because this is an ideal or an accident of association but because it is a truth. Psyche and Cupid confirm this in the myth. At the story's end, they are no longer furtive lovers, but open-eyed individuals in love's dance.

The story of the poem, then, is that of Psyche's way back to Cupid, to Eros. It is the story of Psyche's instruction writ large, for if human and god (Cupid is divine) can be punned in myth and poem, what cannot be punned in myth and poem? Or put another way, where else but in the poem can such a pun take place, where else but in a poem are all significations a kind of play, and new combinations and associations, even contradictions, made manifest?

~

So the poem begins, and Pindar's words invoke, not new sense, but the most ancient space of poetry. Pindar's words, the beginning of a victory ode, posit this ritual space, Apollo's lute overcoming even the thunderbolt of Zeus, and the Pindaric poem itself, though appearing to be a celebration of a chariot race, is actually in praise of the founding of a city. Indeed, Pindar's ode may be taken as disguised epithalamium, as peculiarly appropriate to Duncan's purposes, if we pun the notion of a city, the wedding of many with many to make a community, with the notion of a marriage where one and one also form a community.

Immediately following Pindar's lines, Duncan refers to the nature of the process he has undertaken. To enter "poetic" space is to take the "god-step at the margins of thought," the "quick adulterous tread at the heart." To enter the poem is to leave the reasonable, logical and secure world behind one, to walk the boundary, the "margin" of what one knows, "adulterous" because one is, in a sense, forsaking an original marriage or relation with comfortable understanding and sensible rationality. The old relationships with earth, with home, with sanity are temporarily being suspended; what makes this "adulterous" is that one is never out of relation with the safe and the sane (that is, one must constantly return to earth), but in the space of the poem one is, so to speak, "cheating" on this daily normality. There is also the sense that in the poem one is being infused, hence adulterated with new possibilities and imaginings.

This poetic space coincides with the space of Goya's painting, with the very space of myth itself. Here reality is only the materiality of imaginings, the canvas itself less a depiction than a prophecy:

> A bronze of yearning, a rose that burns
>   the tips of their bodies, lips,

ends of fingers, nipples. He is not wingd.
His thighs are flesh, are clouds
    lit by the sun in its going down,
hot luminescence at the loins of the visible.

                     (*OF* 62)

The scene is timeless and only vaguely referential to the "real" world, for the two lovers "are not in a landscape./They exist in an obscurity." Such a space—and this is the burden of Duncan's *The Truth and Life of Myth*—is not fanciful and imaginary in the pejorative sense, is not the sentimental and delightful space we think of when we think of the fairy tale. Rather, this is the space of Instruction, the space in which Psyche can begin to learn. Here, what the human, and even the god at times, flees or tries to avoid, the pain and suffering of life, are miraculously transformed into lessons. Psyche at this point, Duncan reminds us, "is ignorant of what Love will be," Cupid is violent with discovery, and yet, now, every difficulty is useable: "Jealousy, ignorance, the hurt . . . serve them." The space of the poem, of the pun, is transformative space; reality has lost its literal fixity, and—as with the Buddhist notion of *sunyata*—word, emotion, physical entity are seen as the projection of one's mind. Only in the poem do they attain this playful character and permit us to see them with irony and detachment. In such a space, to call once more on the Buddhists' understanding, pain and pleasure are revealed as ornaments which it is beautiful to wear, treasures from which one can learn.

The second section of the poem begins with the words "This is magic"; the realm for poetic activity is established and "Psyche is preserved." Here, every understanding and connection is true in the imagination. The spiritual company of poetry, the old and dead poets, with "their faltering,/ their unaltering wrongness that has style" are the guides through life and world. They are a force, a conservatory, "a plenitude of powers time stores."

And again, as in Pindar, the strummer of the lute, the poet, contrasts the timeless possibility of the poetic world with the literal, the rational and expedient as figured in political and economic life. When the politician, the pseudo-statesman determines reality, when "The Thundermakers descend," the language, and the intersubjective trust which language engenders is destroyed. For we regard the poet trustfully, in contrast to the dissembling office-seeker, as the one who stands by his or her word or vision. Thus when politics and political realism hold sway, the pun which co-exists between poem and world, made possible by the agency of poetic language, deteriorates. Language is eroded, and the marriage of an individual with his or her imagination, which depends not so much on shared understandings but on shared soundings of words, is threatened. The language itself decays or is obscured and destroyed in the very thunder or clamour of war and suffering: "injured" becomes "in-jerrd," the precise auditions of the tongue are jumbled and confused in one's hearing: "damaging a nuv. A nerb./ The present dented of the U/ nighted stayed" (*OF* 63).

Such a state of affairs is itself a violation of the politician's contract with his constituency. In the poem, this is given as an excoriation of our presidents:

> Hoover, Roosevelt, Truman, Eisenhower—
> where among these did the power reside
> that moves the heart? What flower of the nation
> bride-sweet broke to the whole rapture?
>
> (*OF* 63)

This litany of failed leadership going back to Lincoln's time only ends in Whitman's vision of loss over that fallen leader: "How sad 'amid lanes and through old woods'/ echoes Whitman's love for Lincoln."

Against the obfuscations, the heartless politics of violence and war, Duncan's poem poses poetic activity, the clear hearing of words in their various senses, the space of imagination, as a bridge between humans: "It is across great scars of wrong/I reach for the song of kindred men". For it is in this song that redemption can occur, that one can properly invoke, as Duncan does in the poem, Whitman's "The theme is creative and has vista." True loving statesmanly conduct, Whitman's "the president of regulation," would transform the reductive politics, and the so-called dialogue of political language into the productive and celebratory marriage of peoples and their leaders, again, into an epithalamium of creative possibilities.

∾

Still, although Psyche persists, she has not been reconciled with Cupid. In the myth, soon after Cupid has been exposed by the lamp and flees, Psyche sets off to find him. Let us consider this journey in the light of punning. The pun has "worked" to the point of Cupid's departure, so to speak, because Psyche has only known Cupid as a lover. In this, there was ratio and mutuality. Now the sight of Cupid means Cupid is no longer "lover" but "Cupid," and that Psyche is no longer "lover" but

"Psyche". The earlier pun has been destroyed, and since Psyche can no longer be just "lover" for Cupid, she must come back to him as Psyche. For the logic of a pun, like poetic logic, as Blanchot indicates, requires that the aspects of a word or name (in reality) be fully available so that their absence can result in the "presence" of the literary usage. To know completely is to be able to transcend; this is the function, as Heidegger points out, of limit and boundary, not so much to enable one to contain but to traverse. In other words, for Psyche to properly lose or absent herself in love, she must first know the totality of her "presence," *i.e.* herself. Powerful and authentic love comes not when we know the one we love (Pgymalion's projected image of a beautiful woman masked as another identity), since that is an impossibility, but when we know ourselves. This, the myth seems to counsel, is the paradoxical and contradictory nature of love, that it may not depend on the object of our love but on this *always onesideness*, which makes us capable of giving love in difficulty or without feedback. In the myth, irritating, barb-shooting Cupid is the instrument of Psyche's instruction. And it should be noted that the myth, and Duncan's poem, do not deliberate on the character of Cupid. Cupid is, for both myth and poet, what he was (as Eros) for Socrates and Rilke, an always troubled and troubling figure who creates love, who wanders between lovers. And yet one may infer that the character of Cupid is given so little exploration in both poem and myth because Cupid is the beloved, the one never to be fully known by a lover. To look at love in this way would be to reformulate Duncan's remark on "sin" in a positive manner: the acceptance of "Love Itself" is not so much in the acceptance of love as in the desire to love.

Psyche's journey in the poem is the journey to self-knowledge. The tasks given in the myth, the sorting of the seeds, the gathering of the golden fleece and the descent into the Underworld for Proserpina's box, are recast as figurations of the poet's tasks. As in the myth, the tasks are humanly impossible, but, for each one, some sort of "divine" intervention occurs. For in the poem, what rescues Psyche (as it rescues Ezra Pound in his briefly touched-on fate, the "man upon whom the sun has gone down") is the ancient order of poetry and imagination, the order which transforms all reality into myth and legend:

> The light that is Love
> rushes on toward passion. It verges upon dark.
> Roses and blood flood the clouds.
> Solitary first riders advance into legend.

This land, where I stand, was all legend . . .

(OF 66)

Here, the literal, masking as knowledge, "Scientia's lamp" which shines
on Cupid in the moment of exposure, is a debasement of true knowledge, is "the outrage/ that conquers legend". The poet must overcome
this outrage and restore legend. Psyche, in her discovery, knows Cupid
only in this debased form, a form which parallels impersonal "objective"
science, for she does not yet know herself. To know only in this way is
insufficient; love and marriage, the myth and the poem instruct, occur
only at the end of knowledge, at the end of the self's painful soul-work.
Psyche must learn "passion, dismay, longing, search/ flooding up
where/the Beloved is lost." And because the poem is itself a soul-way, a
path, the poet too can learn. Thus, the movement of the poem is a linking, a punned identity:

> . . . Psyche travels
> life after life, my life, station
>   after station,
> to be tried . . .

(OF 67)

Poet and mythic figure are drawn on toward self-knowledge and the goal
of love, love that is selfless and possibly self-destructive, the love of a
"Rilke torn by a rose thorn/ blackened toward Eros./Cupidinous Death!/
that will not take no for an answer." For this is the ultimate love,
Duncan's "Love Itself" which, like the space of ritual and myth, is a
space of great, open and unreasonable, unconditioned risk.

∾

The poem. The myth. The space of the pun. Psyche has been prepared,
the marriage bed of the imagination prepared, which is outside of Time,
beyond time and time-boundedness, for all is punned in this space, and
myth is as contemporary as science:

> Oh yes! Bless the footfall where
> step by step the boundary walker
> (in Maverick Road . . .
>
>   that foot informed

by the weight of all things
   that can be elusive
no more than a nearness to the mind
   of a single image . . .

         Oh yes! this
most dear
         the catalyst force that renders clear
the days of a life from the surrounding medium!

                                             (OF 67)

Walter Benjamin in his essay "On the Mimetic Faculty" points to the
psychic ground of this activity: "Man's gift of seeing resemblance is
nothing other than the rudiment of the powerful compulsion in former
times to become and behave like something else." In Duncan, this
"compulsion" is of the largest and most comprehensive order. As he
remarks in *The H. D. Book*, "We have begun to find our identity not in a
personality but in a concept of Man so that all the variety of persons
Man has been may be inhabitants of what we are as we impersonate
him."

   Thus the last section of Duncan's poem is itself a kind of participatory cosmos, "the catalyst force" in which past and present times, micro
and macro dimensions, notions of individuality and generality co-exist.
This cosmos is neither true nor untrue; rather, it is the field of possibility, the ever-creative and generative ground in which the imagination
can enter into the dance of all that is real, all that can be imagined.
Such a poem is the ultimate *persona* poem, not only because everything
in it can be embraced but also because *nothing in it* can be embraced. It
is as if neither the masker nor the mask can be determined as "real," as
if the mask looks back on its wearer, gazing at the beautiful fiction this
wearer has maintained as itself. And on another level, the poem not
only allows the pun to occur but is itself one term of a pun with the reality it names. That is, the reader in the thrall of the poem no longer looks
at the poem from the real world but looks lovingly at the real world
from within the poem. The poem, in its difference from other modes of
discourse and in its capacity to pose alternate or imagined worlds,
works through the reader so that poem and reader and reader's "reality" are, in a sense, one grand pun. And the reader is but one term of the
pun, seeking a coupling with the reality the poem drew him away from.
Is this not to allow the reader to share in Duncan's own intentions
which he sums up thus: "I don't want to master reality but to be its
lover"?

The dance then, because it is performed in the service of the creative, combinative, power of the mind, can imagine an alternative vision to the iron and blood of contemporary history:

> There the children turn the ring to the left.
> There the children turn the ring to the right.
>   Dancing . . . Dancing . . .
>
> And the lonely psyche goes up thru the boy to the king
>   that in the cave of history dreams.
> Round and round the children turn.
>   London Bridge that is a kindom falls.

> (OF 68)

"London Bridge", as in Eliot's "The Wasteland", is the metonym of the industrial, technocratic vision, the "Cupidinous Death" that wants, without interference, the object of love, the aggression and possessiveness of contemporary life. These are brought down by the dance, because in the dance, as in the poem (why, again, dance and poem are so alike), people and things come together and come apart and their individual identities are enjoyed but never possessed.

The final image of the poem is of the children dancing "In the dawn that is nowhere," for the vision of this possibility, like the poem, is achronistic, requiring not a specific historical context in which to occur, but a situation, like the poem or pun, in which reality and fantasy are allowed to co-exist, in which the dream-time of the tribal vision or the Buddhist understanding that "life *is like* an illusion" are what we equally mean by the real.

Thus for Duncan, "the old stories whisper once more," the sacred sites of art, history and religion, "Mount Segur, Mount Victoire, Mount Tamalpais . . . " are the way stations of Duncan's own quest commanding the poet to "*rise to adore the mystery of Love!*"

∾

The philosopher Herder maintained "that each Age has within itself the means to achieve its own happiness and fulfillment". Our "age" is marked, not only by the brooding vastness of its technocratization, but by the immensity of its unearthings, containing "within itself" the rediscovery of past lores and the technical ability to make all of man's imaginative record present and available. No other contemporary poet has more deeply or thoughtfully read this book of our Ages than

Duncan and seen, as he puts it, "the common property of man's myth (as) a resource of working materials, a grammar of rimes."

Like Pindar's odes, Duncan's poem itself is a "mosaic" of these old stories, a hodgepodge of times and places, real and imaginary, enfolded on each other, a tapestry or brocade, a dream-screen, in which threads appear and reappear, in which patterns overlay and obscure other patterns which will surface at another point. And here all correspondences, all puns, metaphors and identifications can be made, for this is the weave of the marriage-spread, the floor on which the dance occurs, upon which any coupling or pairing is permitted, and so all epithalamiums are "true."

(1984)

The Objectified Psyche: Marianne Moore
and Lorine Niedecker

In writing about Marianne Moore and Lorine Niedecker, I take a direction implicit in Wallace Stevens's comments in relation to the poetry of Marianne Moore, that "the function of poetry is precisely this contact with reality as it impinges upon us from outside, the sense that we can touch and feel a solid reality which does not wholly dissolve itself into the conceptions of our own minds" (*NA*, 96). This impingement, "this solid reality," is what I wish to suggest by the term "objectified psyche." That is, we come away from a poem with an experience of the solidity of the vision of the mind which composed it, because in some sense the unity of the poem expresses this solidity as an otherness, a 'not ourselves.' Moore, in writing about Emily Dickinson's work, referred to the poetry as a "notable secret." The poem was something known, that is, experienced, but yet unknowable.

If we concur that both Niedecker's and Moore's poems are important as poetry, Stevens's formulation—as precise and useful today as it was forty years ago—obtrudes radically into any attempt to reduce or define these poets to some ideological spectrum of activity. My method here will be to see what the "notable secret," the residue of their poetry, suggests. That is, rather than examine it from the point of view of social conceptions or conditions, some of which are "feminist," if you like, I will try to explore in what way the poetry presents itself as exemplary writing, as tutelary movement of consciousness. Therefore, I want to chart, in Niedecker and Moore, a movement from the various forms of their *poesis*, their poem-making, to an understanding of what is significant about their work in relation to twentieth century poetry. If, from that significance, certain ideological or political conclusions can be drawn, well and good, and I will try to briefly allude to them. My discussion, however, will focus on how the poets work, so to speak, on the value such work has in terms of contemporary writing and as instruction to the poets' self-definition. For, in this defining sense, both poets exemplify the openendedness in the self-contract of writing, in possibilities of self-making or unmaking, in the dialectical relation of a work to a life or circumstance. True, one aspect or term of the dialectical relation here can be described by many names, "gender" or "gender anxiety," or "writing against the patriarchy," etc. etc., but these terms are perhaps somewhat formulaic in trying to account for the particular poetic strategies *qua* poetry of these poets. If we are concerned with those strategies for "unravelling riddles," as Rachel Blau DuPlessis puts it in *The Pink Guitar: Writing As Feminist Practice*, the riddles of psychosocial or cultural entrapment surely, we are also concerned with how one transforms the givens or mythologies of a culture into instruction. Both of these poets point by their praxis through and beyond the analysis of culture to the unfinishable calculus of writing, which, in the end, is one of culture's hopes. Niedecker, who named this hope for herself as "reflectivism," and Moore's remark to Elizabeth Bishop that "a thing [a poem] should make one feel after reading it that one's life has been altered or added to" (*GOM* 337), propose the parameters I want to deal with here.

~

I begin with that sense of perceived austerity which marks the work of both poets, a feeling that each has imposed rigorous strictures on their poems and their poetics. In Moore's case, this sense of stricture, an often remarked upon 'scientific' feel to the work, has beeen seen as an explicit rejection of emotional sprawl. The poems exhibit, as Marilyn Brownstein suggests in her discussion of Moore in *The Gender Of Modernism*, a constant "tension between manners and their lack." Niedecker too, as evidenced in all her poetry and in her commentary in letters, appears to favor reticence over emotionalism.

Thus, one imagines a guiding notion of decorum, but if such exists either in Moore or Niedecker, it is by no means a conventional decorum. For both pursue a far more indecorous poetics, one which borrows or wrenches materials from their original contexts and employs oddly disjunctive syntax and modernist collaging of these materials. This

indecorousness constitutes something of a rebellious break, not only
with poetic tradition, but with the linear patternings of history and
with the inherited gestalts of imposed totality embedded in terms like
"tradition" and "influence."

Such irruptive gestures are especially radical in Moore whose textual
juxtapositions—more strange than Pound's in *The Cantos*—articulate
new meanings in the poetry, in those white spaces between elements of
language. Moore's poetic disposition, the quiddity of her aesthetic
concerns, is almost always toward the act of composition, toward the
way planes of meaning edge or rub against each other. And yet, in terms
of these poetics, Moore is keenly aware of the existing state of affairs
with respect to her role as woman as well as writer. Moore clearly understood this distinction sociologically as it applied to her in her refusal to
play culture's assigned role or rebel by acting out its antithesis. Writing,
for example, to Elizabeth Bishop about the double standards of her male
colleagues such as Williams and Cummings, she remarked "[they] feel
that they are avoiding a duty if they balk at anything like unprudish-
ness, but I say to them, 'I can't care about all things equally, I have a
major effect to produce, and the heroisms of abstinence are as great as
the heroisms of courage, and so are the rewards" (*GOM* 338). Earlier, in
the same letter to Bishop, she identifies her own heroic quest for a
poetry beyond other people's expectations, for a poetry in which
"significant values" are the result of, as she puts it, an "essential bald-
ness" either of statement or effect.

Niedecker's borrowings and textual importations, as various as
Moore's, appear to constitute a psychic pantheon of identifications. One
senses a longing on her part for the autonomy and freedom to pursue
questions of meaning possessed by the male figures (poet, scientist,
philosopher) she inscribes into her poems. At the same time,
Niedecker's technique of condensation, a paring away of what is not
contingent to the structure of the poem, engenders a radicality of its
own, one which is constantly searching for a metaphysical high ground
beyond the solipsistic longings of the self (or the self as victim). Thus, in
Niedecker as in Moore, the impulse to condense, to be rigorous, can be
likened to the scientist's quest for an efficient or necessary, if non-
personal, explanation. Niedecker's way of "planting her poems," as she
put it, "in deep silence" proposes a contemplative or distancing activity,
a form of isolation or separating out similar to the scientist's experimental set-up. For both poets, the discipline of limitedness not only
surrounds and heightens the poetic act, but becomes the working

dimension of being, a way not of inventing counter-roles against traditions but of outfoxing the need for either role or counter-role.

~

From almost the beginning of her career, two particular motions describe Moore's poetics. I want to locate these in a number of poems to indicate how the poetic process in Moore is a move toward 'objectifying' the psyche, of giving weight and materiality to a mode of relating to the world. The first of these, the more common of the two, I would call transposition, the act of recontextualizing or decontextualizing the materials which enter the poem. In effect, the poet, making a new composition, wrenches materials out of context or reforms them so that they may fit into the composition she is making. The new context alters their meaning as well. Like the German painter Durer, mentioned in one of her earliest poems, "The Steeple-Jack," who, emulating the sea's different guises according to the light and surroundings, "changed the pine green of the Tyrol to peacock/ blue and guinea gray" (*CMP* 5), Moore's poetics alter the 'color' and tone of what is transposed. Such a modality is already part of the Modernist arsenal, among which Moore finds herself at the beginning of her writing career. It is related to the culture's major assault on authority, on forms of hypotaxis. It embraces the paratactical mode of thinking and writing which constitutes one of the major thrusts of the Imagist movement and, to a degree, Gertrude Stein's ideas about composition or even the theory of relativity.

At the same time, as Jeredith Merrin has pointed out with respect to Moore's poem about the sea, "The Grave," (*MMW&P* 155) there is in Moore an ambivalence, an ongoing opposition and revisioning of both the romantic and modernist traditions, the male-dominated poetic legacy. Merrin discuss this in full, providing an interesting reading of the poem in terms of specific Romantic identification of woman with Nature, fear of engulfment by female energies or by woman's presumed merciless, if unchecked, volition. Here, I touch only on the symbolical working out of the conflict over tradition embedded in the poem. That is, I am reading the poem metaphorically as a cautionary tale of a poet's relation (woman poet's relation if you like) to a cumulative tradition resident in the master metaphor of the all-encompassing sea as grave to both humankind and history. The first few lines of the poem read:

Man looking into the sea,

taking the view from those who have as much right to it as
                    you have it yourself,

                                        (*CMP*, 49)

The announced struggle over a marine prospect (based on an actual incident when a man stood between Moore and her mother, blocking their
view of the sea) is also a struggle over modes of interpretation, in this
case, the making of tradition. Vantage point, with respect to landscape
or experience, determines articulation, and the battle over seeing is also
the battle over saying. Moore, who often treats the sea as beneficence
itself, makes it in this poem something like the great abyss of history
from which traditions arise, are threatened and overwhelmed and then
die. Moore ambivalently delineates this grave of poetic modalities:

the sea is a collector, quick to return a rapacious look.
There are others besides you who have worn that look—
whose expression is no longer a protest; the fish no longer
                                        investigate them
for their bones have not lasted:
men lower nets, unconscious of the fact that they are
                                        desecrating a grave ...

                                        (*CMP*, 49)

Moore makes note of the tug of war in the predatory moves one makes
toward tradition. To use or transcend the tradition, to seek with a "rapacious look" is also to be aware of tradition's capacity to subvert and
submerge, to co-opt. Anything less than this alertness, she warns, is to
mistake the sea "as if it were not that ocean in which dropped things are
bound to sink." As well, in the western Romantic tradition, this same sea
is also 'feminine.' In that sense, as the last line of the poem, with its
vision of things immersed in that sea, turning and twisting "neither
with volition nor consciousness," makes clear—particularly to the
woman writer—it is this tradition (perhaps all one has) which threatens
her with oblivion. Moore's poem, a text simultaneously inscribed inside
and outside the poetic legacy given to her, is meant to ironize her own
desire to both dwell in and escape from its confines.
      The other motion profoundly characteristic of Moore's work and her
thought is signalled in her poem "The Hero," Moore's re-visioning of
Emerson's essay "Heroism." Heroism is, of course, a particular kind of
self-denial, an abstaining from certain forms, in order that a self-tran-
scending goal may be achieved. The perspective of the hero *as hero* is
always toward that goal, away from creaturely comforts and habits,

away from the self's acquisitiveness. An almost egoless condition, as Moore writes it out, beyond wanting where "hope [is] not hope/until all ground for hope/has vanished" (*CMP*, 8, 9). The poetic task, as Moore envisions it, can be likened to the heroic act, a sheering away from subjectivity, from personal or even bodily needs, toward forms independent (in Eliot's sense) of personality. The gesture is toward form that is consonant with imagist and objectivist practice, in the sense that the work of art (the poem or whatever) achieves a self-sufficiency apart from the author:

> It is not what I eat that is
> my natural meat,
> says the hero. He is not out
> seeing a sight but the rock
> crystal thing to see—the startling El Greco
> brimming with inner light—that
> covets nothing that it has to let go.

> (*CMP*, 9)

Humility before the matter of the poem, the refusal of the self-regarding demonstration, are, in Moore, a functional poetics at odds with either her reputed shyness or humbleness.

This is made very clear, I think, in the violence of a poem such as "Those Various Scalpels," a poem which can be correlated with the project of both "The Steeple-Jack" and "The Hero" as meditations on the artist's role with respect to tradition, and as an expression of an ambivalence similar to that found in "At A Grave." The poem's first line, an appositive fused to the "Scalpels" of the title, reads: "those various sounds consistently indistinct," linking sound and scalpel, cutting tool and cutting word. Certainly, a feminist reading of this poem, with its couplings of scalpels and scimitars with near-baroque images of women throughout the poem, suggest a richly ambiguous reading of literary inheritance. That inheritance, as used by a woman, must indeed cut both ways. Are these images, the defining and imposed image-hoard the poet must work with

> . . . weapons or scalpels?
>   Whetted to brilliance

> by the hard majesty of that sophistication which is superior
>   to opportunity,

these things are rich instruments with which to experiment.
   But why dissect destiny with instruments
      more highly specialized than components of destiny itself.

(CMP, 52)

The irony of these last lines skillfully registers the subtle terrors attendant on an oppositional poetics such as Moore constructs. The heroics of
cutting through the culture's imprisoning images, ultimately requires,
as she wrote of H.D.'s work, that it be "life denuded of subterfuge . . . the
clean violence of truth . . . "

How, given Moore's collaging poetics, could "the clean violence of
truth" be realized? "The Jerboa," a more typical poem of Moore's in
some respects, shows the intimations of her strategy, of her *ars poetica*.
The poem is in two sections, one subtitled "Too Much," the other,
"Abundance." This contrast by itself is instructive, since it is usually
"enough" which is opposed to "too much.". Moore's "abundance" does
not signal a poetical *via povera* but instead indicates that a deft, aesthetic
objectivity might well produce greater richness of effect, a more pene-
trating look into, as she writes above, "the rock crystal thing to see."

The poem, though it overtly dwells on the desert jerboa (and this
focus is of the utmost importance), is a powerful demonstration of
Moore's modernist poetics, integrating her objectivist mode to the
collage or montage principle. In the poem, the "Too Much" section reca-
pitulates the Roman Empire's triumphs as a complex display of power,
cruelty and conquest. Images of luxuriousness and extravagance are
disturbingly yoked to the Roman *Imperium*, which "could/ build, and
understood/ making colossi and/ how to use slaves" (*CMP*, 10). Mastery of
nature (the Roman art most often displayed in the poem is crude imitation) is "a fantasy/ and verisimilitude that were/ right to those with,
everywhere,// power over the poor" (*CMP*, 12). Introduced at the end of
this section as ironic contrast to the pomp and cruelty of Rome, is the
jerboa, "a small desert rat,/ and not famous, that/ lives without water,
has happiness" (*CMP*, 13). A number of elements are at work in this
juxtaposition, especially the way Moore seeks for a moral category, a
relation, almost as a scientific principle, between form and function.
The anthropomorphized jerboa "has happiness" and "O rest and joy,"
and yet lives in a cascade of absences: "no water, no palm trees, no ivory
bed, tiny cactus; but one would not be he/who has nothing but plenty."
He embodies, for Moore, the integration of form/function values. As
depicted in the poem, the jerboa is the moral spring of an attitude

toward life at odds with the malicious artificiality and plenty of corrupt Rome.

The "Abundance" section develops further this theme, positing the sparseness and uncluttered quality of the desert (the habitat of the jerboa) as the place of the imagination. It is here that Jacob (as poet-figure) envisions "steps of air and air angels/ his friends were the stones." The desert, the open, unconditioned ground, is enabling, "a translucent mistake" which "does not make for hardship for one who/ can rest and then do/ the opposite—launching as if on wings" (*CMP*, 14). The remainder of this section is a highly nuanced mimetic description of the jerboa, the conception of which moves between the poet's rendering and the poet's identification with the jerboa as symbolical artist: "It [the jerboa] honors the sand by assuming its color," and, in emulation of a composer, makes art of its own movements:

By fifths and sevenths,
in leaps of two lengths,
   like the uneven notes

of the Bedouin flute, it stops its gleaning
   on little wheel castors, and makes fern-seed
   footprints with kangaroo speed.

(CMP, 14).

The "solid reality" of the poem, the subtlety of its juxtapositions, the enabling matter for the reader, is both comically and ethically apposite. Moore's radical poetic scalpel enjambs and excises the traditional linear unfolding of history. Its corollary, appropriate proportion, places side by side the minuscule jerboa and the Roman empire. The engendered critique is both social and moral: the artistic consciousness of Rome contrasted with the poet's modernist sensibility searching for values. These values are found or encountered dialectically as oppositions between the overdetermined products of Rome and the unprepared-for intrusion, via Moore's readings in natural science, of the aesthetic and natural order as represented by the jerboa. The handling of the jerboa, set beside Rome, saves the poem from cuteness or mere triviality.

Moore's language, rather than mediating reality, Marilyn Brownstein points out in *The Gender of Modernism*, "attempts a return to physical relation." (*GOM*, 325). Moore writes in the manner of science, so to speak, but with a sense that the relation involved is a matter of language, a way of reaching objects not as physical entities but as related or emblematic to a state of mind. In considering Moore's menagerie of animals, it is necessary to remind ourselves that they are products of her readings. They are observed, not in the wilds or in zoos, but mainly in and through texts and accompanying pictures. Thus, as Charles Molesworth has pointed out (*MMW&P*, 118), they are already half-way toward being emblems (in the Medieval sense) which function as both instruction and symbol.

As Molesworth argues, the pangolin, in Moore's poem of that title, is more than a bit of nature imagery. It symbolizes an occasion for meditation on among other things, grace, solitude, vulnerability and artistic precision. As with the poeticized jerboa, a spiritual quest is under consideration. The textual representation of the pangolin, from its armor to its "fragile grace" and ability to roll "himself into a ball that has/ power to defy all effort to unroll it" (*CMP*, 117), also constitutes a use of language both in agreement *and at odds* with other modernist usages such as found in Pound's imagist "dos and don'ts." That is, it both is and is not the "adequate symbol" Pound sought in natural imagery.

Moore's 'lapse' from the new tradition comes out of her need to provide moral exactnesses to the reader. In this, she is closer to the deliberate artist such as Flaubert or Valery, something decidedly un-American, than to the prolix Pound or Whitman. In this intentionality, the emblem as a method of objectification serves her well. For the emblem is always more and less than objectification. The emblematic designations in the medieval picture books which stand for or project qualities—the English lion rampant as courage, for example—in terms of the work they are meant to do, provide Moore with a method which makes a bridge from psyche to expression while, at the same time, bypassing anything overtly autobiographical or personal. The emblem is almost always a simplified picture of the animal, the artist's purpose being not to accurately "represent" the beast but to instill its particular *virtu* in the beholder. Molesworth in his discussion of Moore's "The Pangolin" notices that she carries the mode further, using the verb "griffons" (a word deeply rooted in the Medieval) with respect, not to the pangolin, but to "man, the self, the being we call human, writing master to this world" (*CMP*, 119). Moore's emblematizing to express both "the heraldic and hybrid" (*MMW&P*, 121), (and in this case, the hybrid is at least partially man and beast) is yet another strategy in Moore's repertoire for linking the aesthetic with the ethical. The highly detailed portraiture in Moore's work, while maintaining the emblematizing function, rescues the particular out of which modernist universals arise without loss of the rich ambiguity of detail. Moore's objectifications then constitute neither a fictive nor 'represented' world, nor do they provide an objective correlative expressive of her subjective state. Rather, their purpose, shrouded by detail into riddle and ambiguity, are meant to correlate the psychic dimensions of experience: the moral gesture with the artistic gesture.

∽

Niedecker, in one of her letters to Cid Corman, imagined an anthology, "a book of short poems, just the essence of poetry, you know," one of her ideal inclusions being Marianne Moore. Surely, the example of Moore's poetry entered into Niedecker's thinking, and certain parallels between the two poets are instructive.

As with many of Moore's reading sources, her masters and influences were meditative men and women Jefferson, Darwin, William Morris, the botanist Asa Gray, Margaret Fuller, and more contemporary strategists of poetic silences such as Corman, Basil Bunting and her sometime mentor and correspondent, the Objectivist poet Louis Zukofsky. From these latter, she learned to use contemplation and the absence of noise not as a defense against the world nor as a form of withdrawal but as a compositional element, a way of forcing the reader's attention toward the precision and subtlety of her verse. Trees, flowers, birds, in particular those of her native Wisconsin, are among her favorite subjects partly because their qualities, their growth and development, occur without auditory fanfare.

An implied poetics, remarkably similar to Moore's can be read in her earliest poems. One of her most well-known poems, cited in Louis Zukofsky's *A Test Of Poetry* reads in full:

> There's a better shine
> on the pendulum
> than is on my hair
> and many times
>
> . . .
>
> I've seen it there.

(*TGP*, 3)

The poem is open to a number of readings. One possibility, as I've discussed elsewhere in *Conviction's Net of Branches: Essays On The Objectivist Poets and Poetry* (53), is to see how the pause before the poem's last line holds two contradictory feelings, love of beauty and jealousy, in suspension, allowing for a fullness of each. But another perspective, one reinforced by other poems, suggests a transference or projection of meaning by Niedecker from self to nature's otherness. This is a disposition found throughout all her poetry, often signalled by a vocabulary of endearment: "friend tree," "older friend sun," "our relative the sun," "my pets, the grasses" and "our rich friend silt." Powerful emotion for Niedecker is resident, for example, in such objects as the "little granite pail" or in "Pa's spitbox," the latter which the *persona* of the poem (most probably Niedecker's mother) wishes were put in a museum where presumably it would enter some archive, *i.e.*, rendered safe. In other poems, Niedecker's ambivalent relations with neighbors, "the folk from whom all poetry flows/and much worse," suggest yet another motive for the constant recurrence to natural things as poetic source. The aim constantly in Niedecker is to disabuse herself of the sin of self-regard by maintaining an attitude toward the world, part of the Objectivist honor code, where 'external' things have a more objective truth value than 'internal' things.

As with Moore's constant collaging of her readings into her poems, Niedecker's poetry, as Corman points out, "appropriates voices more than history." She favors the individual account over history's tendency to drown out the single voice, but even more, what she loves about the historical figures who populate her poems is how silence both enshrouds and energizes their perceptions. She cites Audubon, writing home from England to his wife, "Dear Lucy, the servants here/ move quiet/ as killdeer" and also Jefferson who hoped to "establish/ an absolute power/ of silence over oneself."

This silence provides another dimension to Niedecker's contemplative figures. With them, as with Moore, she is part of a tradition in which the scientist, for example, masters phenomena by observation. But a case can be made, as with Moore's readings, that in Niedecker's poetry, the close observation and silence moves the contemplated object from the controlling discourses of science and history into a realm approaching the spiritual and mystical, a realm in which mastery of the object has been lost because it has instead become the focus for intense, nearly uncontrollable feelings. This too, in its way, is Niedecker's war with the tradition of which she is a participant. As with Walter Benjamin's concept of the "aura" in which the word's loss to history brings a powerful awareness of the ruins of the human condition, Niedecker's intense condensations to proto-scientific first causes are constant calls to put her entire life into question. Stevens's "impinge-ments" from outside, his sense of poetry as "solid reality" beyond conceptions, are worked out in Niedecker through impinging physical realities, pendulums and granite pails and natural objects which, rather than anchoring the life, transport her into its uncertainty.

At the same time, for Niedecker, the act of contemplation weds one to the physical universe. Much of her poetry therefore works from an awareness of interlocked unities, of the interanimation of the living with the mineral, as in:

> The smooth black stone
> I picked up in true source park
> the leaf beside it
> once was stone
>
> Why should we hurry
> home

> (*CW*, 236)

To Niedecker, the natural world is a "true source". For where everything is somehow related to everything else, there is no need to hurry 'home' since home is everywhere, as even the home/stone rhyme suggests.

Often, the intense brevity of her poems, isolating individual words in the reader's attention, transforms each noun into a large scale metonymy until what that noun represents is also capable of standing for the world as a whole. This metonymic/visionary mode is most appar-ent in the longer sequences such as "Wintergreen Ridge" and "Paean to Place", *collagiste* hymns to interrelatedness which skillfully enjamb place, memory and history with snatches of witty or comic commen-tary. In "Paean to Place," remembering her dead mother, she writes:

> I mourn her not hearing canvasbacks
> their blast off rise
> from the water
>   Not hearing sora
> rail's sweet
>
> spoon tapped waterglass
> descending scale
> tear drop tittle
>   Did she giggle
> as a girl?

> (*CW*, 263)

Nature and history's voices are by no means her only subject, for Niedecker observes herself in her poetry as carefully as she does the natural world. Her insistent terseness can remind the reader of Sappho or Emily Dickinson, as in this line from a poem about her dead mother: "Dead/ she now lay deaf to death". And, like Dickinson, she can be simultaneously comic and grave:

> February almost March bites the cold.
> Take down a book, wind pours in. Frozen
> the Garden of Eden its oil, if freed, could warm
> the world for 20 years and never mind the storm.
>
> Winter's after me she's out
> with sheets so white it hurts the eyes. Nightgown,
> pillow slip blow through my bare catalpa trees,
> no objects here.
>
> In February almost March a snow blanket
> is good manure, a tight bound wet
> to move toward May: give me lupines and a care
> for her growing air.
>
> (CW, 173)

Meaning and sound are meticulously weighed in the poem, not for lapidary effect, but to give solidity and objectivity to the most evanescent of perceptions. Indeed, Niedecker's powers of objectification are almost unnerving, as in this brief biographical summation ostensibly reporting her mother's words, but which, in effect, carry her own burden of self-knowledge.

> What horror to awake at night
> and in the dimness see the light
>   Time is white
>   Mosquitoes bite
> I've spent my life on nothing.
>
> (CW, 147)

In the later poems (particularly in the long sequences on which, I believe, scholarly interest in Niedecker will focus), the mystical relation with the natural world is heavily stressed. "Lake Superior" begins:

> In every part of every living thing
> is stuff that once was rock

In blood the minerals
of the rock

In its dense compactions of noun and verb, one of the poem's major figures, the priest-explorer Marquette is seen as having

. . . .grazed
azoic rock, hornblende granite
basalt the common dark
in all the Earth

(CW, 233)

As in Moore, Niedecker's language of science is made to perform visionary duty. Marquette, in a way, pre-figures the poet's own mimetic act:

Ruby of corundum
lapis lazuli
from changing limestone
glow-apricot red-brown
carnelian sard

Greek named
Exodus-antique
kicked up in America's
Northwest
you have been in my mind
between my toes
agate

(CW, 234)

In this passage, the absence of punctuation, a device commonly used by Niedecker, creates a verbal enjambment, a concatenation of material signs, which compress identity between head ("mind") and "toes." The "stuff that once was rock" suffuses personhood as sensation, physical object, historical idea, linguistic pun, and, by virtue of a sense of closure, as poem. Niedecker's noun-packed lines, as with Moore's near-seamless collage of her readings, are only partly in the service of rending a physical object 'out there.' Rather, they constitute representations of fairly complex and contradictory feeling states. Rooted though they are in imagist practice, they more closely approach the spiritual iconography of H.D.'s early poetry such as *Sea Garden* with its mythic projections of the world of classical Greece.

In Niedecker's poem, "Paean To Place," autobiography is constructed as a series of analogies to the rural lakeshore area where she grew up.

Her mother's life and hers are both "born in swale and swamp and sworn/ to water" (CW, 261). The father "netted loneliness" (*CW*, 264). Niedecker, in one of her most telling passages, is

> ... the solitary plover
> a pencil
>   for a wing-bone
> From the secret notes
> I must tilt
>
> upon the pressure
> execute and adjust
>   In us sea-air rhythm
> 'We live by the urgent wave
> of the verse'
>
>   (*CW*, 265)

Niedecker here realizes that her poetics, her executions and adjustments, are dependent on the very pressures, in both joy and pain, which constitute her life. There is in the deepest sense nothing to escape; the urge to make poetry, the *poesis* of "sea-air rhythm," objectify the marks of her pencil wing. In her last long poems, the material of her life— much of it, as with Moore, in the form of readings—came back to her as though it constituted a text. Looking over this work, we can see that her formula is at one with Moore's usages in "The Jerboa" and "The Pangolin." The objectified psyche is self-scripted, marked, as in her Darwin poem, as "holy/ slowly/ mulled over/ matter" (*CW*, 295). It is in the earned effacements of the late work, then, that Niedecker, as with Moore, comes as close as possible to a completely integrated psychic objectification, to a remarkable indivisibility between word, representation and poet.

                                        (1996)

Imagining Durable Works: Lorine Niedecker's 'Wintergreen Ridge'

For Lorine Niedecker, *Wintergreen Ridge*, written in 1967, represented a new complexity in her work, something she was barely able to name, whether it was a seeming loosening of form or, as she said to Louis Zukofsky, an admittance into the poem's structure of what she hesitantly called "reflection," a nearly taboo sort of thing as she preceived it, operating against her sense of Objectivist poetic immediacy and primacy of sensory data. Writing to Gail Roub in 1967, she muses " Much taken up with how to define a way of writing which is not Imagist nor Objectivist fundamentally nor Surrealism alone . . .I loosely call it "reflections" or as I think of it now, reflective, maybe. The basis is direct and clear—what has been seen or heard etc . . . but something gets in, overlays all that to make a state of consciousness . . . (Faranda, 9) In the same letter, she continues, "I used to feel that I was goofing off unless I held only to the clear image, but now I dare to do this reflection."

Niedecker's overlay, the making of a "state of consciousness" constitutes a transformative aspect of her work, one she only thoroughly worked out in "Wintergreen Ridge" In fact, among the long poems both before and after it, "Wintergreen Ridge" strikes as a singular experiment, a "one-off" as the English might say. Looked at from a formal perspective, the poem is quite different from the long sequences which were written around the same time. "Lake Superior" and "Paean To Place," for example, are short lyric sequences, each of which could almost stand alone, separated by spacing or some device like a printer's bullet. "Thomas Jefferson," a poem consisting of nineteen discretely numbered sections, invites a *collagiste* reading, one producing an almost photo-album effect, suggesting it be read as a collection of facets around its ostensible subject, Jefferson.

"Wintergreen Ridge," on the other hand, strikes one as a sustained musical and intellectual act. Niedecker's longest poem, (in *Collected Works* it runs 11 printed pages), is composed in somewhat regular looking tercets. And unlike the surrounding works mentioned above in which each section comes to some sort of completion, "Wintergreen Ridge" does not simply withhold closure, but, as well, throughout its length, uses the possibility of closure as one of its devices, almost shutting down or end-stopping itself in places, only to move on, spilling out beyond the tercet backdrop as it enjambs both sound and idea from stanza to stanza. As well, the poem resists back and forth reading while at the same time breaking with the short lyric mode (Niedecker's most salient way of working) by preventing or at least refusing to confirm as finished its own lapidary images or rhetorical elements that in other poems of Niedecker's have been among the major keys to our reading and hence, understanding of her work.

Thus, instead of the divisions between lyric elements normally found in her other poems, signalled by numbering, by spaces or by asterisks, thoughts and images overrun the tercet stanzas, and are stopped or paused by initial capitalizations. The ground bass of the poem is the sentence with the tercet acting as counterpoint. The formal structure of the poem, then, strikes the reader as being unreliable and hence , pardon the jargon, "undecidable," always about to break out in odd directions or impulses. And yet, the impression given by "Wintergreen Ridge" is that, for all its variousnes of tone, subject matter and even prosody, all elements are subsumed in an overriding voice or attitude (Kenneth Cox claims the voice in the poem is closest to that of Niedecker in her letters and speech), the "consciousness" she speaks of, now something over and beyond the perceptions and even intellections that populate the poem.

Peter Nichols, in his essay, "Lorine Niedecker: Rural Surreal," observes that this transformative moment in the poet is allied to her interest in surrealism, to her "long association of the 'subconscious' with certain 'subliminal' sound structures. Nichols stresses the firmness with which Niedecker insists on the way she is both influenced and makes use of a complex conception of Surrealism, but it seems as well, I think, to look at Niedecker's "reflective poetics" as closer to a classical idea of writing, as classical at least as E. M. Forster's "Only connect." For the major characteristic of the poem is its impassioned propulsiveness rather than any disjunctive or dissociative aspect. This driving quality to the poem, rather than inhibiting (as Niedecker sometimes felt the Objectivist strictures to be), is characterized by a severe, focused psychic economy, one which seems to channel all its energy into the impelling verbal structure.

The title of my paper is drawn from this passage beginning on page 247 and running into page 248.

Man
     lives hard
         on this stone perch

by sea
     imagines
         durable works

in creation here
        as in the center
            of the world

let's say
     of art

The significant properties of this passage are first of all its rhetorical structure, neither a lyrical observation drawn from nature nor a strictly philosophical statement. To refer to Niedecker's term, the passage is "reflective," indeed emulative of the reflective mode, an appeal not so much to the phenomena before one's eyes as to an act of intellection upon the data. The concluding phrase, "let's say/of art," a phrase both judgmental and hesitant, appears to be Niedecker's riff on the traps set for us by the word "art." The phrase, with its less than firm "let's say" strikes the reader almost as an after-thought, as though possibly the imagining of "durable works" were sufficient, and the need to categorize them as "art" a secondary gesture, a caveat to culture or socialization beyond the (perhaps more spontaneous or immediate) act indicated by the word "imagines."

As though expressing hopes for her own poetics, Niedecker writes "Nobody, nothing/ever gave me/greater thing/ than time//unless light and silence//which if intense/makes sound." And "Wintergreen Ridge,' as a work of extension rather than closure, operates formally as an homage to time, to ongoingness, and hence to the imagination's capacity for continuity while encompassing a varied world with all its multiplicity of subjects.

In this sense, Niedecker's term "reflective," has a meaning unique to this poem. Clearly, the activity is not one of mirroring in the usual sense, but of seeming to create a receptivity to a line of thought in her mind as it proceeds through representations, associations and word puns and sounds, integrating these and placing transitions so carefully that any individual instance in the poem appears to belong to both a prior and following line of thought. In fact, as I've suggested above, the general rule of the poem is that to fulfill either meaning or sound forms satisfactorily, the reader's eye and ear must ride past the tercet unit, moving down the steps of the poem to resolve thought or musical phrase.

Take, for example, the passage running from the bottom of page 254 in the *Collected Works*. It proceeds from sensory data, "Scent/the simple/the perfect/order/of that flower/water lily" to a digression on "mind-changing acids" and continues on, in an ironic mode, to a mini-disquistion on "church architecture," the strange ungainliness of contemporary examples, and, on to a reference to Eliot's "Murder in the Cathedral." This association leads to Henry James's father, who "pronounced human affairs/gone to hell." The passage then wanders back to wildflowers and churches where dismembered body parts have been left. With a tone that is at once both grim and comic, Niedecker then tells us about the steam fitter who "lost his head" and suicided himself, birdlike, leaping off a roof, then on to real birds, "Pigeons" and "gulls." To unpack all of the material in this passage would take more space and time than I have here, but often one senses a common plaint against either overdoing, overfettering or even sheltering imagination, whether with drugs, in houses of worship or as gathered bouquets. The image of "Old sunflower" bowing "to no one/but Great Storm of Equinox" on which the poem ends seems to argue for a natural relation or submission of poet to world.

Is this complex counter-response a reaction against some Rimbaudlike prompting to disorder the senses, the very basis of the surrealist enterprise? If so, what we normally mean by surrealism has only a small part to play here. For example, it strikes as inaccurate to describe the passage above as having a sort of loose associational logic. The circling back of such a passage to its original starting point, the whole operation creating a rather elegant arc of thought, these are the marks of a unifying understanding, a kind of recognition of the tensions involved in any act of "understanding." Niedecker has found, not surrealism, but a different poetic paradigm, an "awareness," as she wrote to Lisa Faranda, "of everything influencing everything."

"We are gawks" Niedecker says in the poem, "lusting/after wild orchids." These lines are immediately followed by a "Wait! (with exclamation point) What's this?—sign: *Flowers/loveliest/where they grow//Love them enjoy them/and leave them so.*" Here the words acknowledge desire, even while reconizing desire's limits in terms of community. The cautionary "Wait!" strikes one as a bit of a nudge word, reminding the reader that the poem in its ongoingness falls between two stools, the representational or "direct and clear" of Niedecker's Objectivist inclinations and the slightly more questionable socially constructed sign, the "What's this?—" that ushers in the poetic injunction to look but don't touch. For Niedecker, the inherent tension between the seen and the reflected upon propels the poem, so that in a way—because the verse rests nowhere and grants no final purchase on making pictures or making statements—the thought or the music of thought are the one solidity the poem can offer. Throughout, these tensions between meaning and structure give the poem a kind of self-contained solidity. To move away from the poem, to dwell too much in the imagistic picture or overly ponder meaning will diffuse the driving energy of the language

Kenneth Cox in his comments on "Wintergreen Ridge" sees Darwin as its central figure. Quite fitting in that the form of the poem feels like an evolution, not only of Niedecker's poetics but of the poem in process under hand. In the poem's refusal to organize itself around lyric sound bites, it distances itself from the category of Niedecker's "let's say art," or at least from overt artfulness, anything which would blunt the work being seen for what it is. If this is a retreat of sorts, it is also a powerful step forward in Niedecker's poetics. I would go further and insist that "Wintergreen Ridge" represents a completely new way of thinking in Niedecker's poetry, one that we have yet to understand fully, let alone come to terms with. "Wintergreen Ridge" is, as Cox puts it, "one of the poems that show what poetry might be."

(2003)

Typology of the Parabolist: Some Thoughts on the Poems Of David Ignatow

Our literary forms, even as they offer the critic roadsigns as to where a work is going, suggest at their deepest levels the shapes of more general experience. David Ignatow's poems, particularly the early ones, suggest an urge to convert experience into parables, an urge which gives the poems their almost self-contained "objectivist" form as well as their ironic values.

As we know, the parable is a species of allegory or proverb, often in narrative form, by which moral or spiritual relations are set forth. The usual expectation from a parable is that wisdom will be dispensed, that this little verbal knot will tell one how to live, will define an ethic or a course of action. The parable, by its nature, must be short, pithy and to a certain extent, plain spoken. The parable is, after all, more an object of social or religious contemplation than it is an aesthetic one. It aims at being a kind of medium of exchange or currency.

Parables have little to do with realism or with accurate representation in the usual sense. They are not concerned with the world of flux, with ever-changing relative values, concerns which would undermine their very purpose. They are normally at the opposite end of the linguistic scale from such poetic genres as the epic or the lyric, both of which are embedded in certain notions of time, the lyric in immediacy, the epic in the often mythic story of a life. In this sense, nothing seems more anachronistic than the parable.

And yet, the parabolistic trope in the hands of the modern writer (one thinks of Kafka as the major example) is an especially effective literary device. In a secular age, one marked by pluralistic forms of culture and values and the confusions they produce, the parable reminds its modern readers of truths and certainties no longer obtainable in the present. Thus, more than with any other contemporary literary form, it is best at conveying spiritual loss, loss which permeates every other kind of loss or absence in modern life. Throughout Ignatow's work, perhaps in the bulk of it, we see the parable form, with all its necessary problematics, used again and again. I want to examine in a number of poems how Ignatow masterfully uses the form, how he plays with and ironizes our usual expectations for the form, and how, finally, it seems to become for him the fundamental bedrock of his poetics.

Any glance at Ignatow's earlier poems will show the methodology of the parable already in place. Take for instance his poem "The Sky Is Blue," which, in exemplary fashion, suggests the doubling irony of adopting this trope:

> Put things in their place,
> my mother shouts. I am looking
> out the window, my plastic soldier
> at my feet. The sky is blue
> and empty. In it floats
> the roof across the street.
> What place, I ask her.

> (FH 31)

Now a number of aspects of this poem are directly related to the spiritual condition of the contemporary individual, most obviously, the meaning of "place." While the reader is uncertain as to whether or not the child wants to please the mother, the minute world of the poem, sky above, toy soldier at feet, roof, etc. strikes one as being, in the realistic sense, adequate. That is, surely the boy in the poem knows where his mother expects things to go. So it is not the mother's but the boy's idea of "place" which is at issue. And that throws the mother's demand , and the boy's questioning, onto another plane, one which conflates the emotional drama with the more existential or even theological question of where things of this world belong when "the sky is blue/ and empty" of God (?) or of some other transcendent hierarchical ordering.

A further suggested irony of the poem is engendered in the sense that, here, an adequate "place" for things might very well be: nowhere but within the precincts of this particular parable. The parable-form is, by its nature, a composition; moreover, unlike the effect of being drawn

into the world of a painting (possibly a powerfully decentering experience), the parable as a composition is a contemplative space, establishing its relationship to the reader clearly and unequivocally by saying
"meditate on this, and act accordingly." Indeed, we find a certain
tensionless quality in the picture that Ignatow draws, the soldier at the
boy's knee, the roof floating, etc. So the question of "place"-ment
involves some other kind of question, the solution to which is nowhere
apparent. As a result, "The Sky Is Blue," even as it establishes it, breaks
down the contemplative relationship which the pictorial quality of the
poem has set up. Its highly nuanced and reflective "message" is closer to
paralysis than action: take its words to heart and you will have to start
looking at your own two feet, asking whether or not you are in the right
place vis-a-vis the world around you. Paradoxically, the poem denies to
the reader the convenience of an ethical or social agenda even as it
implies one. In this sense, it is as much anti-parable as parable.

Similarly, spiritual loss is prefigured in the poem "Two Voices," as
flight from literary tradition. Here is the poem in full:

> I'll challenge myself, I said.
> I have read the classics;
> my insides feel they'd like to be outside
> catching air. It was cold
> but sunny. I wore my coat,
> no hat though. Adventure.
> I would invite trouble at once.
> Pneumonia. I'll escape Stendal,
> Baudelaire, Whitman, Eliot,
> each pressing me in turn
> to his heart. In the cold air
> I hardened. Nearby stood a lake;
> I jumped in.
>   "We had to haul him
> out, a block of ice, eyeballs
> in a frozen stare. After melting him
> down, we lost him. He had forgotten
> how to breathe. 'Challenge the weather,'
> he murmured. 'Challenge the weather.'
> And he closed his eyes."

                                                        (FH 15)

Here, the narrator-poet struggles with his precursors such as Baudelaire
or Whitman who bear with them the almost cloying, inescapable
warmth of their greatness and insight, "each pressing me in turn/to his
heart." Rather than capitulate to this prior tradition with its comforting

sense of belonging, the narrator-poet jumps in the freezing lake and is pulled out a frozen block of ice, his last words being "Challenge the weather." Ignatow here sets up a complex ambivalence between the poet's need to reject an older poetic tradition, and the possibility that limiting oneself to contemporaneously "challenging the weather" may lead only to sterility and cold-bloodedness. The rejection of the poetic forefathers—in a sense, the 'wisdom' of the tradition—is again an anti-parabolistic gesture even as it bears with it the risk of psychic death, a frozen soul.

Likewise, the poetics of "The Vending Machine" (*P* 205) are suggestive of a new relationship between poet and muse, one situated, in a debased time, on the recalcitrance of the modern world to yield anything like universality in sentiment or ethics. Rather, what obtains is a stand-off where:

> the machine remains stolid
> and silent. It needs a nickel
> to make it work, and I remain
> stolid and silent.

> (*FH* 41)

If, as in the examples above, Ignatow's poems seem to toy with the parable form rather than attempt to become parables, it is first, because they are written in a period in history when religious and even ethical concerns hold little sway i.e. a period of powerful secularization in all walks of life, and second, even as they fail to attain the status of true parables, they provide a sort of formal means, a kind of containment, as psychic self-defense.

The would-be- or pseudo-parable reverses reader expectations. Instead of wisdom, Ignatow's poems remind us that our received truths probably won't work, that whatever our course of action, we are as likely to end up in folly or disaster as to save our skins. Take for example, the poem "And That Night" in which an undesignated "you" is in the narrator's apartment contemplating a photo of his family "enjoying the sunshine" when a "crazy" killer sneaks into the room and kills him:

> You never
> find out why or who, you just
> lean back and die.
> The sunshine is gone too,
> the photograph gets into the news.
> You bring up a family in three small rooms,

this crazy man comes along
to finish it off.

(FH 12)

The obvious thing about the poem is that it structures the bifurcated nature of contemporary urban life between purposive behavior and random violence. More subtle is the line concerning the detail "the photograph gets into the news" where the private act of bringing up a family and the murder are now replayed for the public, hence, our newest wisdom, *count on nothing*, is dispensed. The "you," it appears, does not exist to raise a family, an act called into question every day by contemporary life, but to ultimately get "into the news." In a deracinated society, this way of living may be the only wisdom, since all other signs point to the futility of action.

Of course, replayability is the signature mark of the parable, except that in modern times we are more likely to find our necessary messages implicit in newspapers rather than in theological or spiritual tracts. In "Moving Picture," which seems a variant on the theme of "And That Night," a newspaper, containing the account of a couple who committed suicide in a house, ends up in mud which is scooped up:

and pressed down
by steam rollers for hard ground
and a house on it
for two to enter.

(FH 60)

The seasonal cycles of nature, which parables continually invoke, is here parodied. The narrator of the poem, focussing strictly on the cycle he is depicting, leaves a great deal out, the motives for the suicide, what the house looked like, for instance, in order that the 'impersonality' of the event be transmitted. Ignatow's language, mostly simple nouns and verbs, his clipped prose rhythms, tends toward universalizing the event depicted. The parabolistic mode (especially Ignatow's inversions of it) require less, not more, particularity. Verbal coloration, specification of individuals and objects, lead us closer to the manners of literature and history, that is, *temporality*, which the parable must avoid.

By parabolizing, Ignatow, then, is able to transform the experience he wishes to register, from the merely anecdotal, rooted in the contingent and temporal, into something unbounded by time. This is not to say that Ignatow's work is without a temporal dimension but that we must discover this by coming around the backside of the poetry, by recognizing, as Ignatow does, the near impossibility of the parable form in contemporary culture. An impossibility, as I've mentioned above, which is due to the very unpredictable nature of current behavior and its consequences.

Yet it is precisely in this regard that the form of the parable is so useful and important. One aspect of the parable mode is that in it things, actions, even motives appear to find their appropriate places. Their meanings and interrelations get correlated. This correlation, a kind of seamless narrative web, gives Ignatow's work its paradoxical aura of completeness—even as it defeats the reader's desires to general-ize from the work.

The traditional parable's efficacy relies on a notion of a unified indi-vidual. In cultures structured around some theological principle, the parable as advice or lesson comes to this individual whose unity is co-existent with the ongoing theology. Ignatow's anti-parables simply invert this equation, as in the poem entitled "Brooding," (P 29) where the individual is described as one of those "old sailing ships/loaded with food and drink for a long voyage/self-sufficient . . . " In the same poem, Ignatow remarks: "We live our whole lives as in a husk,/ like an ear of corn./ The husk is our will." The successful modern city dweller (and by successful here, I simply mean someone who hasn't gone mad) develops this "husk"-ness as defense. and inevitably must read his or her experi-ence parabolistically. To survive, experience must be converted from discrete "slices of life" or from seeing one's actions as merely one of the cogs in the great interconnected wheel, both of which suffer dispersal of meaning. The parabolistic form enables experience to be viewed as a self-sustained object of contemplation, even as the form risks falling into solipsism. Against the impingements of urban culture, which constantly threaten identity, and hence meaning, the parable-like story, the minimalist fable, gives a certain limited self-identity.

~

The mode which I have been describing appears in one form or another throughout Ignatow's work, both early and late. For this reason, Ignatow's poetry tends to be one of typologies rather than particulari-ties, typologies in which the formal organization of the poem, word choice, sound form and rhythm, are all in the service of a poetry striving for a certain atemporal self-sufficiency, as though timelessness (and universality) could only be achieved by confronting squarely the impossibility of timelessness or of an order of generality in the present.

In this sense, Ignatow's techniques have some connections to Zukofsky's notions of objectification and sincerity, and the more complex idea of "rested totality," the perfect realization of which would be the totally independent art object, something not only impossible, but perhaps not even desireable. Ignatow's poems, as they approach a version of Zukofskian "rested totality," are sustained by the ironic tension between two contradictory impulses, the "timelessness" of the parable form and the impossibility of the form's meaningfulness in a secularized pluralistic time.

Behind Ignatow's parables are awarenesses of the solitude of experience, of the failure of subjectivity to mediate between individuals through some sort of Platonic ideal of form and, finally, of the singular, unshareable nature of one's death.

In this regard, one is especially struck by the tonal qualities of Ignatow's later work where the parable-maker is no longer simply looking to find the repeatable signature of experience but instead, as though fearful of a self-enclosing solipsism, steps further back from experience itself into the poetics of self-hood, one step towards an infinite regression which aims at transpiercing the timely/timeless paradox, emblematic of the parable form.

Exemplary of this later tonality is the volume entitled *Treading The Dark* dedicated to his friend and poet, Stanley Kunitz, and containing poems to a number of poets and friends who have died. It is as though Ignatow's self-examination here must begin in, and be sanctioned by, bearing witness before and to one's tribal elders and ghosts. With an admixture of *apologia* and *ars poetica*, the narrator of the poems tries to edge closer to the paradoxes he has previously described, as in " From the Observatory:"

> Each step is to and from an object
> and does not echo in heaven
> or in hell. The earth vibrates
> under the heel or from the impact
> of a stone.
>
>   (*TD* 4)

This is the classical starting place of a poetics inscribed, not under eternity, but on an earthly plane, one that must deny itself a theological resonance, even as it is written in the parabolist's stylistics of eternal truth: the use of simple common nouns and a highly depersonalized context, that is, not 'this happened to me,' but that 'this happens'.

These poems are linked as well by a certain continuity of imagery which makes of the sequence yet another twentieth century path of negative capability. For instance, the third poem in the series invokes the sun as a "flame of doubt." And the next poem, ". With the Sun's Fire," deploys its imagery under the light of that doubt:

Are you a horror to yourself?
Do you have eyes peering at you
from within the back of your skull
as you manage to stay calm, knowing
you are being watched by a stranger?

Be well, I am seated beside you,
planning a day's work. We are contending
with the stuff of stones and stars,
with water, air, with dirt, with food
and with the sun's fire.

(TD 5)

The poem wants to abolish any possiblity of solipsism but can only do so by a splitting of the poet's allegiances between the materiality of the physical world and the self-embrace which would put its own gesture in question. Parable here seems to edge closer to the very paradox which would disallow it, hence the admonishments to "stay calm" and "Be well."

The vantage of the next poem in the series is, again, that of interrogation: "Examine me, I am continuous/from my first memory and have no memory/of birth. Therefore I was never born/ and have always been?" This is a complicated, almost buddhistic statement, further complicated because the understood "you" of this poem, the recipient of the imperative question, is never clear. The poem hungers to find a witness to its narrator's self-involvement, for it is only by being witnessed, by becoming an affect for others, that the envelope of self-enclosure can be broached. "Explain me," it pleads, "as you are that I may live/ in time and die/ when I am dead." It is in the poem, "The Two Selves" that the "you" in the preceding poem is seemingly identified as the other self—a consciousness or a self-consciousness—which is the witness and so becomes a consoling figure for the poet:

I existed before my mind realized me

and when I became known to myself
it was with the affection for warmth
beside a radiator.

So you began for me . . .

(TD 6)

For Ignatow, then, the divided self, often represented as a dialogue, at
times comic, at times combative, but always acknowledged, remains the
source of his poetry. In "A Discussion," one of the later poems from the
volume *Whisper To The Earth*, we overhear two voices:

So there was both order and disorder in that house?

I don't know whether that actually was the situation and I can't believe it
can exist, given the same condition for both in the same place.

Then must we say that we don't know whether there was order or disorder or both?

Right.

And we don't have any solid answer to go on?

We're in the dark.

And all is as if back in the first chaos.

Right.

And we have to live with it.

Right.

(WE 77)

Wisdom having been dispensed, this is where parable—not yet poem—
must end. But we have been made already aware, with Ignatow, that this
kind of wisdom is itself yet another cage. And so more must come, as it
does, just a bit later:

As for your ambition to become a watchmaker, did you become such a
person?

It left my mind as soon as I became interested in something else.

And so you lost one idea of order through your own thinking and found yourself thinking of another kind of order.

I have forgotten what that one was.

(WE 77–78)

Here anti-parable and parable coexist, and the poet's earlier prompting, "Examine me, I am continuous . . ." (*TD* 6) circles back to resolve itself in limited yet tonally authentic resolutions, that is, poem by poem.

Ignatow's poetic profferings of wisdom, his philosophizing, are, as we have come to understand them, forms of autobiography. These modes of parabolizing inform all of his work. Yet we sense also a rueful understanding that, in essence, this choice of a form has less to do with stylistics than a deep need to make sense of his own life. Plato, in the famous parable of the cave, suggested that what we take for life and reality is only the play of shadows. The contemporary poet, writing outside of a single coherent belief system, has little else but these shadows to work with. One feels that, among his contemporaries, Ignatow is especially attuned to the music these shadows make. Indeed, as if echoing the platonic theme, in a kind of summing up of *Leaving the Door Open*, Ignatow's austere poetics remind us that the poem itself is a kind of shadow, that, taken deeply, it arises out of the enigma of human existence, out of something as paradoxical as the shape of one's own shadow:

> You are unhappy with the way things
> have turned out for you and for others
> close whose lives touch yours
> and turn it from its path in the sun.
> You are now with your back to it
> and looking down at your shadow
> stretching before you
> at your feet, long, dark and sad,
> you make of it a matter
> for philosophy.

(*LDO* 35)

(1994)

William Bronk's Poetics of Silence and Form's Vertiginous Trace

In one of William Bronk's early poems, originally published in 1955, some anxious children in a car ask "Where are we now?", to which the poem's narrator replies, "Pretty soon, pretty soon," (LS, 26) suggesting that the answers we would like to hear are not always there. The narrator goes on, in this poem entitled "Some Musicians Play Chamber Music For Us," to instruct the reader that the worlds we seem to share are created worlds; like pieces of music, they are "composed, wholly composed" (LS, 27). The tone is muted, the language spare, unable to alleviate either curiosity or uncertainty, yet the voice compels, even consoles; it is a strangely humane whistle in the dark.

Such an effect pervades the entire corpus of Bronk's poems and essays, for Bronk's is a poetry of the epistemological limit, of a message formulated by a border guard on the outer reaches of our shared assumptions. The natural world, Bronk would insist, is a world we can never know; it is, as he notes in "The Gulls of Longbird Island," in another early collection, the "stuff of stubborn stuff/indifferent to what we do/or fail to do" (LS, 22).

Against this recalcitrance, Bronk has fashioned a remarkable body of work, one which suggests that the recognition, the taking in of this fundamental estrangement, illuminates and clarifies the human situation. To make clear such an understanding, Bronk employs, with great tact, a language of logic and paradox, a language which eschews imagery in favor of direct statement of thought, of the unadorned meditations of experience which look on the page, like the clean syllogisms of a logician. There is implied a distrust of the usual devices of ornament or analogy, of metaphor, of anything which might remove the reader from the exacting and naked process of realization. "Language," Bronk warns, "is the hypnotist," ready to lull us into a trance, against which there is only the poet's refusal to falsify, uncomfortable as it may be. As he puts it in "The Inability,"

> She wants me to say something pretty to her because
> we both know the unabettable
> bleak of the world. Make believe, she says,
> what harm? It may be so. I can't. I don't.

(*LS*, 193)

Bronk's view of human limitation is neither solipsistic nor pessimistic. Instead it offers another way of looking at our common humanity, not in some imagined concurrence of shared knowledge, but in our need to construct and reconstruct worlds, in our attempts to appease a common metaphysical hunger. This, the poems show mainly by indirection; their terms of conflict, be it love or language or the natural world, are subsumed in a voice which seems as compassionate in its registrations as it is clear, as in "On Being Together":

> I watch how beautifully two trees
> stand together; one against one.
> Not touching. Not awareness.
> But we would try these. We are always wrong.

(*LS*, 189)

All of Bronk's work moves toward silence as both unanswerability to the meaning of experience and as an opportunity for further growth. In Bronk, silence is not the absence of sound but that which makes poetry possible, the ground of necessary speech. In *The Brother in Elysium*, his prose meditation on Thoreau, Melville and Whitman, Bronk writes "Silence is the world of potentialities and meanings beyond the actual and expressed, which the meanness of our actions and the interpretations put upon them threatens to conceal . . . . Nothing is worth saying, nothing is worth doing except as a foil for the waves of silence to break against" (*BIE*, 80). "Silence," he quotes from Thoreau, "is our ever inviolable asylum" (*BIE*, 80).

For Bronk, silence is the return to groundlessness, to an experience of the unconditioned, since all substance, name or sound is a kind of figuration, a partial instancing of existence. It is the ultimate estranging condition, yet paradoxically, the ultimate familiarizing condition as well. Any utterance out of silence can only falsely or incompletely name or inscribe, yet naming is the only way to articulate the unnamed ground of silence.

Silence as Bronk transmutes it, in a sort of lineal refinement of Thoreauvian thought, is "a refuge from the finality of experience" (BIE, 128). "Asylum," "refuge" and "finality" are, in a sense, cautionary words. That is, we can imagine that for Bronk, once utterance is ended, once a gesture is made or an action concluded, there must be a place to regroup, to rethink. A human life goes on and on, and no singular act or thought suffices to define it once and for all. Silence is the site of imaginal possibility, the arena of regrouping, the uncertain or skeptical ground of existence.   .

Silence, then, for Bronk is neither quietism nor passivity but the necessary ground of continuing. Bronk, a late Yankee poet, insinuates an idea of action into an older Eastern or Hindu thought which was one of the underpinnings of New England Transcendentalism. In effect, Bronk seeks to make the contemplative act dynamical by showing how, for him, the structure of silence leads to or is at least dependent on the structure of poetry and vice-versa. Concerning this theme, many signals abound in the work, but some of the clearest are to be seen in the section of *Life Supports* entitled *Silence and Metaphor*. The first line of this section annunciates the theme: "Here is silence, it is everywhere," (*LS*, 161) which then serves as an introduction, paradoxically, not to blank pages but to ones filled with poetry. The poem, as though exfoliating the nature of its own dilemma, continues: "under the noise, silence is what we hear." The second poem of the section, "Utterances," replays this interaction between noise and silence along the axis of metaphor, i.e., poetry:

> Everything is, almost in the utterance,
> metaphor—as we measure miles, and miles
> are meaningless, but we know what distance is:
> unmeasurable. But there are distances.

(LS, 161)

Speech denotes but even as it denotes it instantiates distance. We are never farther from something than when we name it in a poem, than when we attempt to realize a conception about something or someone:

THE WORLD

I thought that you were an anchor in the drift of the world;
but no; there isn't an anchor anywhere.
There isn't an anchor in the drift of the world. Oh no.
I thought you were. Oh no. The drift of the world.

(*LS*, 189)

Such a poem makes a gesture, as I described above, toward the philo-sophical syllogism as if the processes of rationality and logic could lock out unease. But the quest for certainty, that momentary reprieve from thought, is inevitably thwarted by the tone of the utterance with its "oh nos", its incantatory repeats of "anchor," "drift" and "world." Repetition, as Yeats reminds us, has a childlike, wish-fulfilling quality, and Bronk's rhythmical positing of words that are ultimately contradic-tory or at war with each other ("anchor" vs. "drift," for instance) shows forth a voice given over to its misgivings.

There is a circularity or spiral like motion of thought to Bronk's poet-ics, one which the poems enact on both the rhetorical and ideational level. Take for example:

QUESTIONS AND ANSWERS

The inconsistences of experience
deny us, not life, but the sense of what
life may be about. About what?
Who, what where are legitimate
as questions. Desire is question. They are desire.
It has no answer; no more have they. But desire
is undenied and asserts itself in one
voice or another. Its questionings insist
as if answers were what it wanted, whereas
it wants only to keep on asking: what?

But we quiet it, giving it answers: things
we make up which are not true.
Hunger, hunger! What does hunger want?
To be stilled or to go on hungering?
Well, of course, it wants both and neither one.
Questions answered, the inconsistencies
keep nudging us to acknowledge their untruths.
Our oaths lie to our experience; ease

discomforts us. We go on with life
alive only as the shape of life is foregone.

(LS, 219)

The poem, in fact almost all of Bronk's works, counsels a kind of renunci-
ation, not of the world, but of our constant need to over-conceptualize it.
There is in Bronk's work an austere beauty, unlike anything else in
American poetry, an asperity which requires the reader to enter into their
quiet thoughtfulness, an act which is already a partial estrangement,
already half-way toward being "alive only as the shape of life is foregone."

Such a foregoing is clearly demonstrated in one of his later volumes,
Manifest, And Furthermore. Take the title, for example, where *Manifest*
proclaims what is obvious, what is clearly apparent. But there is also
that other sense of the word, a listing of the goods, the cargo stored in
the hull, the inventories by which we make ourselves "real" and, often,
manifest (the verb form, to show forth or display) our power (as in
"manifest destiny"). Bronk's ironies are all in the byplay between these
senses of the word, senses which Bronk is able to place in contradiction.
For what the poems engage is our hopes and failures as they are pinned
to the endless catalogs of our materiality, to our physical being and our
being in the world. In this regard, the *And Furthermore* of the rest of the
title, strikes almost like a clearing of the poet's throat prior to attempting eloquence. That is, the nature of our condition being now understood, made manifest, Bronk implies, we can now make an invocation to
the offices of poetry, to our deep need to speak the thing out.

This book is also in a sense Bronk's Winter Tale, including some
poems specifically concerned with winter, with aging, but these, as with
the rest of the book, resonate with Bronk's career-long preoccupations.
The world, tonally and symbolically, like the Mid-Hudson late January
afternoons of Bronk's home, wears a deceptively wintry guise, assumes
a shape covered in snow, barely discernible—or rather, our thoughts of
it are like the snow itself, seasonal, evanescent, a momentary boding of
what exists which like any utterance must die on the air. In "The Winter
Light," Bronk muses "How should we not know/and be alive, not be
deprived . . . we know the light as much/ and even more from gone than
when it is there." (*MAF*, 23) Knowing cannot be known, Bronk counsels,
since it is, after all, an action, one which uses itself up, leaving the poem
as its trace. The book's emotional compass is between the line "ache us
to know" (*MAF*, 3) of its first poem, "Winter Vocative," and the "desire,"
Bronk notes in the last poem, "to say what is unsayable. what doesn't
satisfy" (*MAF*, 77).

What must be spoken of, according to Bronk, is as illusive as ever, even as we vaguely sense it beyond the margins of thought. Bronk's poems have a sort of negative architectonics; they are strategies which aim to de-create rather than construct new edifices. One nervously climbs up a Bronk poem as though it were Wittgenstein's famous ladder, the one at the end of the *Tractatus* that gets kicked away. We begin the ascent I think because Bronk's poems have such a seductive perfection of finish. Unlike much modernist and post-modernist poetry, they look visually familiar, regular in line length, clearly stanzaic; they exhibit none of the discontinuous leaps of print nor the oddities of typography found in Pound or Williams. Their radicality comes gift-wrapped in the standard conventions of the contemporary poem, the voice of an anguished "I" willing, presumptuously perhaps, to speak for a communal "we." The poem "Endings, The End," for example, is a subtle demonstration of how Bronk works:

> I, remembering the false spring when
> red-winged blackbirds cried assertive desire
> in the bare elms and those elms dead by their look,
> hear now, in August, cardinals cry, they
> breeding again, I suppose.
>   It is summer still
> but going to sleep, easy, my reflection is how
> the end is not near, perhaps, but the end is sure:
> desire is all, is its own end;
> what else is to come?
>   I think how all our advance
> is against each other—against, in the end, ourselves.
> Whatever survives us we cannot recognize
> though it may be—unknown—what we are
> and we may be nothing and nothing lost when it comes
> so all right, even so: we have to believe.

> (*MAF*, 10)

At first glance, the poem updates our Wordsworthian retrospects of mind and nature. We are lulled by the first stanzas plaintive and lush sound-forms and repeats. But a second, unsettling, reading suggests that the poem is rather more like a compact toolbox of logic operating slightly against itself. Yet closer inspection shows the toolbox to contain nothing but assorted monkey wrenches. What struck as *frisson*, as a dying fall into nature as teacherly, becomes instead a calculated cate-chism of antithetical pastoral appositions from "false spring" which began with the sounds of red-winged blackbirds to August's cries of breeding cardinals, then on to a "reflection" of an "end" not near but "sure." The last stanza is about the hopelessness, demonstrated by the poem, of human knowledge, yet it urges us in conclusion that "we have to believe." This last line can be played a number of ways, as command or observation or, worse, as *fact*. On reflection, it would seem, we have been led down the path of Romantic nature poetry directly into the maze of a purely Bronkian quandry where belief cancels unbelief and vice-versa.

It is no accident that Bronk's poems derive their power neither from the destruction of some outworn edifice of thought nor from the knowledge that we will replace it with a yet more sophisticated rhetorical structure. Their power comes, instead, by the precision with which Bronk can capture the moment of swerve or trope *i.e.* at the very *bardo* of rhetorical structuring, that momentary gap between the old and the new conception.

In this sense, Bronk is not a poet of ideas. The true "substance" of his poems is the vertiginous trace of temporality, a trace made up of regress after regress of rhetorical pivots, as in:

WHAT FOOT

We are shoes it wears for the time and then discards.
Nothing wears them again. Memorials,
they show for awhile what foot and where it walked.

(*MAF*, 4)

This poem, a rueful hymn to belatedness, suggests the obscurity which surrounds the verbal 'monument' of the poem, it's rise into authorship and its quick fade. Behind the poem lies Shelley's "Ozymandias," where the wanderer-poet discovers in the desert the immense pedestal with its broken feet and ironic inscription. But Bronk overwrites Shelley with a deeper, more cutting irony: the failure of memorials is not only that they do not last against time, but that their meaning can never properly be read; they record not what they mean but what was not meant to be recorded, our own unease with records of all sorts, with chronicles, with literature and with monuments.

With Bronk, the question (or the impossibility) becomes not one of cheating death but of cheating a certain disgust with the literary act itself. Here, we feel the weight of the poet not as a presence behind the language of the poem but as an exorcist, one who would like to throw off both language and reality (which in Bronk is nearly always our conceptions of reality) in order to experience the immediacy of his own life. Bronk's poetry is an attack, a series of stratagums, on his own self-consciousness.

As I suggested above, such an attack is a moment-by-moment affair, an act of verbal trickery and verbal contradiction. It won't work unless the poet is sufficiently seduced by his own sentiment, by a deep feeling for the world and for his own linguistic representations of that world. "I love what is wasted, don't yield the way," (51) he insists. No simple nihilism here. Rather, over and over again, in Bronk's poems, we read him falling in love with the world. "Earth is like home . . ." he writes in "Friends Of The Earth" (*MAF*, 18). But he almost immediately follows this with "A planet is home?" The question relates not to the earth, but to the fictive orders of language, to the way Bronk, the poet, has been sucked into his own reifications, and to his own awareness of their simultaneous power of confirmation and denial:

> . . . God bless us! Something is wrong.
> I can't put things together; atoms, too,
> they have their distances, infinities
> in respect of their smallnesses. Balks are built
> into the system, balks are the base of it
> — our system, our way to materialize.
>
> (MAF, 18)

I think Bronk truly and deeply means that "God bless us!" But he means it doubly, i.e. as both a cry for mercy and, more importantly, as the discovery of deliverance. The phrase is the poem's pivot, for even as the hierarchical structure of intellection is brought down and its knot of certainties cut, pitching the poet into despair, this finding of something wrong begins to show, indeed, as a blessing. The balk of the poem, the hindrance or the false move (as with the baseball pitcher's manuever which gets the batter on base), the irruption of dissonance into the soothing engines of conceptual thought, is deliverance itself.

This delivering moment is syntactical before all else, by which I mean it can only be registered in language or thought by two disparate terms of existence crossing each other's paths. It's signature in a Bronk poem is the point or points in the work where emotion, which takes sides, seems to drive on through the intellect. It may occur within a line or through a process of lines which culminate in the poet's refusal to go along with the intellectual analysis he has himself constructed. In "Friends of the Earth," (*MAF*, 18) for example, it is the question mark after the word "home," turning a manifest-ly commonsensical notion into a philosophical wedge. What the reader gets is not the grand competition of large-scale systematic ideas but a little granular irritation in the molecular structure of his or her thought sufficient to open the mind to an infinity of potential balks.

Of course, this is what Bronk has been doing all along; his is one of the most sustained careers against closure in all of contemporary poetry, and in this, he is infinitely more signficant as a poet than a bus load of avant-garde experimenters. "I do nonsensical things," (*MAF*, 21) he proclaims and irradiates with truth all our programmatic and presumed "sense."

(1989–1993)

Armand Schwerner: The Semiotician of Self Work

"Grant your blessings that confusion may dawn as wisdom". So wrote Gampopa, the 11th century Tibetan codifier of the buddhist teachings, and so, like a dialogue across centuries, does Schwerner's poetry seek to respond back. That is, in its marvelous range, in its tactful infusion of esoteric materials, in particular those of a buddhist nature, Schwerner's work seems to be one of the few blessings that transform contemporary confusions into major instances of wisdom. Or to put it more precisely, confusion, wisdom and poetry, as well as humor and delight, are in inseparable consonance in his work.

Consonance, a reader may ask? For to the casual observer, Schwerner's poetry—*The Tablets* are exemplary in this respect—looks like nothing less than a collection of well-travelled meteorites, gouged out and pock-marked, and still smoking. The poems gape with dislocations, abrupt terminations of thought and image, enjambments of what at first strike as totally 'other' material. In addition to poems which display no regular metric structure, there are a significant number of pantoums, the rigorous formalities of which are stratified by mysteriously beautiful, if disparate, lines. The very plug seems pulled on western culture's overriding and over determining intelligence. For the reader—and the reader can only 'read' it into the poet—confusion dawns, is, well, *is*.

The reader, then, who may be in need of a reference point, is well advised to turn to the poem "snow" in Schwerner's *Selected Shorter Poems* which is at once Schwerner's poetic honor code, descriptive methodology, *apologia*, and most intriguing of all, a defense against defense itself. For Schwerner means to shun more typical modalities of poetry, not in order to exhibit unconventional poetry, but to escape the comfortable harness and haystalls of contemporary poetics. Most of all, to be exposed, as he writes in "snow," to his own fear and processes:

> I don't invent, find them in poring over the wastes
> of the miles-long snows of habit, find the tiny outcroppings
> whose thrusting greys and blacks and ochres seem real and I
> skeptical geologist call the work poetry and make my measures limp
> to catch the whiteness the intermittences . . .
>
> (*SCP*, 123)

So in a crucial sense, a first, somewhat bewildered, take on Schwerner's poetry is appropriate and even essential. For what this poetry takes to task is the notion of wisdom, and wisdom-poetry, as something rational, purposeful, even beautiful, in other words, the idea of poetry as a conventional form of discourse that can be manageably worked into our usual modes of thought.

But if we mean by wisdom that which is transformative or consciousness altering, something which will destroy the ossified mindset of both the spiritual journey and the poem and thereby liberate both, then one of our blessings is surely Schwerner's poetry. At the same time, it is necessary to assert that Schwerner's work will be seriously misunderstood if we lump it in with the collective avant-gardisms of the day. No, Schwerner's meteorites are mini-terrains as far removed from the icy constructs of the language centered schools or the halls of the totally aleatory as they are from the overplowed farmlands of academia. They fit nowhere in the current crop of modalities, the "shopping centers of traditions" as Schwerner refers to them in "snow", and by that signal their literary as well as extra-literary importance.

Schwerner's poems are as much about departures toward as they are about departures from. Each poem, and this is true of *The Tablets* as well, is at least partially founded on that curious fulcrum, perhaps first encoded by Rimbaud, of the self aware of its non-self. Such awareness in Schwerner however, is less occasion for *angst* than for celebration. In the first poem in sounds of the river *Naranjana & The Tablets I–XXIV*, "'the waves are the practice of the ocean'" with its zen teaching title, what is announced is not dread but the dropping away of the inauthentic, the releasing pleasure of its loss, where "here, happy outside of pursuits" poetry again becomes possible:

> I can make and offer the fluid confirming of this verse. . . .
>   my heart bearing you up as if, in a high-pulse
> of endlessly heavy white

two floors of Atlantic separated you from me

(SRN, 3)

Such a state of mind (is that the term?) also animates many of Schwerner's love poems, as in the very beautiful "the pillow" where the physical act of love is transposed into a resonating gratitude:

I'm so grateful to have lost
what I used to believe was my attentiveness and fall
into my confusion with a gardner's trust . . .

(SRN, 8)

And while Rimbaudian dissolution of self has been a dominant trope of modern and contemporary poetry, its appearance in the very heart of Schwerner's work is unique. For Schwerner is less dissolver than semiotician of this self-work, a sort of Heisenbergian hierophant, sensing and testing the vocabularies of spiritual journey and authenticity. Like Pound's Chinese historians in *The Cantos* who leave blanks, the gaps and dislocations of Schwerner's poetry are the interactive spaces of a risky not knowing. Thus his modes, in sharp contrast to the willful disordering of the senses, are an embrace of awareness and an accommodation of ever larger inclusiveness into what we might call new states of being. In such poetry, attraction, affection, personal love are deeply felt animators, the goal, as in the "pillow," less possessiveness than receptivity:

. . . I never understood
why incredible star distances come inhabit me
when my little body protests against itself

(SRN, 7)

Openness here becomes generative, the poet's construct a celebratory trace, as in "Piazza Fumie," of the fusion of inside and outside, a sort of affectionate bow to the entirety of the phenomenal world:

connections at random found as real
as history and present as child's play.
hello.

(SNR, 16)

In Schwerner's work, this randomness is no mode of production but an occasion for interpentration, the "found as real" authentically moving, the poet another 'antennae of the race' upon whose ear falls everything from the cadences of other poetries to the rhetorics and metonomyies of history. The poem "breathing in & out: Leonard

Crowdog and Wallace Black Elk", for example, with its stunted fragments of speech and autobiography enclosed between the lines "I am
the evidence of this Western Hemisphere", implicate, with Blakean
rigor, a century of mistreatment. The overhearing or "found object"
quality of the material in the pantoums and in such poems as "Milagros'
song" seem to rub against the psyche like a rasp on steel; the ugly gran-
ules of history, the *dura mater* of personality, fall through the interstices:

> inside the sun, tumor, the name of the sun, which follows me —
>   why is grass green? why do stars shine?
> through the window fall moldy dream cones of pine trees
>
> insect storms of triangle points, blunt insult trapezoids
> corrugated stone tissues filled with anger in a mine
> the idea of the uncaused liberates like dissolution

(SNR, 13)

The Tablets, Schwerner's masterpiece, some thirty-five years in the
making, is an immensely varied and parodistic work. Its central focus,
for those unfamiliar with the poem, is Schwerner's "scholar- translator",
possibly the most comic character (in both the Chaplinesque and
Dantesque senses) in contemporary poetry, busily, hurriedly, distract-
edly engaged in deciphering the tablets of an ancient proto-Sumerian
"civilization". This "civilization", which has inscribed the stone tablets
with everything from religious hymns to metaphysical shopping lists to
poignant and searching poems of love and spirituality, is in a sort of
binary apposition to the deductive and anxiety-ridden mind of the
scholar-translator. Apposition and not opposition because in
Schwerner's hand this is no mere struggle of the archaic versus the
modern, but an intertwining and interpenetration of the two. The intention is toward what is both useful and authentic in the present. As
Schwerner remarks in his notes to the Tablets:

> Eliot and Pound structured ironic and tragic commentaries by
> confronting past and present. Why not go further, I thought, and recreate
> the past itself, in a series of subjectively ordered variations suggestively
> rooted in the archaic? And, more, why not augment the confusions
> between illusion and reality by the further invention of a scholar-transla-
> tor whose fictive but oppressively present self would add a dimension of
> narration? .... The final question is When are a man's discoveries tech-

niques subsumed in his vision; and When are his inventions gimmicks straining to support a petty order of limits?

(TT, 134)

The Tablets, of course, brilliantly explode such limits by claiming neither the modern nor the archaic as privileged ground. Consider the beginning of "Tablet XXIV":

> no wisdom no ice no forest no segment no foolishness no cave
>   [no knowledge harmony
> of rabid openness ++++++++++++++++++++ the cities sigh
> under the fullness of too much (heavy cream). I+++++++
> the ruminant anxiety that the old question
> is the new question. among the craftsmen I busy myself
> among the veins, identifying ores, laughing
> with the tailings, underneath the bed of brilliant metal
>   [families
> another *underneath*, as well as another *below*
> below my anger about the ridiculousness
> of trying to remember . . . . . . such a delight . . . . . . a light

(TT, 67)

Here the lines and such terms as "no knowledge" and "no wisdom" coupled with "harmony" hold the usual meanings in a kind of fluid suspension, an amniotic sac of hope and fear threatened by the tablet-narrator's needle-like vectors of intentionality and resignation. The scholar-translator's overlay of "untranslateables" (++++) and "missings" (. . . ..), of inappropriate guesses "(heavy cream)" compound the uncertainty until the tablet itself is a figure or exemplum of the vastness of human longing, a desiring of "a light", itself less definable than acknowledged as something shared, as in the last line: "circulation++++++++++ sky-veins, and very slowly with many people". Multidimensional, self- contradictory, immensely moving and humorous, *The Tablets* ought to be received not in the spirit of exegesis but in the spirit of delight and play by which humanity re-envisions and so continually recreates itself.

The title of one of Schwerner's poems, you will recall, is 'the waves are the practice of the ocean'. If Schwerner's work is a releasing or letting go of the self-imposed limitations and reductive thinking by which contemporary poetry has constrained itself, it is also that "departure toward" which I mentioned above. As the waves are the practice of the ocean, so the operations of mind and body are 'the practice' of the poet, a practice, as the Buddhists (whose thinking colors so much of this work) remind us, is rooted in the notion of our own and the world's impermanence. In Buddhist thought, and deeply and lovingly in Schwerner's poems, impermanence is the key to realizing the truth or "suchness" of reality. In the latest work, in particular the long poem "sounds of the river Naranjana", the acceptance of impermanence and confusion becomes a mirror of this understanding.

The poem, in its length and variousness, one of the most moving evidences of Schwerner's transformative openess. consists of eighteen alphabetically lettered sections, and makes use of an enormous number of technical devices, both traditional and experimental, ranging from symbol and metonymy to the musical analogs of sound poetry. (Schwerner's ear—he is as much musician as poet—is an unfailing organizer of these diversities). The poem is something like the river of the title, not merely flowing but incorporating and changing as sections roll, one into the other:

> . . . .what I hear keeps changing, the flute
> becomes a garbage truck, the velvet grasp
> of your hand on my balls becomes winter, the materiality
> of my knee and my ass dissolves into a joke, what I know
> forgets me again and again, how I love loss. I want
> my absence to fill me, what falls from me then?
>
> (*SSP*, 114)

Yet the poem strikes one as far more than a registry of Heraclitian flux; its tendency is toward binding up the riverlike perception of life into healing recognition, into moments of attention and resolution where: "now when you walk you walk" and where, as in the lyrical Section "p", the "red-orange balsam tree" returns that bow to the world I mentioned above and "its slow/ power invites you and remains itself". If the poem is epiphanic, and its most moving passages suggest epiphanies and losses of all sorts, it is also one of our most powerful and contemporary hymns to the visionary perspective it has achieved:

> . . . you wander
> in the alien sounds of your names, listening
> for the river Naranjana, the release
> a slow green walking throughout your bodies
> after the effort fails. you have gone that far in your surpriseable
> |readiness . . .
>
> (*SSP*, 118)

~

Looking back over Schwerner's career, we see that long before the advent of our current post-structuralisms, now thoroughly commodified and defanged in any number of prominent poetics, he was busy with the central and unanswerable question of being, the question, as he ponders it in his late notes to *The Tablets*, of there existing "no nuclear self . . . no *unendurable* inward or outward Babel of tongues, there is merely Babel." A way of perceiving Schwerner's career-long arcings above these matters, less a 'project' than an attempt at constant clarification and wisdom transmission, may be discerned by contemplating some of the parallels between *The Tablets* and Schwerner's marvelous reworking of Sophocles' *Philoctetes*.

First, both works ought to be considered from the point of view of 'translation.' My justification for bracketing the word with inverted commas comes from Schwerner's prefatory note to the Greek drama. As he puts it: "The translator, *carrier-over*, owes the play-language and himself an immersion in the extensive field of those possibilities" (*TWJ*, 36). This immersion has something to do, not only with finding an alternative to stuffy or outmoded language in other translations, but to exploring the "possibilities," the "play-language," of what the text might say to us now. Play, not as gamesmanship or fashionable flutter but rather as a mode of seeking framed by the parameters of Sophocles's conception. Thus Schwerner employs a contemporary economy of language, one which favors the close-to-the-bone conversational idiom over the speechifying tropes of the Loeb, the Columbia, etc., breaking with, wherever possible, the overly ornate and formal sentences of most previous translations. His aim, as he puts it in his note, is to foreground "the various embodiments of subtle and shifting psychological states [which] evoke constant recognition." Philoctetes' psychology serves well for this evocation. He is afflicted with a foul-smelling, suppurating and often disabling wound in the leg. Unable to stand the stench of his wound, his fellow companions and warriors have rejected him, abandoning him on the uninhabited island of Lemnos. There, he is at the mercy of wild beasts and violent weathers. These depredations of Philoctetes' mind, the painful psycho-physical condition which finds him half-mad and vulnerable, lie at the heart of Schwerner's translation. Here, the exposed fluidity, the "shifting psychological states," of what we normally call "character" is situated in Philoctetes being buffeted between enormous terrors and almost vainglorious hopes. In

Schwerner's version of the drama, Philoctetes's suffering serves to remind the modern reader of how the self's desire for certainty puts it very much at the mercy of narrative seductions.

How is this thematics exposed? In Schwerner's translation, the wound, foul-smelling and driving others away from Philoctetes, is both social and literary fact. Philoctetes' hurt, his disease and misfortune, in spite of the fact that he has been a great warrior and hero, leave him open to prey by a dissembling Odysseus.

Sophocles's play indicts the cruel side of the ancient Athenian idealization of perfection, that abiding matrix of Greek art and culture, which forms one of the bedrock elements of the play. Schwerner's version seems to concentrate more keenly on Philoctetes' pain, his confusion and vulnerability, as the truth-function of the drama. Odysseus, who believes that "only stratagems will work" and who is convinced of "the tongue's ultimate power," is trying to author a fictive world, using Achilles's son Neoptolemus, to gain Philoctetes' bow, a necessary part of his armaments against Troy. Philoctetes is doubly victimized in the play by these dissemblers, first Odysseus and then Neoptolemus who, acting on Odysseus's suggestion, convinces Philoctetes of his good will toward him. The translation deftly captures Philoctetes' capitulation to Neoptolemus' blandishments:

> how wonderful, waking to brightness with you
> near me, concerned about me
> I never hoped for that, never dared.
> the Atride, those courageous captains
> had no heart to accept my cries
> and my wound. I afflicted their eyes, I insulted their ears, my hurt
> was foul in their nostrils but you have a noble nature my son

(TWJ, 72)

And throughout, we readers/observers are absorbed, not only by the piteous condition of Philoctetes and by his hope of release, but, as well, by the spectacle of his feverish turnings as reason gives way to deceit, rhetoric and sophistry. Philoctetes struggle becomes for the reader a recognition which dissolves the hungers it so vividly portrays into self-knowledge. This struggle, which has many similarities to the emphases of *The Tablets*, strikes me as Schwerner's point, even if, at the play's end, the sudden appearance of the god Herakles alters, with a kind of Greek rightness, the resolution of the drama.

Let me carry these parallels a bit further. Schwerner's consummate work, *The Tablets*, is one of the great ironic workings of the scholarly quest for self-knowledge, a masterwork of what we might call "experimental scholarship." Ordinary scholarship proposes the fact, usefully disentangles it from its ghostings, in order to work it into discourse. The anthropological enterprise, both imitated and ironized in *The Tablets*, derived its authority through narrative structure. But everywhere *The Tablets* refuses the gesture of narrative authority. There are no 'facts' as we know them in *The Tablets*; rather, a reader finds only a slippery slope of speculations and guesses invoked by the anxiety-ridden Scholar-Translator who, like Philoctetes, is trying to make sense of the versions of reality proffered to him. And also like him, the Scholar-Translator too seeks for the "truth" of the structures he partially creates ('hears,' visually) from the marking on the tablets:

> In addition I am worried that I may have mistranslated part of the preceding Tablet, a combination of dialogue and narrative. . . . There is growing ambiguity in this work of mine, but I'm not sure where it lies. . . . On occasion it almost seems to me as if I am inventing this sequence, and such a fantasy sucks me into an abyss of almost irretrievable depression, from which only forced and unpleasurable exercises in linguistic analysis rescue me

> (*TT*, 31, 32).

The Scholar/Translator, abandoned on the pitted and scarred surfaces of the tablets, his Lemnos, is ravaged, like Philoctetes, by his uncertainties and by the linguistic inventions which he only half-authors with the tablets' markings. For the ghosts and echoes which surround and invade the work are not voices from the past (Schwerner has emphatically stated, the past of this work is "invented"), but imported phantoms whose function is at least partially to render the tablets meaningful to the Scholar/Translator.

Clearly, the parodistic flavor is already an ironic commentary on the anthropologist's goals. But the Scholar/Translator's inventions are more/other than scientific guesses—or their parody. Instead, they are the projections, mindscapes, of his and our anguish over matters involving our connection to the spiritual, the sexual, the cultural, etc. As 'translations,' they seem to bind up a past into recognizable configurations, affording some occasional surcease to the Scholar/Translator. In actuality, they form a kind of pantheon, an unstable collection of gods, goddesses, rituals, a series of proto-golden ages by which we bind up neural anxieties. In this sense, the Scholar/Translator seems to be performing *our* work, *our* questing, seeking to becalm himself by creating some form of tranquilizing story, some encompassing 'translation' of the archaic culture under hand which will give him certainty by explaining the present.

Thus *The Tablets*, like Schwerner's *Philoctetes*, are cautionary tales about our hunger for chronicle, history and the dangerous precincts of the spiritual, dramas of selfhood/non-selfhood which depict the exacerbated psyche at those precise and telling moments when all its fears and hopes have gone awry. The Scholar/Translator, again like Philoctetes, persists, and this is the creative side of the exacerbation. For the fictiveness of the real, its ungraspability, becomes the shadow-existence of the real under the mind's play, the perpetual irritant or wound which demands invention and so is, ultimately, the opening for poetry. And here, it might be added, Schwerner, making this opening the working space of his efforts for over thirty years, has anticipated such thinkers on language and dread as Blanchot, Bataille and Lacan.

It is rumored that Sophocles, unlike most of the other Greek dramatists, desisted from acting in his own works, possibly because he felt that the mind's play as exhibited in his characterizations, were clear and 'true' enough to be a part of anyone's thought. Schwerner's work strikes me as imbued with a similar confidence. His ventriloquisms, which abound in the heteroglossia of *The Tablets* and in translations such as the *Philoctetes*, are about bringing to the fore what he has referred to as the "availabilities," the sense that our potentials of being, our desirings, are the very structure of language, the tropes of both epic and lyric poetry. Nothing is left out. *Sub specie aeternitas*, Schwerner's powerful—and greatly good-humored—writing and performance pieces keep reminding us that all narrative lies seductively on that very human plane between our overheard infernos and paradisos.

Which brings us to Schwerner's Dante collected in his *Cantos From Dante's Inferno*. Like his *Philoctetes*, Schwerner's translations from Dante's *Inferno* attempt two interrelated tasks, to rescue the translation from the nostalgia which surrounds all translations of great works and, at the same time, to create a powerful figurative linguistic object, one that brings the powers of the original into the present. In this Inferno, Schwerner's aim, as he noted in his interview with Ed Foster (*Talisman* #19), is to invoke "a direct confrontational sort of adventure" with Dante, an adventure which seeks to avoid the recycling of former English or American versions into the work. One notices immediately that the standard three-line approximation to *terza rime* of most verse translations of the *Commedia* has been abandoned, to be replaced by a prosodically tighter form that assigns narrative to the left side of the page, juxtaposing it with speech and oration on the right. This lineation, unlike other translated versions and with perhaps a Bakhtinian dialogics in mind, creates a new set of formal implications, not previously foregrounded in other versions of Dante, between the interiority of narration or rumination and the externality of speech. As in *The Tablets*, where the archaic is posed against the contemporary via the commentary of the Scholar/Translator, there is a lineage of destabilizing practices, ones which make the reader rethink the work from a new vantage.

This impulse to re-envision is, well, Dantean, emulating the precursor's break with prior form, his incorporation of a whole range of formerly unheard voices, demotics and tonal ranges embedded in the Italian of his time. So too with Schwerner's American/English which is not so much colloquial as infused with the polyvalent, reflexive potentials of present-day speech and writing. Schwerner's working notes in the book to a number of the *Cantos* are remarkable prose-poem-like forays and recuperations into English. They provide a fascinating exploration of word-choice, tone and, finally, artistic judgment as he brings Dante into our time. The "Notes to Canto VIII," for example, contain this meditation on Dante's "*anima fella*" mistakenly shouted at Dante standing with Virgil by the boatman crossing the river and found in Schwerner's line 18. Schwerner's entry reads: "literally *wicked, foul, impious* etc. *Wicked soul, foul soul* etc. evokes the rhetoric of 19th c. melodrama. But *gall* seemed interesting: (Outrageous insolence, effrontery.—Middle English, from old English *gaella, galla*—See Synonyms at temerity; also abnormal swelling of plant tissue caused by insects, microorganisms, or external injury; v.t. to irk or exasperate; vex)—thus *galled soul*." (*CDI*, 61, 62) Schwerner sees these words as "relevant in their relative distortion to the reader's sense of the oarsman's character and cry, a sense intensified by the hieratic contempt implicit in Virgil's utterance" "Over the stinking waves you can already/glimpse what's coming . . .". (*CDI*, 33) Hence "galled soul—which takes the measure of the oarsman's demotic *now you've had it* . . ." The kinetic energy of the work is released via these strenuous etymological exercises which lies behind each word.

Clearly, Schwerner's untimely death before he could complete the entirety of the *Inferno* makes these translations something of a work-in-progress. Undoubtedly, there would have been revisions and rebalancings as more Cantos came into being. Still the absorbing idiosyncratic

power of what we have here, the great pleasure one gets out of
Schwerner's play with both form and diction, reminds us of his peculiar
brilliance as both poet and translator. To use one of his own favorite
words, Schwerner has given us a translation full of "availabilities," entry
points and registers of our hopes and understandings, leading us,
compellingly, both forward and back to the figure of Dante.

∾

Schwerner's many 'translations from numerous works,' *The Philoctetes*,
the Dante work and, of course, *The Tablets*, appear to involve, to borrow
Schwerner's own words, "an intention to carry over" a prior work or
prior existent into a present articulation. Clearly the vocabulary
employed by Schwerner of 'translation,' 'version' and 'working' suggests
some sort of source, a well or excavation from which something is to be
drawn or worked or re-envisioned, something to be concretized, made
transmittable through the text which Schwerner then produces. Yet
looking at the new additional end notes to The Tablets, "Tablets
Journals/Divagations", notes which are part autobiography, part confes-
sion, part *ars poetica*, it is clear that the notion of a prior work or text as
the basis for the work is at best an elusive one.

In "the air of Performance at Liancourt," a late poem incorporated
into "Tablets Journals/Divagations," Schwerner formulates the problem
of his work in this questioning way: "What is the nature of the recurrent
hope/for the seizure of the irreducible?" (TT, 140) Such a hope may be
vain; as he puts it, "the sense that whatever could be findable will not be
findable . . ." (TT, 142)

"Tablets/Divigiations & Journal" can be seen to be divided between two
basic sections, those notes composed before and while working on *The
Tablets* and those notes he wrote after completing Tablet No. XXVII, written under the knowledge of his illness and death. The two sections are
signalled as different and separate by a gap in the text and by an epigraph
taken from Louis Zukofsky's "A"-12 and centered on the middle of the
page at the beginning of the second set of notes. It is these latter notes
that I take up here. They appear in print for the first time (see pp. 139–158)
in the National Poetry Foundation edition of *The Tablets* published in 1999,
the year of Schwerner's death, and constitute a back-glancing meditation
on the thoughts and poetic gestures that have gone into his work.

The first entry of this new section reads "All concepts are misconcep-
tions" (TT, 138). Schwerner has made this his 'headline,' so to speak, its

cautionary import addressed not only to the reader but to the author himself. In this sense, the entry points two ways at once. First, and for the reader: if, in the matrices of the act of translation, a source text exists (as with Philoctetes, Dante, Michaux, Amerindian chants), any reading, by the reductive process of reworking, is already a misreading. The letter is, alas, the letter, but the mind is yet something else. Neither literalism nor poeticizing (by these I mean a spectrum of possible approaches to translating) will render what cannot be found (the *mis-* of misconception) by forming a fixed idea of what the text says. This is also the central path of *The Tablets*. The Scholar/Translator's work, in fact, is a textbook of misapprehensions and misreadings, which, on the level of parody, puts us through a number of lesson plans, deliciously serio-comic, on what fails when Western Civ. meets the big Other.

One doesn't perceive the words; rather, Schwerner maintains, "the words perceive you, in their variousness" (*TT*, 142). Schwerner defines the *Tablets* as "a grammar facilitating the arrival *into* a word through some conduit, to abolish Option by inhabiting utterance." It is, "the self-undoing genre crowded with doing" (*TT*, 142).

In "Tablets/Journals & Divigations," Schwerner describes these as the Scholar/Translator's "morphemalgia," a wonderful word which can be unpacked in a number of directions, "word pain," "shape-shifting pain," with echoes of something obsessive or annoyingly chronic like neural-gia. Knowledge for the Scholar/Translator is not the successful capture of something prior. He will not restore the linguistic Hanging Gardens of Akkadia to us, but embrace instead a "singular confusion of pronouns here. I do not know who I am when I read this. How magnificent."

The second entry of the Journals/Divigations, which reads: "Is it possi-ble to live without a zone of comfort, of solidity?" (*TT*, 139), enlarges the platform of confusion. The question interrogates the Scholar/Translator's possible magnificence, his celebration of his muddled-head-edness by an ironic take on the over-romancing of "confusion." For confusion is requisite but also potentially trivial, self-indulgent and even dangerous unless it plays over a more serious ground. *The Philoctetes*, for example, is the story of a man who has too easily surren-dered to confusion spun out by Odysseus and his minions, and, as Schwerner notes of the original, is only saved by a *deux ex machina* of a descending god.

≈

As noted above, one of the influencing factors on Scherner's poetics is his Buddhist studies, among them Gampopa's chants, his four dharmas, recited at every meditation session in the hopes that "confusion [may] dawn as wisdom." And part of the poet's task is how to save confusion or its more enlivening counterpart, "play" from triviality. Schwerner quotes, without comment, from Cixous's *Three Steps on the Ladder to Writing*: "Writing is learning to die. It's learning not to be afraid, in other words to live at the extremity of life, which is what the dead, death, give us" (*TT*, 139). Death and terror of death are a foundation for play and confusion because they point toward a groundless ground. The powerful Body-Declensions of the later *Tablets*, "CROUCHED-DYING" and "LYING-DOWN-SICK," are likened by Schwerner to the way "the Indian artist shrives himself, does special ablutions, etc" (*TT*, 142). They are, he says, "a kind of speed-up of this process [of shriving], made a very part of the utterance world."

The Scholar/Translator, that complex imaginative entity at the center of the *Tablets*, is a psycho-spiritual-physical presence, as much inflected by materiality/de-materiality as the work itself. He abides in "the weather of his work," as "a gauzy pillaging ghost" (*Tablet XXVII*), his discoveries, according to the "Tablets Journals/Divigations," embodying "a reflexive Medusa of the seemingly knowable." Indeed, when all the self-cancelling effects of *The Tablets* are summed up, when the dance of strategies is exhausted (as in a sort of Philoctetesish swoon of rhetorics) "all that's left," Schwerner reminds us, "is pattern (shoes?)" The word "shoes" is comic, deflationary but marvelously accurate, for what else are the patterns but shoes, items to take the walk with, the endless walk of walking (see Schwerner's poem "The Work, The Joy and the Triumph of the Will."). Walking toward our deaths.

Schwerner quotes from Lou Nordstrom's *Toward a Philosphy of Zen Buddhism*: "Whether we speak or remain silent, the ultimate reality in its suchness can never be indicated." The Scholar/Translator echoes the thought: "The word is never quite the thing, nor is it ever quite not-the-thing." To continue the Buddhist-ness of this: we're on a Mudymakaya slippery slope of learning how to give up absolutes. The capaciousness of *The Tablets*, the metonymic fictive or fugitive Ur-civilization that it presences, or, if we take up Schwerner's Dante which transmutes the descent into the circles of Hell as something like endlessly recursive Bakhtinian dialogics, these are problematics which we can learn from. That is, seeing the work as teaching. Schwerner: "The pain I felt when I interrupted a lyric song by any of my unknown archaic speakers by intercalating—or rather by finding necessary the presence of—the Scholar/Translator's discursive, often apparently irrelevant comments, often wrongheaded inventions which nevertheless brought the reader into a consideration of the essential ambiguities of syntax, grammar and translation, a kind of undependable groundlessness of appearance" (TT, 157).

Comedy, even Divine comedies, are composed of shoes (who remembers Mandelstam on Dante, the verse as embodying the physicality of the stroll, like the Scholar/Translator's peregrinations with form, context, work-thing, we all stroll toward our underworlds). Or, as Schwerner hears it in Beethoven's 7th, the second movement, "Tiny motifs. Notes the same same same same, but what harmonic sound! He was I guess already deaf, or on the way" (TT, 157). In a lineated poetic fragment which ends the Journals, Schwerner asks:

> How, did he disown
> the experience so
> as to leave fermenting
> Space
> for composition.
> Being? Arriving?
> How did he hear what he
> listened to, to transcribe
>   as he was also making it?
> Where was the Space?
> Where is mine?
> With good karma we earn deafness
>
>   (TT, 158)

"With good karma we earn deafness." This seems, given what has come before, a rather extraordinary closing line for the Journals. There are many ways to read this, for instance, as an obverse of a Shakespearean "the rest is silence." Death here as a beginning to notice back, to back read as it were, over the motifs of Hamlet. Or—which may amount to the same thing—that the life of awareness is in the play and replay of tiny motifs, the wearing out of shoes (the Buddhist monk's wearing down of his sandal leather), the endlessness of inventiveness, of new tries and assays as evidenced throughout all of Schwerner's work. "There's no old or new in it," he says, "as long as I'm in language's changing weathers" (TT, 157).

                                         (1995–2000)

Towards our Mallarmé

Mallarmé's effects as a poet are now so diffuse in the practice of contemporary American poets that he is almost impossible to find. Like so much in the progressivist climate of contemporary poetry, Mallarmé is neatly atomized and dispersed in everything from the proto-symbolists to post-structuralist and language poetry. As with Shakespeare and with Dante, Mallarmé has been absorbed into the DNA codes of poetic culture. To find him would now require a violent anatomy lesson upon ourselves; worse than amputating a limb, it would mean removing and isolating a part of each cell that makes up the body poetic.

And yet, at the same time, Mallarmé has become a victim of the technological approach to poetry. The force of his work, his vision, inseparable in Mallarmé from the technical moment of his craft, has been decontextualized out of existence. A poetic opportunism has cannibalized the poet into a thousand partial and exploitable gestures; Mallarmé *entire* can be treated with indifference.

Into the midst of this climate, a climate which eats up dead poets and spews them out as 'poetics,' comes Henry Weinfield's brave and elegant construction of Mallarmé in English, one which tries to restore a wholeness to the poet even against the formidable odds of translation's innate reductions. The stratgems of this construction are clearly marked. Foremost is Weinfield's decision to recoup in English something of the sonic force of the poems by the use of meters and rhyme schemes which approximate Mallarmé's poem-by-poem metrical designs. Yet this is less a desire to follow the conventions of verse form than to give us something akin to the embodied voice of the poet, which not only has its peculiar accent, history and occasion, but in which we will hear the striving for the incantatory quality that Mallarmé sought in the poetry.

Weinfield, in his Introduction, describes this attempt as one of rendering the "'music,' or 'musical essence,' or 'spiritual essence'" of the
poetry (*W* xi). For Mallarmé, the musical and the spiritual dimensions of
the poem point toward the unsayable or Ineffable, as he called it, that
quality which constitutes the unparaphraseable aspect of the poem,
that which makes poetry poetry. The poet's duty, as he put it in a letter
to Verlaine, was the making of an "Orphic explanation of the earth," in
which all of reality was to be rendered as a kind of inspired music (W
xiii).

Many translations of Mallarmé tend to emphasize the 'spiritual' over
everything else, unduly solemnizing the poetry until it reaches our ears
as abstracted high-minded drone. Weinfield's versions are quite the
opposite; deeply inflected and often acerbic, they remind us of
Mallarmé's problem, that of the genuine difficulty of voicing a new
poetry, of the resistances which it encounters both within the poet
himself and with the public. In this way, Weinfield's translations do us
an enormous service by conveying a sense of how such resistances are
themselves part of the shaping forces at work in the poem.

As Weinfield envisions his project, Mallarmé must be rendered as a
'dialogic' figure, one whose work must be heard in the conversation of
the poetry of its time; its ideations are at one with its tonalities, its
emplacement in the argument of French poetry. Perhaps an example or
two will indicate the liveliness and historical sensitivity of Weinfield's
efforts. Let us look at the first two stanzas of "Salut," a poem Mallarmé
chose to be placed at the beginning of an edition of his collected poems,
Poésies, although it was written in 1893 after he had turned fifty:

> Rein, cette écume, vierge vers
> A ne désigner que le coupe;
> Telle loin se noie une troupe
> De sirèns maint à l'envers.
>
> Nous naviguons, ô mes divers
> Amis, noi déjà sur la poupe
> Vous l'avant fasteueux qui coupe
> Le flot de foudres et d'hivers;

Weinfield translates the two stanzas as follows:

> Nothing, this foam, virgin verse
> Only to designate the cup:

Thus, far off, drowns a Siren troop;
Many, upended, are immersed.

We navigate, O my diverse
Friends, myself already on the poop,
You the sumptuous prow to cut
Through winter wave and lightning burst;

                                        (*W* 3)

Mallarmé originally read the poem at a banquet for the magazine *La Plume*, a gathering of younger poets whose ambivalent veneration of Mallarmé, a veneration which Mallarmé felt compelled to both honor and reject, is invoked throughout the poem. Weinfield's lines, their heightening of the functional syntax embedded in the poem, beautifully capture the need for Mallarmé on this particular occasion to respond generously to the regard of the poets, and yet, at the same time, to remind them, with minimal offense, of the solitudinous role of the poet. A rendition less responsive to the social contract of the poem or one desirous of Englishing or modernizing Mallarmé would reduce its meaning to a transcribed idea and destroy Mallarméan *Idea*, the moment, as defined by Mallarmé, where thought is no longer abstract but totalized, wedded to many factors including those of personality and occasion. Mallarmé's abstraction, in other words, is bloodied, incarnated, not in the ideational realm but in the pressures of voicing and in the presencing of the poem as a response to an occasion. The 'purest' Mallarmé in this sense is also the most historical one.

Which leads us to another remarkable aspect of Weinfield's translation, its hardness of diction. Where a number of different word-choices are possible, Weinfield continually picks the more definitive concrete word. For example, in the poem just cited, Anthony Hartley's prose rendering of the first stanza reads: "Nothing, this foam, a virgin line of poetry only to describe the cup; so plunges far away a band of mermaids, many a one head downwards." (H 7) And Keith Bosley's version reads:

Nothing, this foam, virgin verse
Pointing out only the cup;
So far off a siren troop
Drowns, taking turns for the worse.

                                        (*B* 55)

Hartley and Bosley both lose the demonstrative force of the word "Thus" in Weinfield's third line. Hartley's "mermaids" prettify and erase the Homeric tonalities invoked by "Sirens," tonalities which are, as

Weinfield makes clear in his notes to the poem, an essential element of its structure. Likewise his use of the word "designates" is far more forceful than Bosley's "Pointing out" or Hartley's "describes." Bosley's "Drowns, taking turns for the worse," strikes me as imposing a facile value judgment on poetic fate while Weinfield's "Many, upended, are immersed" maintains the crisp imagery, the 'objective' or transportable datum which keeps a poem alive in translation. Throughout the translations, Weinfield's diction seems inspired by Mallarmé's mischievous *elàn*.

But I am not trying here to write an exercise in comparative translation. Rather, the issue it seems to me is one of not allowing or easing a transparent passage of Mallarmé into English, but of reminding an English-speaking reader that, no matter how much Mallarmé is a part of our poetic landscape, he has entered it as another, as an *Other*. Some measure of the force of his work lies in its foreignness, its entrainment of another culture and poetic tradition. Weinfield, in other words, has not normalized or colloquialized Mallarmé for us but has instead reminded us of the geographical and chronological distance between Mallarmé and ourselves. The effect is bracing, that of a living figure swimming back up to us out of the palimsests of our poetry into which he has been interred.

In addition to Weinfield's masterly translations, part of the magic of the unearthing lies in Weinfield's notes, marvels of empathetic unfolding. Forming a running commentary that occupies fully half of this volume, the notes resemble most a series of remarkable études, part scholarly but also, in their quick leaps of thought, part poetic as well. As such, they are less definitve interpretations of Mallarmé's poems than insightful responses aimed at setting forth and clarifying the ambiguities of each work, the historical matrices surrounding it, coupling such explications with other critic's discussions. At once reticient and informative, they seem to prompt the poem to do its own speaking. In this sense, the notes are one of the best readings of Mallarmé we have.

Valéry noted, in this poet whom he worshipped, that Mallarmé was "the least *primitive* of poets and yet that "he restored the most powerful impression to be derived from primitive poetry: that of the *magical formula*." This is a matter of abrogating time, even as time remains the field out of which we must receive a poet. But then it was Mallarmé himself whose work makes visible this short-circuiting loop in time which we call tradition. This is most clearly signalled in Mallarmé's homage to Gautier, "Toast Funèbre." Mallarmé's poem, as Weinfield tells us in the notes, is no ordinary elegy. It is, instead, a reversal of the usual sentiments on the death of a poet, the everlastingness of his lines or his firm place in culture's memory bank. Gautier's death, the poem announces, is a "fatal emblem, thou, of all our happiness!" (*W* 44) Now I read this image as foregrounding, perhaps shockingly, not the memory of Gautier but the actual fact of his death as not a blot on our happiness but inextricably bound up in it. The juxtaposition puts us *in media res* with the complex occasion of what a poet's death means to another poet, to the field of activity we call poetry. Weinfield's line dramatizes this strange, disturbing conjunction of the line's thoughts far more effectively than Bosley's normalizing "O fatal emblem of our happiness!" (*B* 131) As a strategy for putting us immediately in touch with the poem's subject before we fall into the typical sentimentalizing mode of the elegy, Weinfield's opening line is nothing less than brilliant, comparable to Mallarmé's own "Ô de notre bonheur, toi, le fatal emblème!".

For Mallarmé, the legacy of a dead poet is not in what he said or wrote but in what he has left unuttered by virtue of the poem, "the irascible wind of a work that he did not say." The *Neant*, the empty space of silence around a poem, and which belongs to the poem, is pregnant, the birthplace of the next poem, conditioned by what the poem said, but unconditioned as well because it is the space opening and intermixing with the unconditioned, the Absolute in Mallarméan terms. Gautier's death is a closure, but it is also fertile and productive, the source of the poet's happiness because it is the source of poetry to come. As Mallarmé put it, in a letter to Sara Sigournery Rice, recalling Gautier, "after the death of that great poet, there is nothing but Poems." (*L* 117)

The cultural sociology of the trope enacted in the Gautier poem is, of course, inscribed in Christian resurrection themes as well. (Mallarmé, on the verge of making what to him were his most important discoveries in poetry, likened himself to "having died and been reborn" (*W* xv). But endings and their poetic remains are also profoundly located in various mystical doctrines of gnosis (a word like "emblem" serves to implicate them in the Gautier poem). Such conceptualizations are Mallarmé's footpath to the poetry.

Such a pathway strikes me as being very clearly laid out in "The Demon of Analogy," one of Mallarmé's most important prose-poems. The poem is a play on the *nul* of *Pénultième*, the abolishment or zeroing out, as by death, which yet leaves a residue of poetic possibility. For this possibily to be realized, however, the dead must be acknowledged as dead, or as Mallarmé formulates it in the poem, "*La Pénultième . . . est morte*." "*Est morte*" ("is dead" or "has died") performs elegiac duty over the "*nul*" much as "Funeral Toast" mourns the death of Gautier. Weinfield's note to the poem reminds us of Mallarmé's idea that "the otherness of the poetic process makes poetry analogous to prayer." (W 247) The residue, the *ultième* or last remaining, the living, momentarily silenced by death, are to voice poetry again.

The fullest expressions of Mallarmé's art are to be found in the late sonnets and in "Un Coup De Dés," his final masterpiece. Weinfield's translations of the "Plusieurs Sonnets" grouping are among the most brilliant in the volume. Let us be clear: neither in the original nor in any translation can these difficult works be made to yield up their meaning unambiguously. Powerful translation is not normalizing or mastering but a kind of surrender to the otherness—extraordinary in Mallarmé's case—of the work. The most a translator can aspire to is to restore the vivacity, alacrity, the very shock value of the disjunctive syntax and radical imagery of these poems, thus imparting to the reader an experience similar to that of a French reader encountering them for the first time. To see Weinfield's skillfulness at work, let us do another comparison with Bosley, since Bosley's *Mallarmé: The Poems* has been a standard version of the work for many years. Here are Bosley's first two stanzas of the first of these sonnets:

> When with fate's law the dark was threatening
> One old Dream, wish and woe of my spine's column,
> Stricken with perishing where roofs are solemn
> It folded in me its undoubted wing.
>
> Pomp, O hall of ebony where a king
> Is charmed by laurels writhing on a tomb,
> You are but empty boasting by the gloom
> For hermits' eyes dazzled by visioning.
>
> (B 167)

And the Weinfield version:

> When the shadow menaced with its fatal law
> That old Dream, desire and pain of my spine,
> Grieved at being swallowed in night's black maw
> It folded within me its indubitable wing.
>
> O deluxe, ebony hall, where, to beguile a king,
> Celebrated garlands are twisted in death:

You are but a proud lie composed of nothing
In the eyes of the solitary dazzled by his faith.

(*W* 66)

Now it will be seen that Bosley's version more closely follows Mallarmé's own rhyme scheme, ABBA, while Weinfield adapts an ABAB scheme. But the fact is, as close readers of poetry know, end-rhyme is a less than subtle poetic device. Cadence, especially as it evoked by word-order, is a much more sophisticated communicator of a line's meaning and intention. And it is here that Weinfield's ear and sensitivity to nuance provide us, what seems to me, the much superior translation. Mallarmé's first two lines from the above read: "Quand l'ombre menaça de la fatale loi/Tel vieux Rêve, désir et mal mes vertèbres" are beautifully rendered in Weinfield, the first line "When the shadow menaced with its fatal law," almost a conduit between the verbal worlds of French and English. Bosley's "fate's law" and "dark," his "threatening" rather than "menaced," the cognate deployed by Weinfield, as well as his anachronistic "wish and woe" in the second line, these register not as translation but as secondary over-reading, as though his main desire were to explain Mallarmé. Weinfield, on the other hand, continually rises to the occasion of the original; his two inner lines of the second stanza, "Celebrated garlands are twisted in death:/You are but a proud lie composed of nothing," are especially striking, rising to the level of the best of poetry in English while at the same time remaining wedded to Mallarmé's vision and thought.

"Un Coup De Dés," Weinfield reminds us, "occupies a singular position not only in Mallarmé's oeuvre but in European literature as a whole." (*W* 264) This extraordinary work is the closest Mallarmé came to the fulfillment of his dream of the Great Book, something that would gather and transmute his entire theoretical considerations of poetry into poetry itself. Mallarmé's own Preface to the poem, as Weinfield reminds us, reveals the poet's "awareness that the poem enacts the very crisis of modernity to which it responds" (*W* 265). This crisis, as Weinfield puts it, is the question "of how to establish meaning in an essentially meaningless universe—that is, in a universe from which the gods have disappeared, with the result that meaning cannot be transcendentally conferred" (*W* 266). Weinfield guides us suggestively through the poem, pointing out the links between format and thematics, the poem's relationship to other poetry of Mallarmé. It is a *bravura* reading of the work while at the same time preserving its essential mysteriousness and beauty.

"Un Coup De Dés's" unusual across-the-page format and multi-font typography have made it an extremely difficult poem to print properly. In Weinfield, both the original and the translation are laid out with extreme care, as close to Mallarmé's original intentions as can be achieved, something that in ordinary paperback format could not be accomplished. Indeed, one suspects that the extra-wide page of the Weinfield/University of California Press edition was expressly conceived to accommodate the poem. This version including Mallarmé's preface along with Weinfield's extensive, thoroughly researched note to the poem (possibly the very best reading we have of it in English), are in themselves major achievements, crowning this meticulous and beautiful book.

Mallarmé's tutelary presence, his importance in the intellectual life and letters of France, remains powerful to this day. It is to be found not only in poets like Char or Ponge but in more contemporary poets like Jean Daive or André Du Bouchet and, as well, in a whole range of thinkers as diverse as Bachelard, Derrida and Bataille. To the extent that American poetry and poetics have been influenced by such writers, Mallarmé is already present among us, even if piecemeal, muted and obscure. Pound referred to Mallarmé as "almost a mantram, a word for conjuring" (P 420). Eliot saw him as part of "that familiar compound ghost," the voice of Europe (A 271). Such ghostings are fine, implicit in any cumulative transmission of culture. But they are also unconscious taken-for-granted habits. What we have needed is a Mallarmé to converse with. Weinfield's translations, in their completeness and in their powerful reconstitution of Mallarmé's voice, now give us Mallarmé as a presence, someone whom we can think about or approach, possibly for the first time.

(1996)

Part III

The Poetics of Unspeakability

Our paradox: the Holocaust displaces literature, and literature tends to displace the Holocaust. The reasons for this paradox are rather complex. There is, first of all, the sheer recalcitrance of the Holocaust as a subject, its unspeakableness as against poetry's futurity, or, as Gerald Stern puts it in his excellent Foreward to *Ghosts of the Holocaust: An Anthology of Poetry By The Second Generation*, a collection of poems written by the children and relatives of Holocaust victims and survivors, "Isn't it in the very nature of poetry to always reserve a place for hope?" And then, hasn't the Holocaust dealt something of a blow to the literary act itself? For what we label as "postmodern," whether it be an art object such as a poem or an idea or a sensibility, while it may be the product of any number of historical trends, is quite likely to have as its *primum mobile*, its underlying and secret foundation, our knowledge of the Holocaust. It is the one event, well beyond the impact of any literary theorizing, which seems to have flattened the earth of meaning, to have transformed its surface into the slippery incline of contemporary letters where words and referents skip past each other, where, as the German critic and philosopher Walter Benjamin (himself a victim of the Holocaust) pointed out, we have lost the ancient ability to tell each other our stories. John Felstiner, in his essay "Mother Tongue/Holy Tongue," on the translation of Celan into Hebrew, makes the similar point that "European history has broken the signifying grasp of language" (154). Furthermore, as Felstiner tells us in the same essay, a contemporary poet charged with a Jewish perspective and dealing with Jewish matters, with recent Jewish history, is continually reminded of the severance that now ironically animates his efforts. That is, the almost nuclear bonding of the poet with the materiality of his trade, that basic trust

[151]

embodied in the *davar*, the Hebrew word for both "word" and "thing," has been fundamentally violated.

Such an effect (or is it more correct to speak of the word's *loss* of effect?) to blank out the future, to blunt narrative before it begins, to deny witnessing, to overshadow meaning with meaninglessness, is surely the burden of a number of poets in *Ghosts Of The Holocaust*. Poem after poem, resonant with Benjamin's insight, recounts the termination of personal histories and reminds us of the clipped threads that bind the past to the present. Only a kind of historical aphasia, it is clear, will allow speech to continue. In one poem, for example, by Anne Ransinge, the narrator interrogates her dead mother killed in the camps, "And did you think of me/That frost-blue December morning? . . . When you knew it was the end,/The end of nothing/And the beginning of nothing,/Did you think of me?" (42). And in another by Richard Michelson, a concentration camp artist, sheering away from unbearable truths, emulates the very act of displacement as he hears the cries of his fellow victims "but will not document their pain. Apples/he draws instead, knowing each line could be his last;/still he must see Palestine" (41).

Concerning this nullification of narrative, Stern notes that "the history [of the Holocaust] precedes the poetry . . . a history heretofore undreamed of . . . indifferent to Literature." The word "indifferent" in this context gathers many meanings. There is, given the incredible shamelessness with which the Holocaust was carried out, a desire to see the event as lying on the borders of the human, steeped in human motive, determined and willed as any war. At the same time, there is also a deep desire to place it in the category of a disaster, something like an earthquake or hurricane, whose victims have only a passive relationship to its occurrence. Here tragedy, if it exists in the specific Aristotlean or literary sense, does not have a good outcome. For the second casualty of this indifferent history, after its overwhelming human toll, is the triumvirate of Western thought: reason, continuity, causality. It is in this way, and not merely by an excess of horror, that the writer or poet is impoverished.

The poets collected in *Ghosts of the Holocaust* thus labor under the severe conditions imposed by the very subject matter they wish to deal with. Do we evaluate this work? If so, how? If we are thinking of immediate relevance to literary art, we must also note that these poets labor as well against a massive accumulation of Holocaust literature, one in which virtually every poetic manner and trope, from rhetorical outrage to surreality, has been tried out, worn out, at least a dozen times. And then, with but few exceptions in this volume, these poets write at some remove. We will accept, we will grant as a *donnée* and call it literature or testimony, what is written by any survivor, simply because we are curious or account it a miracle that one could survive and tell. In this, Celan's difficult poems, those verbal black holes of literature, represent an outer limit of witnessing, of the lengths we are willing to go, of the language we will tolerate at the extreme borders of testimony.

We will have less tolerance perhaps for the writer at second or third hand who indulges or exploits a subject, the very name of which already constitutes a horrific extra-literary effect, bound to push certain buttons in the audience. Tact is essential, but what this tact should be is very much a question.

For a number of poems in this collection, those dealing directly with the events of the Holocaust, tact is implicitly attempted by the use of framing devices such as a persona or by working off of a photograph or a memory held at a distance. The late Charles Reznikoff carried this method to an extreme in his long poem *Holocaust*, made up of citations from the Nuremburg Trials records. The aim is to force a participatory, even judgmental, act on the part of the reader as he or she comes to terms with the presented materials. Yet curiously, poems of this sort collected here, charged as they are with the visualized or embodied atrocities of the camps, strike me as the weakest in the anthology. It may be be that, after forty years of such image bombardment, one is simply inured, or that one feels the poet, rather than making meaning, is borrowing it indulgently, in a kind of stock way, from the data bank of history. The effect, for this reader at least, is to be repelled, to want to resist, to see the poet's gesture as similar to the use made by a movie maker of some absurdly inappropriate mood music to hype up a trivial event on the screen.

Perhaps more important, I think, is that our psychic needs concerning the Holocaust have changed. Our hunger now is for analysis, for historical reflection, a hunger which drives us toward Primo Levi's precise equilibrations of death camp life, to any number of recent books, to films such as Claude Lanzmann's *Shoah* or Max Ophuls' *Hotel Terminus*, works which have to do with two things at once, historical causality and the adjustments of modern memory. Reading the poems in *Ghosts Of The Holocaust*, one wonders whether the mainstream modalities of current American poetry make it the appropriate medium for such a retrospect. Somehow the conflation of domestic experience with memories of the death camps, as rendered by our thoroughly tamed imagistic techniques, feels forced or inauthentic. I find myself mildly bemused and irritated by the simple-minded yoking of Auschwitz and contemporary politics or socio-cultural issues such as feminism or the ambivalences of assimilation.

The poems that work most effectively, even artlessly at times, are those where the tendency to sentimentalize is directly faced, where the poem, even as it speaks forth of intense grief or outrage, still has a claim on us for its vulnerability. Evelyn Posamentier's "Being Modern In Jerusalem," for example, illustrates with a quiet coolness the demands placed on poets who write about the Holocaust. The narrator of the poem, whose relatives died in the "final solution," is visiting *Yad Vashem*, the Israeli Holocaust memorial; beside her, a teenaged American girl, weeping, asks:

> *"why aren't you crying?*
> *all your grandparents,* she sobbed, then wept
> again & again
> for the other millions of voices.
> soon she pulled herself together
> & snapped my photo with the instamatic.
> gisela, your daughter
> has seen this snapshot of
> her daughter: cool in the desert
> light, solemn & new, sunglasses concealing
> my eyes.
>
> (61, 62)

Here, the calibration, the adjustments to history needed to survive, between sentiment and resolution, seem effectively caught. The subtext of the poem's captured moment is the unarticulable incommensurability of experience, a silence which in this case is doing the work of language.

Silence, aphasia, underly the modalities of a number of other poems, among them C.K. Williams' complex and powerful "Spit," which draws an implicit parallel between the modern poet and the tongue-tied Moses, and so strikes the difficult hairline balance of memory and art. In a like manner, Stephen Berg's poem on the poet Robert Desnos, who died in Buchenwald, is one of the few in the volume that intensely recreates the tension between despair and joy, dread and hope. The poem is a moving, surreal weave of images where future and no-future dance around each other while the imagined Desnos goes on doing the most human of things, comforting others. Here, the poem's Desnos tells us

"the last smile is smiled first/and I am both of them/on the last mouth."
(29,29) This is, of course, fable barely intermixed with realism. Often, it
is only art that can sustain these imaginative realms simultaneously,
and in such a way as to blur where one leaves off and where one begins.
In the face of monstrosities, often there is little else one can ask of the
poem.

∽

Primo Levi's *Collected Poems* published in English translation in 1988,
some seventy pages of poetry set off against the many volumes of his
prose, unlike the poems in *Ghosts of the Holocaust*, must in some sense, be
considered as survivor testimony. The greatest number of the poems—
and the strongest—are related to his concentration camp experiences,
but there are also delicate love poems, playful meditations on animals
and sea creatures and minor celebrations of the dailiness of life. If
poems were not his most favored medium (in one place he refers to his
verses as *nebbich* poetry), they nevertheless embodied those virtues of
clarity and communication which he felt were of absolute importance
to the modern writer.

The poems show a certain lyric amplitude, often in the face of their
subject matter, indeed, in the face of Levi's suicide, and so therefore
demand an accounting which *must* be at odds with some of my observa-
tions made above. For it is these peculiar lyric qualities which make of
Levi, camp survivor and witness, something of a paradox to the contemporary reader and critic. In a time when criticism speaks not of authors
but of an "author function," when the notions of history and self are
questioned as ways of entering into the interpretation of texts, Levi's
personal *hegira* in Auschwitz touches everything he puts on the page.
There is a strong tendency to project Levi's camp experiences into every
aspect of his work, as, for example, in his poem "Monday," a touching
lyric on the inevitability of death which begins with the lines: "Is
anything sadder than a train/That leaves when it's supposed to." (11) The
image immediately conjures the trains which carried the victims to the
death camps. Such a response is common while reading Levi. It speaks
volumes to the power of the *Shoah*'s reach into ordinary language, to the
capacity of the event to disperse or do violence to the literal sense of
words.

Yet even more paradoxical, if Levi's prose and poetry are our
evidence, is the fact that Levi lived out an experience which, according

to a number of thinkers (Adorno immediately comes to mind), cannot be communicated. Instead, at the most, the camp experience guarantees a certain difficult, exclusive or privileged voicing, and hence, tends toward a privileged language such as Celan is thought to have invented to "communicate the incommunicable." On the face of it, Levi seems to have resolutely refused such a point of view and instead remained insistent on communicability, on a certain stylistic classicism, a view of the writer not as a maker of difficult fictions but as a testifier.

Raymond Rosenthal, the translator of Levi's *The Drowned And The Saved*, places Levi in the line of Galileo and Machievelli and, inferentially, among the "classicists" of English prose such as Swift and Defoe, or, more recently, Orwell, writers whose linguistic stance was indivisible from their ethical one.

For Levi, the ethical stance, as implied in his own words, is only indirectly related to the formal problems of literary production. Instead, as he often declared, his chief aim was clarity. "Judges are my readers," he insisted in an essay in the *New York Times*. He went on to summarize the imperatives of his craft as follows: "since we the living are not alone, we must not write as if we were alone." Writing, then, is not a solitary act but a pathway back from the dead to the living, away from an autolectics performed on the edge of the abyss and toward the need to function as witness. In his reflections on the death camp experience in *The Drowned And The Saved*, Levi contemplated the disastrous fate of those in the camps who suffered, what he called "linguistic deafness and dumbness." The failure to understand a simple command shouted by a guard or the import of a petty regulation led to suffering and hastened death by blows or worse. The impressions of such experiences left their permanent mark on Levi and colored his view of writing.

For Levi, the inability to communicate was not a given but something built into the design of the camps themselves, and he feared that this inability was being subtly built into the design of contemporary life. In this sense, his reflections not only bear witness but perhaps ought to be taken as cautionary paradigms against what he termed the "fashionable theory" of "incommunicability."

Levi's reflections sit on the mind of the reader; it is difficult if not impossible to discuss his work solely in the grey neutrality of metaphor and image, of literary device and craft. What seems necessary to seek out, if only to satisfy one's own inclinations and sense of reading, is how, in Levi's case, tendencies, personal history and the very otherness of experience conspire in the form of the work.

Levi's poetry is an excellent place to start, for in it, the natural analytic tendency found in his prose is only partially muted by the lyricism. One senses in his poems that the nodules of extreme experience and literary device are co-emergent. Take for instance the matter of vocabulary. It is useful, for example, to compare the diction of the first two poems in *Collected Poems*, "Crescenzago" and "Buna," one written before Levi's camp experiences, the other after, times which, as many camp survivors tell us, would appear incommensurable.

The place Crescenzago of the first poem is an industrial area, a place of factories and workers' lives; Buna is, of course, the infamous I.G. Farben works built at Auschwitz by, and for the employment of, slave labor. What is so striking, however, is how, for Levi, the two worlds are conflated by a continuity of language, a *res linguistica* of word, image and thematic. Crescenzago is a place of "smoke ... so black and poisoned/The wind is afraid its breath will be cut off." (3) Here, "when the factory-whistle blows at dawn," the workers go out to "keep/the grim black stonecrusher panting ..." The motifs of the Buna are striking similar: the factory "smokes from a thousand chimneys,/A day like every other awaits us./ The whistles terrible at dawn." (4) Both poems treat of the monotony of labor and its crushing effect on love and companionship. Placed as they are, side by side, at the very beginning of Levi's book, they imply something terrible: the Holocaust is not an aberrant moment, an ahistorical event in the human continuum, but rather something far worse, a logical extension, an ever-present possibility, of certain tendencies of modern social structures. As a result, it is "speakable," and the duty of the survivor is first of all to see that it is prevented by retelling and talking about it. According to Levi, were it simply an unaccountable fact, an abnormality outside the province of history, witnessing would be of no value. But language betokens. Levi's poetry suggests that an unbearable bridge of words exists between camp maker and camp survivor, that a possibility (a frightening possibility no doubt) exists that there can be total and communal comprehension of an event like the *Shoah*. Levi, we are reminded in the pages of *The Drowned And The Saved*, made it his business to see that in the German language translation of *Survival in Auschwitz* "nothing should be lost of its harshness and the violence inflicted on the language" (172).

For Levi, the law of the writing life could only mean autobiography, its testimony to be received not only as fact but as moral imperative. In "Shema," (the word means Hear!) the poem whose title he gave to his first collection of poems, he writes of the camp victim, so weak and deracinated by his condition that he is unable to remember his life or his humanity. Yet the poem is more than descriptive, for it is addressed to us, to those "who live secure/ in your warm houses." (9) It concludes with a curse on those who forget. In a later poem, "The Survivor," Levi felt compelled to delve into the fact of his own survival with its attendant guilts and remembrances. Like Coleridge's "Ancient Mariner," which the poem cites, Levi's journey was from horrifying experience to speech. In such poems, we recognize the arc of the tribal poet, a modern *vates* whose clarity is demystifying, but a painfully inverted one, where horrors rather than glories are the tales of the tribe. One imagines that this clarity is addressed to a time beyond contemporary memory, beyond, as well, the time of that contemporary thinking which defines language as a prison house of incommunicability. For Levi, words continually marked the road out of that prison house. What impelled his poetics now strikes me as an attempt to reach beyond the ordinary confines of literature. His muse was as much futurity as it was history. When asked if there was not a desire to forget Auschwitz, he warned, "Signs do exist that this is taking place, forgetting or even denying . . . Those who deny Auschwitz would be ready to remake it."

～

Forgetting and/or memory? The function of an art such as poetry, suggested Walter Benjamin, was to transform historical content into something like truth. For Benjamin, literary works were "hieroglyphs of redeemed life," rescuing individuals and even whole epochs from the darknesses of chronological time. Such a project of redemption strikes me as being at the very center of some new work by Jonathan Morse, a historian and essayist whose recent book, *Word By Word: The Language Of Memory*, comprises a phenomenology of history, an analysis of how historical information is deployed and of the subtleties engendered by our use and misuse of memory. Morse's view of history, both informed by and in agonistic struggle with much contemporary thinking about literature and history, strives for nothing less than the recuperation of a lived historical consciousness (and conscience, one might add), an attempt to restore time and event to active force against the distancing effects of "official" or, to use Morse's term, "virtual history."

"Virtual history," history as mere archive, constitutes, in Morse's analysis, that highly conditioned view of the past that fits seamlessly into the culture's current agendas, political, social and economic. It is language half asleep, shorn of its prior, often fearful dynamic, occulted into symbol or buzzword so that it may seem to arrive in the present from a golden or idealized past. "Virtual history, an exclusively verbal construction," Morse insists, "has nothing to do with life or death: it is a Grecian urn of speech, waiting to be spoken by the human, forever young." ("Young," in the sense of being without a past.) The language of virtual history is, at present, all around us. It invokes words like "liberty," "patriotism," "fatherland" and "nation" as though their meanings were self-evident, transforming them from descriptive language into the engines of mass movements and mass destruction. It conveniently "forgets" what bloody histories are entrained (one of Morse's key terms) in the usage of such words.

Against contemporary forgetfulness, Morse proposes, in *Word By Word*, a genealogical searching that exfoliates history and its usages both forward and backward in time. And while the book covers a wide range of historical eras and subjects, what is pertinent here are Morse's reflections on the historical presentation of the Nazi genocide, on its rendering in art and literature. Morse would have us see that literary art, more faithful, perhaps, to the content of language than virtual history, has become, since the Holocaust, rather forgetful of the psychological motivations deeply rooted in the vocabulary of its gestures.

The gist of Morse's argument is to be found, I think, in this particular passage:

> Consider, for example, the event of our time which most demands to be recorded in tragedy: the mass exterminations of the Hitler era. Writers have tried to record the significance of that event, but so far all have failed. Their own ways of thinking in words have subverted the effort. We think we want to speak tragedy, but so far we have been able to utter only sentimentality, pornography and lyricism. We are trapped in literature, with its clutter of associations extending across time and space; that is, insofar as we write in language we are part of the culture which enacts and is enacted by that language. The Holocaust, however, belongs to no culture. It was a definitve rejection from culture: a decision, made within history, to draw a terminus at history's edge and say, *Beyond this there will be no more.* Tragedy demands an ideal elemental form, but the Holocaust has deprived the ideal of its light and air. There are no words to write its history.
>
> (100)

Literary or cultural *praxis*, says Morse, cannot reach to the *non-* or *anti-culture* of genocide. In reading imaginative works dealing with the genocides of the Nazi era, Morse implies, we become keenly aware of literary activity, of the blips of metaphor or image scattered through a work. But far from enhancing our appreciation of the text or of an author's cleverness, we tend to feel embarrassment or shame towards ourselves and towards the author who manipulates us. Some bond of truth—or fascination for that truth—has been cut in favor of something we call Literature, and we are irritated by the misplacement of our concentration, by the inappropriateness of any linguistic gesture which calls attention to itself.

What Morse fears, as he writes in "Words Devoted To The Unspeakable," an essay in *American Literary History*, is that, with respect to the Holocaust, "the beginning of fiction is the end of memory's meaning. Reduced to an effect of the imagination, the experience of the Holocaust drifts, a cloud of special-effect smoke, into the bad novel that we call historical narrative." Are the appropriate poetics for the unspeakable, its very unspeakability? This seems to be what Morse is counselling.

For Morse, the banishment of literature, it would appear, is a concomitant of any rendering of the Holocaust. In this, he seems to answer Stern's questioning of whether poetry can be adequate to genocide, with an almost definitive "no," a moral "no" at that. And yet, in *Word By Word*, in a passage immediately following on the one cited above, he brings us to the possibility of a text which might exist, as he puts it, "in a state of wordlessness." That is, a text so written that only an immense effort of mind can make its words allusive and associative, *i.e.*, *literary*, and by so doing, thwart our desires to turn it into literature. If I read Morse correctly, the texts which most approach a "state of wordlessness" are clearly documentary or at least texts which adhere to something like Roland Barthes' idea of a zero degree writing, freed from personal nuance or gesture.

Among such texts, Morse would cite the scientific and management *minutia*, the day-to-day communications, engineering orders, purchasing requests of the genocidal machinery. Indeed, such communications were documentary not merely in fact but in intention, as is clearly shown by the penchant for euphemism and circumlocution. For their purpose, even while trying to define something or to conduct business, is to enter into the realm of science as datum while at the same time trying to protect the ethical and psychological state of mind of the authors and readers of such works. Here, for example, is a text which Morse cites, used in Lanzmann's film *Shoah*, a portion of a letter written by a man named Just, probably an engineer, concerning the design of the Nazi killing vans:

> ... The manufacturers told us during a discussion that reducing the size of the van's rear would throw it badly off balance. In fact, the balance is automatically restored because the merchandise aboard displays during the operation a natural tendency to rush to the rear doors, and is mainly found lying there at the end of the operation. So the front axle is not overloaded.
>
> 2. The lighting must be better protected than now. The lamps must be enclosed in a steel grid to prevent their being damaged. Lights could be eliminated, since they apparently are never used. However, it has been observed that when the doors are shut, the load always presses hard against them as soon as darkness sets in. This is because the load naturally rushes toward the light when darkness sets in, which makes closing the doors difficult. It would therefore be useful to light the lamp before and during the first moments of operation.
>
> (119)

In this passage, the poetics of the unspeakable has been reduced to, as Morse puts it, "a language of picture words: words recording their data without connotation, words as wholly devoid of prior significance as the silver halide crystals that make up photographic images . . . .a language whose own formal properties organize the chaos of light and dark into significance." (110) One thing is clear; only history and memory can establish the significance of such language, only knowledge of the years 1938–1945 can "translate" them for us. Without history or testimony, without a future to look back from, the Rosetta stone of these words are so much chicken scratching.

And yet *given* that such translation takes place, that we become aware through it that the euphemistic text disguises horrors beyond horrors, a blackened miracle occurs: an incredible law of inversion begins working on us. Everything about this text transmutes itself by virtue of an almost schizoidal and saturnine *poesis*, and we are again confronted with imponderables that almost every 'poem' presents to its reader such as: who is voicing this and what is the psychology, not of the text's deviousness, but of its author? In this way, *contra naturam?*, the words end up demanding the same interrogations as the lyric.

Morse's harsh formulation of a poetics for what cannot be said, therefore, strikes me as offered in the service not only of truth but of literature as well. For he has not foresworn meaning so much as once again recalled to us the direction from which meaning arrives, neither from 'the outside' as intertextuality or as the voiceless and inarticulate testimony of things nor from 'the inside' of purely private pain and private unreason. Meaning arises rather from the juncture of, from the middle place where human need and inhuman data meet. So we know why Celan was not silent and why Primo Levi, who had sworn to tell, spent his entire writing life bent on organizing that foulest chaos into patterns of the most striking light and dark.

(1990–1994)

Diasporic Poetics

To begin, this, from the *Zohar*: "Woe to the generation lacking in shepherds, when the sheep stray, knowing no direction."

I started to write poetry in my late twenties. As with much which had preceded in my life, I blundered into poetry, neither a lover of poems nor aware of their transformative power. As I came toward poetic and personal awareness of my Jewishness, paradoxically through my own deepening sense of secularization and then by way of my turning to poetry and philosophy, it was a few articulations *as poems* which kept faith with the sea changes of my life. Scraps of poetry, like philosophical maxims, became my shepherds, my word paths for entering what seemed to be a latent version of myself. One saw the word, words, as having a two-fold power, first to draw one's attention, to cause one to be at an instantaneous remove from the actual dailiness of an activity (this has always been, for me, the subtlest yet least examined meaning of the Book), and, second, to be a haunting. In this latter case, the ghostly powers of words resided, incarnating themselves in one until they were no longer capable of being recognized as mere objects of attention. Via the poem, words were physically incantatory, orders of possession, dilators of consciousness and its apprehensions.

The poets who first nurtured my growth in poetry, I think here of the Jewish Objectivists, of Charles Reznikoff, of George Oppen, Carl Rakosi and Louis Zukofsky, struck me as being married to their aloneness, as to a bride. Little noticed by the public or the academy, they wore the public neglect of their work as prideful badges. These were the poets whose books I carried on my own *hegira*, my wanderings, as I tried to find the forms my words and acts must take and be taken for.

I remember it was Oppen's words: "Truth also is the pursuit of it . . .

We must talk now. Fear/ is fear. But we abandon one another". from his poem "Leviathan," which, when I was beginning to find my way as a poet, pulled me from despair and confusion. Language, these words told me, could be a thrall, a moral animator—this was power and danger— in the life of one who took words in, of one who was a reader. To reformulate Eliot's famous comment in "Tradition and the Individual Talent," the dead poets are not only "that which we know," but "that which we desire." In this sense, any powerful mastery of words occurred under the signs of or even within the strictures of another's poetry, rather than within the free play of language.

In a sense, to be a supplicant before words, before combinations of words, was to gather two intimacies at once, that of the very things words named, the trees, the rocks, the persons and images, etc. and that of a *renaming*: that construct of the poem which collocated all these names of things and yet held them in some new order and relationship and so constituted a new name. Here, in renaming, tradition and freedom co-existed side by side, forming a continuous juncture which ran directly through the poet. It was this juncture which I felt to be my rootedness in Jewish tradition, and like the living root of a plant which one unearths from the soil to examine closely, there were areas where the cellular structures of the root exchange minerals and nutrients and water with the earth, a boundary membrane where what is dead and what is alive are indistinguishable.

~

Isaac of Acre, the 13th century Spanish Kabbalist, writes: "He who is vouchsafed the entry into the mystery of adhesion to God, *devekuth*, attains to the mystery of equanimity, and he who possesses equanimity attains to loneliness, and from there he comes to the holy Spirit and to prophecy." In this passage, one can identify not only a sacred journey of the soul but also a kind of *poesis*, for to come "to prophecy" means ultimately to come to speech, to poetry, to utter both hope and dread. The loneliness that Isaac of Acre speaks of is thus, to my mind at least, deeply connected not only to the severity and isolation of the spiritual journey but to the often wearying aloneness from which the poetic act seems to spring.

Reznikoff, in particular, was a Jewish *flaneur*, a diminutive figure in dark suit and tie, and yet, an isolato endlessly walking the streets of the city, milling with its crowds or divagating into the suburbanlike precincts of Flatbush and outer Queens but always sensing his apartness. "I am alone—and glad to be alone," he writes in his poem "Autobiography: New York," linking himself both with the diasporic witness of an alienated consciousness and with those moments of the Jewish mystical tradition, as expressed in Isaac of Acre's words above, which acknowledge a fundamental and unbridgeable separation of God and man, but yet allow man to glimpse God, momentarily, as it were. Perhaps Reznikoff espied God on a sidewalk in Brooklyn, espied Him sardonically as kind of modern *deus absconditas*: "This pavement barren/as the mountain/ on which God spoke to Moses—/suddenly in the street/shining against my legs/the bumper of a motor car." Or possibly Reznikoff experiences the religious moment as truly fleeting like that instant of deep love in Baudelaire's poem when the poet sees and falls rapturously for a woman who passes quickly on the street, is swallowed up by the city, never to be seen again.

Louis Zukofsky too, made the Jew's peculiar burden of aloneness one of his major themes. In *"A-12,"* that beautiful weave of a father's love for his son, he asks plaintively, "Where stemmed the Jew among strangers?" And answers himself: "Speech moved to sing/To echo the stranger." With a kabbalist's intuition of the power of wordplay and pun, Zukofsky seemed to reinscribe family history, religion, philosophy and the poetic tradition as so many instances of an almost sacred sonic attentiveness. Everywhere in Zukofsky, this attention was manifest as a kind of love both for the objects of his devotion and for the weight and tone of every syllable by which it is rendered. In *"A-11,"* his prosodic masterpiece of family life, he enunciates his poetics as "our /love to see your love flows into/Us. If Venus lights, your words spin, to/live our desire leads us to honor." Naturally such care has a religious dimension, a resonance of acting under the eye of God. "There is no one," his poem's Rabbi Pinhas says, "who is not every minute/Taught by his soul."

Zukofsky, in his major prose work, *Bottom: On Shakespeare*, formulates the poetics of Shakespeare and, implicitly, the Objectivists, as "favoring the clear physical eye over the erring brain." In a poet like Rakosi, such a trust in sensory perception is, as in Zukofsky, a religious imperative. In his poem, "The Vow," Rakosi proclaims this trust outright: "Matter,/with this look/ I wed thee" (222). And in his haunting "Associations With A View From The House," he writes, "It is the great eye,/source of security./Praised be thou, as the Jews say, who have engraved clarity/and delivered us to the mind" (237).

What I felt from these poets who taught me so much was the power of perception, the happenstance of authorship, the impingement and penetration by the world into our would-be discursiveness, our self-involved chatter.

The gloss of eyes across and over streets, as though the city were made of languages, inscribed in the ages and designs of buildings, in the oddities and samenesses of people one passed . . . a collection of languages, written and rewritten. From so much utilitarian secularity, one might derive a non-theological theology of language, as if to say: thank Whomever (ironically of course) or whatever has designed this world. For I find new languages daily; I find that not all is written out, and that therefore I too am allowed to speak and write.

Further, there is, in the life of the writer, those moments of being sickened with one's own work, one's very words. At such times, I have risen from my desk and hurled myself out into the city, evicted myself from the precincts of my own logorrhea, partly as break or diversion, but also to be in touch with the languages of others. Thus, to gloss, to go over, as an eye savoring the textures of the world, is also to be compelled into utterance, and so to provide interlinears and commentaries.

Commentary, therefore, is first eyes before words, a searchlight of eyes on texts which invoke disturbances and consonances in the reader. Commentary, too, is never synonymous with the text; it always remains apart. And so it stands, in the idealized version of interpretation, in *devekuthic* relation to the text. The commentary adheres to the text, and —whatever its virtues as a text in its own right—never enters into mystical union (one in the other) with it. George Oppen, in his late poems, expressed such adhesions as a kind of poetic radiation. In a poem to Louis Zukfosky, who he regarded as one of his poetic fathers, he identified the poet as a lighthouse turned back on the coast, searching out the edges of the continent, illuminating the particular commonness of Americans, and ultimately of humans, as figures of differentiation, as ways of acknowledging the fundamental conditions of apartness. This recognition of difference, a refusal of sentimental or too easy identifications at the heart of all of Oppen's work, accounts for its probity. Such a voice struck me as embodying not only a full and tested knowledge of our lives, and our way of thought, but also offered us hope that such a knowledge was our ultimate value, a value out of which not only truth but compassion could be found. Oppen, the "meditative singular man", seemed to stand, like the lighthouse image at the center of his poem, on an isolate and prophetic vantage-point in which

... to say what one knows and to
limit oneself to this

knowledge is

loneliness turning and turning

lights

of safety for the coasts

(NCP 256)

Oppen's entire poetic oeuvre was for me an endless efflorescence, a singular linguistic act of the truth of boundaries and boundedness, not only on the level of nations—where the inability to tolerate aloneness was most destructive in our time—but on the level of the singularity of individuals and on the level of consciousness relating to the non-human world.

～

The Jewishness of the Objectivists was manifest in a variety of ways, in their textual practices, in their love of visible objective fact and, most significantly, in their questioning relationship to a Jewish God and Jewish dogma. On this latter point, I remember the powerful effect of reading and taking in Zukofsky's placing of Spinoza at the center of the early sections of "A" and of Reznikoff's skepticism (in his Poem "Hanukkah" he writes: "the rebellious Jews/light not one light but eight —/not to see by but to look at."). Equally powerful on my consciousness were the meditations of Rakosi and Oppen on the uncertainty of the theological point-of-view, its transmutation in their work into a phenemonology of near-secular spirituality.

The impact of reading these poets was to reinforce my own question of my relationship to Jewish thought and culture. Briefly, the way had been prepared in some sense by my family history, for it was my grandfather, a rabbi from Bialystok, whose strictness drove my father from his house at age fifteen, making him, at best, an uneasy participant in Jewish life. And my mother was a professed atheist who on the High Holy Days and only at my father's strongest pleadings, went to the Temple.

Most powerfully, it was my growing sense of a kind of diasporic consciousness in these poets, one created by the dis-ease and difficulty with which they approached their heritage and by the cultural and poetic apartness under which they worked. The question of how one's poem relates to one's Jewishness is, for me, deeply inflected by my reading of them. In fact, it was they who led me into a re-engagement with Jewishness and with the philosophical and linguistic aspects of the tradition.

But first, let me be clear: obviously, from the view I have espoused above, there no such stable category as Jewishness. That is, if the commonplace of Jewishness, of Jewish thought and poetry, involves textuality and commentary, it is also true that the poetics of Jewishness involves the undoing of text and comment, that textuality is a kind of traveling away, of departing, of heresy. As Gershom Scholem puts it, an enacting of a "counter-history," or, as I echoed in my own memoir writing, a "counter-memory." I would allow this trope as a very Jewish commonality, one that is best seen as an attempt to unlearn when that which one has learned imprisons like a bondage or a reflex.

The Objectivist poets to whom I am indebted wrote against history's grain, wrote their poems as a kind of counter-memory, not out of any desire to reject their pasts, but to find their own specific gravities within more general traditions, to find those stories that belonged to them. For these poet, there was that other diaspora—within the larger diaspora of America and its culture—of their own estrangement from the familiar: their sense of distance from the life around them, their need to give witness to this distance, the need, as Zukofsky put it, "to sing/To echo the stranger." The texts of America and of American-Jewish life as well as those of the inherited literary traditions of their time were to be revisited in this way. This is what diaspora meant, not alienation, but a need to re-engage the old texts, the old familiars and circumstances. John Taggart, in his brilliant meditation, "Walk-out: Rereading George Oppen" maintains that "Insofar as Oppen's work may be considered Jewish, it is a differing Jewishness or, to adopt one of Oppen's own terms, it is an antinomian Jewishness." The diaspora invokes not rejection but a rethinking, a travelling with tradition in a new, even if oppositional, way.

Thus, if it appears that in the work of the Objectivists, commentary circles back to origins (or let us admit—commentary *does* circle back), for these poets, it does not merely lodge with prior thought but displaces it, though never totally. To be human, to be humane, is necessarily to grow by traceries, to be revisited so that we may visit, so that we may visit our own experience even as we are revisited.

Ineluctably—and perhaps this is where my relation to the Objectivists and my Jewishness intersect—I, too, participate willingly in such a return not only to origins but to the modalities and thoughts of the poets who have shaped my work.

Let me follow the dynamics of such traceries through a poem that I have written, bearing in mind that the poet exegeting his own poem is involved in a perhaps suspicious act of commentary, trying to account for something not entirely of his own making. Here is the poem:

DIASPORIC CONUNDRUMS

—*Call me not Naomi, call me Mara*—

And now this man is fatherless
because he had a father,
and Israel is no more.

A line encircles
deserts beyond Jerusalem,
and he who was given a name
has lost the right to silence.

The man had a mother
because he had a mother,
and Israel never was.
Jerusalem, the golden,
city's mirage
shimmers on desert sands.

How could this be real?
Who will raise up
a name like Ruth,
put a name,
like a child, onto the air?

The dead are dead.
This is certain.
This is what was written,
why it was written.
This need not be said.

This poem was written almost unconsciously at first, as though in a haze or fever. A number of things were on my mind, all of which in one way or another entail diasporas: the story of Ruth in the Bible (the poem's epigraph is from *The Book of Ruth*, I,20)), that very post-modern idea that the word is displaced from the object it refers to, that the word *is* exilic, and, as I have written elsewhere, that whatever my religious inclinations, the world has labeled me a Jew (or as Celan puts it, the Jew has nothing which is not borrowed, least of all the name, Jew).

For me, as I'm sure for others, the essence of poetry is naming, naming in the sense that the poem is a name for a thing or state of affairs which did not previously exist. For Oppen, such naming was a "test of sincerity, the moment . . . when you believe something to be true, and you construct a meaning from those moments of conviction." In this, poetry repeats the Adamic act; it bears the force of original conjunction. Walter Benjamin, for instance, sees the name as a "primordial form of perception in which words possess their own nobility as names." Elsewhere throughout his writing Benjamin suggests that this form of perception does not simply correlate words with the things of the world but creates an immediate and powerful relation between the two, short-circuiting conceptual thought. But what about re-naming or, as I"ve tried to suggest above, what about when we revisit naming as re-naming? I'm thinking here of what textuality and commentary, at root, actually consist of. The original Adamic field of play can be seen as namelessness, as a silent and unlettered cosmos. But if it ever did exist, this undifferentiated namelessness is no more. It has been replaced in the contemporary consciousness by the totality of Adam's act, by Babel or, as the Kabbalists insist, the world and all its forms are already, albeit secretly, a form of *Torah*, lurking as a written out and inscribed universe hidden behind apparent phenomena. Adam, then, was the first textualist, possibly, by that, the first Jew in the Bible.

But let me refocus on the poem. First, its epigraph, which came into my head and was the seed-phrase of the poem. In the story of *Ruth*, Naomi has suffered an incomprehensible and overwhelming fate. She has lost her husband and sons, and is burdened with two step-daughters. In her anguish, she cries out "Call me not Naomi, call me Mara, for the Almighty has dealt very bitterly with me." Naomi is here testifying, heart-wrenchingly, to the perceiving function of the name. "I went away full," she exclaims, "and the Lord has brought me back empty." Given her experience, she is no longer a "Naomi," (something pleasant or good), but a "Mara," which is the biblical word for bitterness.

We know that Ruth's conversion, the sense that Judaism is more than a tribal or blood kinship religion, lies at the heart of the story, as well as its foreshadowing of the rise of David. But what most struck me in this instance was Naomi's demand to be called by another name. Name changes are among the most significant phenomena in the bible: Abram to Abraham, one of the most important, as well as Jacob's change of name to Israel after wrestling with the angel. Naomi's fall into ruin, her changed condition, requires this self-renaming.

Yet another way of looking at Naomi's story might be by way of the notion of sympathetic magic. That is, if we keep in mind Benjamin's phrase concerning naming as a "primordial form of perception," then the experience of Naomi, the bodily and emotional stuff of her coming to bitterness, that is, the non-linguistic or opaque and hidden aspect of her suffering, is revealed to us by her name change. What has happened is neither synonymity nor mere gloss but the transformation of physicality into language. The diasporic journey, as embedded in this exemplary story, is first physical, experiential and, yes, is signaled to the reader by physical means. "Mara" cannot be pronounced as "Naomi."

In this sense, the story of Naomi's name-change is a prologue to the rest of the poem. For my poem seeks to address the conundrums of inherited names as fixities and the relation of these fixities to the self, to poetry and to nationalisms and nation-states. Each stanza expresses a linked conundrum. And the conundrums are diasporic, quite simply I hope, because they are written from the viewpoint of someone (me) in the actual diaspora, someone who embraces the diaspora as the condition of his Jewishness and of his poetry. But as well, I've tried to intuit here, as I did in the Objectivists, a sense of the transmigratory aspect of words and names, of naming and re-naming, one which floats or drifts into wandering on the polyvalence of words as though one could send a word towards a meaning it did not begin with, hence disperse it, place it in diasporic motion. Emmanuel Levinas calls Jewishness not a metaphor but a "category of understanding." He suggests what this understanding might be for a poet when he writes: "*Is it certain a true poet occupies a place? Is the poet not that which, in the eminent sense of the term, loses its place, ceases occupation, precisely, and is thus the very opening of space,* neither the transparency nor the emptiness which (no more than night, nor the volume of beings) yet displays the bottomlessness or the excellence, the heaven that in it is possible . . . " (63)

Levinas's thought is not concerned with the so-called nomadic tendency of the Jew or of the Jewish poet; rather, it testifies to the dynamics of the word-experience phenomena, to the poet as transmuter of a worked-upon physiology into language, the re-namer. Implicit in this line of thought is that the poet is not perceived as an experimenter with language *per se*, for there is nothing more confident than the experimenter in the laboratory who can objectively manipulate materials (language in this case) in a fanciful manner. On the contrary, Levinas's poet is anguished and exposed; he "loses place," "ceases occupation," that is, does not perform but is performed upon by experience, by adversity, by love and history.

Again, I sense that I am wandering. So let me return to the first stanza which is about the son ("this man") maturing towards ethicality by moving out from under the father's name (the conditions of the father's world and his social realm). The son becomes a refugee or emigrant from the name, which is, basically, a diasporic movement. To put it backwards (which is what conundrums do), the son does not fulfill his own hopes or potentialities while under the father's name, a name which roots him in place and identity. But he must have a father, he must have a reference point or cause to exist, in order to become fatherless. There is no hope of fatherlessness without there first being a father.

Likewise, and recent history is very clear on this, Israel, as a project of the Jewish people, can become either simply a fixed geographical place and/or the term of an ethical process beyond conception as only a nation-state. Franz Rosenzweig in *The Star of Redemption* refers to the solution to such a dilemma in the separation of ethics from coercion. Coercion is state business, is about maintenance and fixity. In my mind, the existence of Israel, given the recent, tragic history of Jews, had led to a conflation of hope with unbending rigidity, of self-protection with an overzealous notion of defense, security and opposition to compromise. But Rosenzweig searches for a sense of self-restraint of power, a withholding which he, as with Levinas, is convinced is the Jewish secret of survival and eternity. When the son is fatherless, that is, when he moves out from under the father's name, he also moves out from the idea of fixity, of Israel as fixity. I'm not speaking poetry here as much as I'm suggesting the possibility of an ongoing prophecy.

The conundrum of the second stanza, linked to the first but also autobiographical, is that there is an obligation by having been given a name. If the name represents an authority prior to understanding, it may be questioned—indeed question is required. One of my favorite thinkers on religion, Ludvig Holberg, wrote that if a man learns theology before he learns to be human, he will never become a human being. One could paraphrase: if one learns to be a Jew, or a fundamentalist or an avant-gardist, etc . . . The received name is dogma incarnate, not experience. Thus, the obligation is to grow, to move out from under the name, and to express that movement as a new understanding. The poet's work can be seen as an undoing or at least testing of the parent's or father's authority, for one who would aspire to poetry, to identify naming as renaming. Naomi-Mara is the paradigm of this poetics.

Now the mother of the third stanza does not give a name to the child; inherited names come by way of the father. This situation is paradoxical. The mother's love is so seductive and all-embracing for the child that to stay within its confines may be to obliterate the possibility of creating an Israel. The idea of redemption for all humans, the Jerusalem of the poem, can only be a mirage unless one accepts discomfort and struggle by foregoing the child's sense of security which the mother represents. And one supposes that this makes the poem even more of a conundrum since we all have mothers and fathers whom we love. We are always living in the dynamics of being placed between their love and compassion and our own strivings. A further conundrum is that since a mother's love does not come by way of a name or authority, it need never be abandoned. The idea of the selflessness of love, often represented as a mother's love, is just that, non-centered and free of coercion. Love and compassion, without name or reference point, are always possible, even when one is renamed. Again, the story of Naomi-Mara is instructive. It is the renamed Naomi that Ruth embraces as her mother.

The fourth and fifth stanzas are questions and admonitions put to myself about the writing of poetry, and, in a personal sense, about self-growth. The name, in the act of renaming, in poetry, is, for me, a kind of seeking. And given the above three stanzas, the fourth one, with its sense of difficulty ("Who will raise up/a name like Ruth, put a name,/like a child, onto the air?"), suggests a wish for courage or means to write, a desire, perhaps a hopelessly wishful one, for the substantiality of naming. The fifth stanza constitutes an injunction to not write like the dead, for "The dead are dead./This is certain./This is what was written . . . This need not be said." The implicit injunction is to avoid being involved in mere repetition, writing, as it were, under the father's dictates (sometimes mislabeled as tradition). Of course, we must write *to* the dead, but about our present and our hope for the future.

The question put here is how a particular Jewishness informs a poetry—and especially, how it might inform this poem. I hope some of those specifics, those interrelations between prior texts and commentary, the reflections on sources and concerns, are clear. But a deeper question might be how one is informed (if that is the correct word) by Judaism? Though I was born into a Jewish family, I was not raised in a theocratic state (despite the efforts of my stern rabbi-grandfather). What informs me and my poetry has been the path, to some extent self-created, which I have taken through the particularities of the Jewish tradition. These particularities, to borrow from Oppen's poem above, have been "lighthouses" to me, at times deeply and seductively beckoning, at times warding me off from dangerous rocks and shoals. Equally important, I would acknowledge that there is a powerful sociology of exposure at work in me as in everyone.

Put more generally, one's writing can been seen here not only as a possible record of what has happened but also as a kind of becoming. For becoming begins in exposures and antecedents: those poets that I read, the life their words would lead me to. This is very much in keeping with the Jewish notion of revelation which begins in overhearing the revelatory nature of the text before one's eyes, its imports and prophetic hopes. One's own writing, then, can be looked upon as a kind of commentary on one's antecedents in much the same way that Talmud and Midrash are commentary on the Torah. That model of commentary (Blake would call it, "not Generation but Re-generation") is what I always have in mind when writing or when reading. Furthermore, I have a strong suspicion that this modality, as I learned it through the Objectivist poets, is far more than merely my idea of how one approaches the making of a poem. For in truth, we circle out, we are impelled by experience into the diaspora and, lo, we have fathered our own fatherlessness.

(2001)

Journey to the Exterior of the Symbol

Semite: to find a way for myself
                    —GEORGE OPPEN

Is what I am setting down here concerned with travel, with going on a trip, a voyage, *voyeur* to see? To be a tourist. Well that, we know, may involve the banal vicariousness of the subject rather than his or her object. What is more unspeakable than to feed at the trough of another culture, to acquire photographs, beads, charms, geegaws, to hoard sights and smells, to expand on the confirmatory slide show of one's memory bank? Will it do, at death's door (which I often imagine to be the boarding gate in the corner of an airport passenger lounge), to shuffle photographs, go over one's atlas with a magic marker, ticking off in dayglo red, France, Burma, the Galapagos? Before redemption, Walter Benjamin tells us, every day must pass muster as judgment day, including the final one. Will mine be spent undergoing the transit of recollection?

This I know: certain images, correlatives or correspondences, somehow, after the fact, speak to me. I will let the cofferdam of memory open, the torrent flow by; the heteroglossia of potential remembrances will cling to the mind, in effect, mark their own passage, these hard turds of experience which it is almost a sadness to evacuate. Give me back the memory. For my travels, if nothing else, will give me eyelets and hooks, reference points of there and there and there. The tour is in a sense a chronicle against non-existence, a scroll of sometime being, the filled-out bank check against my own dying.

Possibly the literary model can be useful. We, who go on the tour, have not yet reached a state of Literature, by which I mean that we are not yet as characters in a novel whose lives and actions demonstrate significance at all points forward and backward through the spans of a book. In the best fictions, a character's 'reality' is co-terminous with his or her 'symbolism'. At best, we travellers have reached the life of the Prologue or Exordium, in that there is both the need for and the possibility of meaning, and that the tour is chosen so that we may complete ourselves, eradicate our lacks in Time if not in Being. We will compel our *as-if* histories toward fullness; our durations on the tour then are meant to be philosophically satisfying, to be no less sufficient than necessary. Emerson referred to this as "the superstition of Travelling"(at the same time as he was reminding Americans that "the soul was no traveller").

Memory. I even store an image of sucking at my mother's breast. Let me make this clear: I don't see *me* doing this, but see her, the long slope of her shoulder, the curves, the aureole, the black hair flowing like a torrent down her shoulder. Hence I am easily capable of sinking a paltry twenty years back into the memory hole. I still taste by mere induction the dust of the powdery rocks of Spain that lay beside the roadway, and feel the bright sun as I came into the hilltop town of Frigiliana, walked to the cafe for a *vino de terrano*. I am now going to sit in the cool darkness, listening to the click of the dominos. The man next to me accidentally drops a coin onto the sawdust-covered floor. I watch him take another coin off the bar and holding it between finger and thumb, grovel in the sawdust for the coin he has lost. The one in his hand will 'attract', will guide him to the other, he tells me.

Like that coin, I will travel. I will be pulled out of my self-made pocket. I will voyage not for the 'new' but for myself, for the self I do not (nor perhaps want to) know.

If so much happens on my travels: separations, break-ups with old friends, the weird self-involving metaphysics of identity, does the coin of personality by the act of transfer become something else? In the Orient, where all spiritual transformation is a path, a journey, still one returns to the self-same self. So travel, the tour, is also the recombinant acquisition of one's lost or emptied heritage, is a reminder that the vessel is incomplete or inferior, indeed, that its very inferiority is based on its having missed something.

At the very beginning, wasn't there also a key? The freighter which left from New York had been at sea for eight days, a loose, various, unplanned time for the passengers, people wandering in and out of one's cabin, parties and song through the nights. And then one morning, with the coast of North Africa a smudge on the horizon, to be called into the dining room by the ship's pursuer who returns our passports and hands each of us our cabin room keys and says, "Here, you'll need these now that you will back among your own kind".

Characters in a novel? They are stamped with such immensities of assurance, such consistency, that even their innocence or lack of fore-knowledge is simply another of their traits. And I must admit that we see, in our travels, those 'hip' tourists of the world whose coolness would seem to express a certain self-confidence of Being, the sort of confidence which a living of life-as-literature might embody. One does not deny that particular book, but finds it trivial, for close inspection shows this confidence in the service of presuppositions, of bestowing a kind of honor on indifference among those who carry their cultures forever with them, who, if we look closely are indistinguishable as they sit at their cafes or on their beaches in no matter what country of the world.

The truth of the matter is that few serious tours are taken with confidence (and by this mean that the absence of confidence concerns one's self, not what is to be seen). My subject is this very lack. To be a tourist, to venture forth, yet to be aware of emptiness and anxiety as the root of the search itself. To be, as Baudelaire put it, "one whose desires are shaped like clouds", whose characteristic way of being in the world is not in the sense of attainment but in the paradoxical continuities of the search.

Now the contemporary tourist is certainly not on the way to Canturbury or Mecca. His pilgrimmage is without an identifiable locus, without an imagined state of grace. Rather he or she is in the grip of an almost biological panic which is curiously eased by travel. We hear travel's relief almost as a sigh. Isn't this what we hear in Rilke's first sentence of the *Malte Laurids Brigge* as the poet-narrator first arrives in Paris: "So, then people do come here in order to live." He espies the Hotel de Dieu, whose inhabitants go to meet their Maker, the ultimate trip. As long as you are dying, you are living; as long as you are dying, you are still on a journey.

Concomitant with Rilke, however, came Freud's accomplishment: the inward world falls victim to science. If Rilke could imagine an ultimate parity between what lives and what feels and thinks, in Freud, we find displacement—the hand of God toward which the dying moved was just another opiate of travel. The journey must be borne with the knowledge of rationalizations. So one senses, no matter where, that one does not belong. Freud transforms the wanderer into the stranger, the one who is 'alienated'. The contemporary tourist then is suddenly some admixture of Sisyphus and Tantalus (whom we remember were visitors too of a sort) driven by knowledge he cannot shake, by feeling which cannot be eased. Such a seeker is terrorized most especially among what are referred to as *Peoples*, those with ritualized lives, a sense of place or duty; particularly among their monuments and scenery, he feels humbled and even dishonored. For these have an adamantine hardness; they are more like strangely distorting mirrors than objects; their inaccessibility reminds him that everything about his own culture reeks with motive and reason. Its faiths and concepts are a mere means of holding fast to a world which through science has become a kind of *perpetuum mobile* swimming in seas beyond the net of Eros as do now our distant and unseen constellations. Even matter, as the physicist insists, is, in itself, simply another guise for symbol. The tourist is swamped by his own historicity, his awareness that every strangeness in his culture can be defused, identified and cataloged under a multiplicity of systems—every act of his has been determined on its calculus of thought.

What can save this Tourist, this one who wants to mean but who has lost every prop of a faith or culture? Perhaps the question is ill-put and should be, what is meant here by *to save*? The world of our thoughts, the world of our World, is a mediation, and the desire to travel, the reason for the Tour, at least for those who by conscious effort have placed themselves outside the museums of received ideas, involves a bald-faced metaphysical contract which acknowledges this present state of affairs.

For what is clear is that travel, once envisioned as pilgrimmage or aspiration toward a visonary or symbolic entity, no longer conforms to these ancient forms of spirituality. These older forms now seem tainted with limitation, with determinisms. It is, rather, as though the modern traveller catches the wafting odor of himself as he faces into the wind ahead. The tour, real or imagined, already smacks of failure, and the lucky voyager, like the religious aspirant of the Orient, will find he has made the journey he need not have taken. Thus, Benjamin travels to Russia to find: "More quickly than Moscow itself, one gets to know Berlin through Moscow." The only way to travel, he remarks, thereby indicting the metaphysics of the exercise before he begins, is by "having chosen your position before you came".

A priori or *a posteri*, the result of travel is quite likely to result in foregone conclusions: written in the distant desert sands was your very name. Baudelaire recognized that his wanderers, even in their love of the quest itself, carried their own excess freight, their incredible propensity for psychic projection. One of his traveller-narrators realizes: "as if in a shroud/ my heart laid buried in this allegory".

Still, to come upon oneself, symbolically transfigured, is both a kind of life and a kind of death. Because we encounter the "new" (life), we also encounter our rigidities, our fixities of mind (death), and it is the mediation between the two that make transformation possible. As Elias Canetti puts it, the traveller "wants to know something about other alien people. The path through the jungle goes step by step, the number of daily miles is carefully recorded. All the forms in which one later discovers new things are prefigured in these." Every traveller or writer must come finally to a kind of death, and, superficially, travel would seem to be merely another way of dying painlessly—hence travel's inherent propensity for being falsely used.

Canetti seems to suggest that we may look at the act of writing as we do the act of travelling. Consider that writing, like travel, involves life and death and so is like a kind of travel or tour, but of a more exacting nature. Where do words have their births, their deaths, their short lives, except as they are buried in their use in art? How, for instance, does the line or poem appear, the dialogue or scene of a novel? The writer takes a trip, a trip into the white space of the page, he sets down letter, syllable, word, sentence, moves from one to the other, as though across an Antarctic waste, the intensity of the white background giving a figuration to the word. But we should not perceive this 'whiteness' as some purified space upon which the pristine minted word will be set down. The word does not suddenly acquire visibility in this white space, but rather, like a voyager, has crossed or been wrenched beyond a border, the old contexts in which it occurred. It travels with this baggage much as we do, and the page is merely the possibility of recognizing the plenitude of the word, and in a sense the materiality which is both friend and enemy of the writer.

The past, the 'community of memories' of which we are all constructed both out of our experience and out of our readings arrives also in similar fashion. Travel presents unfamiliarity— but not enough to render us speechless; rather the Other often suggests, as William Bronk refers to the Inca ruins of South America, an "algebra of cats"; the very uncertainty which arouses in us not silence but an astonishment impelled into speech or writing. One of the deepest and most unanswered of questions is why awe leads *ultimately* not to silence but to words. One reason, to borrow a term from Clifford Geertz, is that what we do not understand we will attempt to make grammatical. When we travel, to place or to page, we will try to imagine a syntax for ourselves, a way of being which is like the way a noun has its appropriate place within a sentence. In cultures close to our own we often achieve something close to this. In Paris, for instance, one might feel like an italicized English word embedded in the French discourse. But it is questionable that the true traveller could find a perfect syntactical relation to the patterns around him or her, or that it would even be desirable. Without the edge of difference, why travel in the first place?

The word then, like the traveller's weight, does not so much stand out on the page but leaves a footprint. Its density is there for all to see, but only its travelling to the page, only its placement, its inscription has given it again its totality.

So we journey, and man—the cliche runs—is a symbol-making animal. This is but a half-truth, for as I see it, man is also a symbol-escaping animal, and to achieve this he has had to journey to the exterior of the symbol, to experience the boundary of its contours, to break with its borders. *Now the words constellated on the page, a tiny island in the icebound seas; Now the letter tops, a city's irregular skyline seen from a distance.* And since these words are stand-ins for myself in their temporal evolution, are they not a kind of knowledge of myself? Do I not, as I gaze over my own words circumambulate my very ruination?

Otherwise the writer is the victim of the symbol's limitations, enclosed in the prison of its dimensions. When Eliot perceives that the symbol is the way of relating to reality, is it not in this fashion that he means it? For if we are unable to transcend the symbol, to pass beyond its limits, then it seems evident that there is no art, no thought, no growth, only the movement of counters, the manipulation of already received images and ideas, the tidy mechanisms of an inhibited survival.

Precisely because the unknown is unknown we cannot aim at it. In every true instance of travel, we will shipwreck on our own perceptions. Like Columbus, we must discover America rather than India, we must travel with an eye for our own obliquity. I am reminded of the ever-creative nature of our endeavors by Wittgenstein's remark, which is in its way about the kind of travel I have been suggesting here: "In the actual use of expressions we make detours, we go by side roads. We see the straight highway before us, but of course we cannot use it, because it is permanently closed." So we travel, not to find Spain or ancient Greece or the mystical East but something that belongs to no one but ourselves. This the act of writing witnesses and confirms.

(1985)

Poetry Without Credentials

For One Who Would Begin

Yet good
Is converse, and to say
The heart's meaning, to hear much
Of days of love,
And events, the doing of deeds.

—Holderlin

A place, a room. Paper, pencils, tools of this craft. They sit on the desk before one, inert, valueless. We could do almost anything with these; we could hurt, be hurt with our own words, our own tools. But for an instant we have just looked at them. We looked without thought, without content or purpose. We are going to look again, to trick ourselves again into a neutral looking. This time the sense is that they are placed there, that they solicit us . . . yes, we are meant to use them, to 'converse' and to 'say'. *And already* we are in a world of poets, of poetry, of art, of all things which accrue, which are encrusted on this world: passion, fame, career. Already we are thinking of a world, imagining a world of hopes, of fears, which for some will contain enormous dread, for others, enormous possibility. A moment ago, the paper and pencils were just there—it seemed so simple; but we have begun to move off, to fantasize, to project . . .

Or we have been sitting in a chair, reading a book of poems. Suddenly a poem has touched us. Eyes smart or laughter overwhelms. For a moment all we are is that feeling, that laugh. It lasts only a moment. We turn the book over, read the book jacket about this poet's life. You see, we had to leave the moment, had nearly to invent a curiosity. And now we are reading the fly leaf: how old was this poet when he or she began? What prizes, honors, lovers, what place did this poet live in? A world begins again: every nerve, every muscle suddenly aches: the ache of the poem and the ache to be a poet merge.

Still, we are left with paper and pencil, we are left with ourselves. Everything we have just thought of, everything we hope and dream about is "out there." The paper and the pencil which no one else is using—they remind us of our solitude, our loneliness which nothing else will fill. The "out there" surrounds us, threatens us, entices us, but it is not here.

It is not here. Not here as the paper and pencil are here. We could admit that we are outside, excluded from the inside of "out there," and if we are not "out there," what are we inside of? What of this bereftness, this sense of loneliness where a line of poetry can whelm us? We have nothing, absolutely and fundamentally nothing but ourselves, our tools here. Perhaps from here, poetry can begin.

It can begin then because now we have seen what is before us clearly. We have seen it for what it is, an intention. We want "out there," we intend to get out there. We intend to begin; we intend to write poetry. *Then we have already begun to write it.*

Perhaps at this initial moment the very words poet and poem *since we are not,* since we are not, since we have not—must be dispensed with. All we actually have is our intention, our decision. Whereas every time we use the word poet or the word poem, we begin to fantasize, we begin to create that which we have not created.

Recognizing this, it is possible to look at these words very clearly, more clearly than we have ever done. No matter how we say them, construct them in our minds, they remind us how absurdly alone, how removed we are from them. There is us and those words. All we are is naked intention, our intention which cannot reach, which can barely point. What is there is our intention; but its goals as we have thought of them are outside of it. If we can see this and grasp this then there is nothing to condition, nothing to qualify about our intention. *Poetry can actually begin.*

It is not as though we could start purely—that would be the greatest hoax of all, in fact is most often our major hoax. But that we could become aware of everything which comes with our intention to write a poem, this is important: to acknowledge all that, and that yet the intention is there, almost as though it were counterpointing, justifying everything else.

How rich we are with turmoil, with lust and the juicy desires for recognition. How extraordinarily interesting is this secret life, the life ue have held back while proclaiming our urge to write a poem. And what irony —have we actually believed no one was like us in this regard, that others who called themselves or were called "poets" arrived full blown in their purity?

It is possible that poetry could be rooted in acceptance of our state of mind as it is rather than in some abstract "subject" we think poetry ought to be, in the notion that poetry is an activity which will get us to some goal. The poet Basho, after years of self-scrutiny arrived at this:

> What is important is to keep our mind high in the world of true understanding, and returning to the world of our daily experience to seek therein the truth of beauty. No matter what we may be doing at a given moment, we must not forget that it has a bearing upon our everlasting self which is poetry.

We could say to ourselves that, yes, there is this mind's life, this actual world I am in, and there is also all my hopes and fears which are synonymous with it, are fantasies generated by it, which comprise my "daily experience" and yet there is still this intention, this "unconditioned" intention when all is said and done, and it is out of this tension between what is totally conditioned and unconditioned out of which poetry might arise.

What Is Poetry?

In 9th century China, about the time that Tu Fu and other poets worked in the bureaucracy, the labels "artistic" for poetry and "practical" for prose existed in a particularly dramatic way. The fact was that in China, prose was considered an unfit medium for anything but the transmission of facts or the carrying out of minor business matters. Poetry, on the other hand, was the medium for consideration of the *Tao* of government, for serious thought, for generals to inspire their armies with, for the bureaucrat/poets to inform and persuade the Emperor. In this sense, poetry was not a diversion from the on-going business of the day, but a way of entering into its deepest levels.

If we are willing to look at poetry as neither a product nor a diversion, if we are willing to take it as seriously as the Chinese, we may begin to have a glimpse of it as a method, a method of awareness initially, but then, as we probe more deeply, as a method of communication.

The desire of the poet, says the late Louis Zukofsky, is not to show himself but to show his world. If we are to enter our worlds, poetry—and by this I don't mean a particular verbal product—must inevitably arise. To repeat from Basho's statement above:

> No matter what we may be doing at a given moment,
> we must not forget that it has a bearing upon our everlasting self which
> is poetry.

There is something movingly unequivocal in this statement, uncompromising in some fundamental way. Our life, Basho insists, is poetry. He is not talking about some category or class of people who write poems, rather he is talking about the very ground of our existence. In suggesting that whatever we are doing we *are* in a sense, poetry, he is implying that the label of "poet" with its freight of self-conceptions and imposed criteria (at least as it has evolved in the present), is unnecessary. The opposite of role or criteria may be, if we are willing to completely release these notions, recognition and friendliness, recognition toward our state of mind and our intentions.

In this context, the question "what is poetry?" need not arise. Or it might, with some sense of humor, which is the same thing; it might even become a question one imagines Basho asking: "what is not poetry?". Because we have recognized and are able to give up the urge to play a role, to impose ourselves on others in that fashion, the possibility arises that whatever is going on in our lives—where our focus is and must be—is communicable, communicable because it is available.

When we say our experience is available, we mean it is just there— it is—in viewing it this way—completely unconditioned. Shorn of the urge to impress or confirm, the exact nature of our experience, its particularities and textures, are available.

I say available because at this moment we have yet further understanding to make. There is much talk among people about "expressing" themselves, its value, etc., but the very word may be a kind of block, a kind of trap. It implies that one is unfulfilled unless one is engaged in expressing oneself, making art, making poetry. There is some essential truth in this idea; the urge to art is universal, comes up in many forms, and there is no culture, civilization, as far as we know, without art. (Indeed, the recognition that culture exist is often only made through its art.) Heidegger, in an essay on the poet Holderlin, suggests the very ground of expression: "Who is man? He is the one who has to bear witness to what he is." It is this consciousness, Heidegger insists, that defines man. What Heidegger says seems as unequivocal as Basho. Man is "the one who has to bear witness."

In this same essay˜ Heidegger refers to Holderlin as the "poet of poetry," the poet who seeks to understand what it means to write poetry. He goes on in the essay to quote from a poem in which Holderlin says: "since we are an exchange of words/ and one can hear from another." Here, with the use of the word "since," what we have previously seen as an intention has also about it, as Holderlin suggests, the character of necessity. Basho and Holderlin meet in the idea that there is both a need to express, to witness our lives and that the ground of our lives is poetry— is, in other words, expressible.

The poet, then, is the one who is willing to bear witness thouroughly and completely. Yet how does one witness? Like the man called to court, he must tell the world "to the best of his knowledge." This is a useful way to look at oneself as a poet because as witness *qua* witness one's aim is not to draw attention to oneself unnecessarily, but to present the facts of the case. A witness whose concern is accuracy doesn't particularly care whether he is thought good or bad; he has no stake in how his language is perceived by others except in the sense that it is perceived, that it is understandable. In this attempt to make things understandable, it is possible that our language, our art of language, can become something transpersonal. When this happens, the witness, the poet in this case, is no longer a private person; he has made his experience felt.

To go back to the problems created by the distinction between expression and communication: we know in ourselves of the need to express ourselves. We might ask ourselves as poets: why does our job not end there? I'm just doing my thing, not hurting anyone, etc. Yet there is some hypocrisy in this attitude. We who supposedly "just express" ourselves nevertheless want this expression to be heard, to be validated. Both our need to show our work and our need to keep it shyly hidden, are acknowledgement of the power our own creations have over us. When we think of expression only, we are thinking of confirmation; we have lost the sense of the witness, of someone who has no stake save in the clear presentation of his or her experience, of someone who has only a sense, a desire for clarity, as he or she/speaks.

The witness is making an effort to be clear, to present it all; perhaps even that part of it which might leave the witness in a bad light. This effort we could look at as a gift. We could see that what transforms expression with its overtones of self- involvement into communicatIon is this sense of gift. We are no longer doing something for ourselves, (or, in a strange way, for someone else for that matter); we are trying to communicate without fear of what has actually occurred or what is occurring. In the moment, in desiring to see and say clearly, we are involved in the giftedness of communication. Perhaps that is all poetry is.

Giftedness

Often, our desire to give a gift has little to do with actual generosity. Our motives for giving may involve seducing someone, easing guilt, any number of hidden motives. This is true of the reasons we write.

The question we may want to ask, then, is: what actually do we have to give? Possibly the notion of "gift" and the notion of true generosity meet in the place where we recognize that it is nothing but our unique —I might say exact and precise—experience we are giving in our poems. We are the vessels of our experience. There is in a sense no other experi- ence than our own—therefore, to part with it, or better to offer it up whatever it is about, our shame, our joy, sex, hate, is to make it part of the totality of human experience out of which we learn. For we know that we learn as much, we live as much through other's experience as our own. Our whole world, our way of seeing and being in it, are as much the result of other people's experience as our own. If our experi- ence is uniquely ours, we already have something to offer. There are no credentials necessary to make such an offer, to add to this sum.

Who is the Poet?

"The novelist is one on whom nothing is lost."

—HENRY JAMES

Here we have been talking about "experience." This happens to some- one, that happens, and this someone is us. Yet when we sit down to write, what we are about to put down has already happened, will happen, will not have happened, and certainly we are not *in* the "expe- rience" we are relating—in a sense. We are not, if we look closely, expressing our feeling about an experience.

In this sense, the poet is outside the experience of what has happened, to one side of it at least—his is a view, a perspective of his experience—and by that, he can actually see it, can feel its texture—this is slightly different from being inside it, from being possessed by it. Yet, the poet's possession of his experience is different from the possession of him by the experience. The poet's view is somewhat more spacious, large, aerial; his experience is seen in an open context, its energy, its quality is felt. The great poet, Holderlin claims, is never beside himself, is never caught up in the intensity of the passion, but in the intensity of showing.

Technique

We should dissociate our notions of technique from ideas of development or novelty. Technique can be seen as a means, not of making a new object, but as a means of revelation. We are willing to break with an ongoing order of reality when it no longer conforms to *our experience* of reality, when an urgency to discover what the world is like arises and the formal means sanctioned by the past, *though still operating in the present*, no longer suffice. As long as technique is looking over its shoulder at either art-history or at novelizing the art object, the spontaneous release of the present is threatened.

So technique has about it two aspects which we must be continually aware of: its artificial character, its capacity to distance the artist from experience; and the opposite, its ability to aid the artist in discovering what his or her experience is. It is this latter aspect which the artist will develop. Technique from this point of view is associated with the "gift" quality of communication. It represents a desire for clarity, for transmission—and cuts through the egocentric idea of art as only *expression*.

We must also consider what we mean by "experience." For when we convert that experience into communication, we present it as an order, as a form. This is what transforms our so-called private world into that thing which Zukofsky said of poetry, that it is "an order which speaks to all men."

So, in a sense, we are not talking here about our experience as much as about the idea that our experience has an order (or series of orders) by which it can be grasped, first by ourselves, then by others.

In talking about experience and communication we could make this further distinction: that communication (and by implication,poetry) has the quality of soliciting a judgment about itself. It has taken the risk of stating itself, of stating its version, of opening that version to inspection. Concommitant with this willingness to say how things are is an impled outlook—not a heavy-handed judgment against the world, but a suggestion as to why the work of art is truer to reality than men's conventional notions of their experience. The dynamic by which a work of art moves us is no more than this undermining of the solidified character of our usual world views. Thus understood, communication is more than information; it is, in a curious way, an attempt to set things right, perhaps even further, an affirmation that things can be seen properly. The truth of communication, in this sense, is creative. It is without bias because it has sprung from an actual lived world, unconditioned by any *a prioris*, and is continually undercutting the conventionalized constructs and arrangements of our normal thought patterns. Art introduces uncertainty into our view of things, and communication and uncertainty are indissolubly wed in authentic art. A confirmation of our existing world views in art is a harking back to nostalgia, to the redundant and sentimental view of life: the stuff of soap opera, pulp fiction and their fashionable introversions which go by the term of decadence.

Perhaps it is necessary again to assert that we are talking here, not about an artist submitting to doctrine, whether others' or one's own, but to his or her experience which always has the character of freshness and uncertainty about it since it is ephemeral, arises out of the artist's singular viewpoint and, as it is transformed into expression and communication, is filtered through the mind and body of an historical person.

Communication remains conventional only to the extent that the writer or reader refuses to acknowledge its full character, and instead allows what has occurred—singular though it must be—to be made to conform to existing patterns of thought; in short, one has refused to risk looking at the actual textures and forms of an experience.

Poetry Without Credentials

If we look closely at the effects strong poems have on us, we may discover something quite strange.

The poem 'alters consciousness' it is said; it shakes up and disrupts our certainties. We could say it introduces uncertainty where perhaps there was none before. New truths, new conceptions of world or life are tendered by the poem. Yet we return again and again to the poem to find ourselves shaken up. What is curious about powerful poetry, what is profound about it, is not the conceptions of truth offered but the disruption, the actual opening and experiencing of *what is* when the conceptions have been torn away.

In the moment of that happening, everything we are has a bearing—our experience has led us here—and is also beside the point. The only thing which has meaning is the uncertainty; our attempt to maintain a grasp on the solidity of our views has been undermined.

How strange! What is actually true is not the certainty but the uncertainty. If we are willing to recognize that moment, to live thoroughly in that understanding, we recognize that it is just as we give up our views and our values, give up ourselves and our credentials that poetry takes place.

This is what we mean by *poetry without credentials*.

(1982)

Encountering Oppen

Buddhist scriptures contain a saying: "regard all sentient beings as your parents." The idea, I infer, is to look at every individual and occasion in one's life as an actual influence, a scene of instruction, a mentoring of sorts. So it is under that rubric that I wish to write about the influence of George Oppen on me and my poetry. Which means that, before I get to George, I must invoke the catenary leading to him.

But what is this catenary at the end of which a poet stands face to face with another poet? What chain of *poesis*, of making and reading, of possible personal encounters, leads out of the self and its linguistic solipsisms towards the poem which ultimately must stand apart from its author, indeed, predicates its existence on the author's metaphoric disappearance. Making, on the path to a poetics, is accompanied by undoing, by the attempt to resist, even as one is using them, the seductions of everything prior: personal history, nostalgia, conventions and traditions, and by trying to refuse what Oppen called "the trick of gracefulness," the deceptive enchantments of language, of abstract formalisms, literariness or harmonious forms.

The uneasiness of poetic interrelation, of "influence" (as Harold Bloom might inflect the word) lies buried in the factorials of poetic learning. Every transmission from 'mentor' to student abrades the self's inertial desires to maintain the fiction of its own "gracefulness," of its own completeness. Possibly that is why, particularly in the twentieth century, we have whole ranges of poets who would prefer being mentored by an impersonal theory, by the dictates of a *zeitgeist* or school, all of which appear to be authorless (i.e. where authority is diffuse) and so less messy, less psychically unsettling.

In this essay, I have tried to grasp hold of the emotional and intellectual undercurrents of my early relationship with Oppen, to lean into that relationship and the psychology of it. This then is a record of youthful but also useful uneasinesses.

~

"Truth also is the pursuit of it"—this line was from George Oppen's book, *The Materials*, which I found among others, in the blue footlocker I had dragged across the Atlantic at the beginning of an expatriate hegira. My friend Ernie, who had studied with Louis Zukofsky at Brooklyn Poly, had suggested Oppen's work to me, along with that of other modernist poets, William Carlos Williams, Charles Reznikoff, Olson, Duncan, Levertov, Creeley.

It was 1965; I had won a small poetry prize from The New School For Social Research, resigned my well-paying job as the head technical writer for a major corporation and taken a Yugoslav freighter from New York to Europe where I planned to live for an extended time.

In that footlocker were other books, Dante, Shakespeare, some contemporary poets, notes and manuscripts as well as an old Hermes portable wrapped in a blanket to keep it from being damaged. I had little idea what I was doing. Here, nearing thirty and on the whim of a minuscule prize, I had thrown a whole career away, had become "hooked," as Oppen once put, on the *sincerity* of the poem, and was truly sailing into the unknown (I had never been to Europe before, and my 'research' consisted mainly of reading Frommer's *Europe on Five Dollars A Day*). I was ripe, split wide with vulnerabilities and longings. It was a mental condition that I recognized in my own attempts at poems, in my efforts to bind disparate words together, words marked sentimentally for me, that I clasped or bracketed into forms the way one applies a bandage or dressing over a raw wound.

Two things stick out from that sea voyage as markers of my state of mind: One was the sound, on the radio in the ship's salon, of the empty airwaves in the middle of the Atlantic, a strange roar not unlike the roar of the sea itself, non-human and terrifying. Signalled by that roaring, the vast jumble of phenomena, the world, made any writing, the use, that is, of the intermediaries of words, a seemingly impossible act of translation. I thought about this in my bunk at night, how little words counted against the strange unknowableness of the world. How everything of true depth to the individual struck me as being *unnamed*, and thereby unsayable even as its shadow in the form of desire swept across one. The other marker of my troubled mental state—I was looking, in the romance of my discomfiture, for such little poetic hints—was that every evening just as the sun was setting and the stars were coming out, the first officer appeared on the bridge, his figure dark against the darkening sky. I watched him, immediately an embodiment of certain masteries, take the sextant from its polished wooden case and "shoot" the first appearing stars and the horizon, thus locating our position on the vast planes of endless water. In those rough and glittering seas, it struck me that only the thin, imaginary line which he constructed between the heavens and the ship anchored us in any way to what was at all human. That line, construed as it was from the symbolic orders of numbers and ratios, was more than mathematics; it was also part of our languages of hope. My education, which had been in the sciences and engineering, made me well aware of the metaphoric nature of our formulae and equations, how behind them lay a search for connections and attachments to the physical world, to certainties and arrestments. In that sense, they resembled all other questing forms of language such as poetry or literature.

Even as the journey across the ocean ended, disorientation hovered over me, a vague fog of personal and poetic choices. It was still with me some months later when I had finally settled in a small house in a small village in Spain. In that house, in the bedroom that was to be my study, I took the books out of the locker, placed them on a shelf, put my papers beside them, set the typewriter on the cheap wooden table which my landlord had given me and looked around. I was unable to begin. Instead, I found myself arranging and rearranging the books, surveying the room, the whorls of its plastered walls. I recall nothing so much as the deliberateness of my actions, as though the precision and repetition of physical gestures, of minutiae would translate my surroundings into familiarities.

There was a bed in the room, covered with a long white spread. It appeared to float off the floor, and all I could think of was to lie down on it, to float away like a child on a nimbus. From the small high window over the table, I could hear some kind of animal thrashing in the yard next door. I climbed on the table and looked out but could see nothing except a thatched roof where the noise came from, above it an absurdly blue sky and the Mediterranean dotted with a few fishing boats. I felt vertigo, dis-ease. Those words of Rilke's, as he recorded his "mystical" experience, "the Spanish landscape, the last I *inimitably* experienced" ran through my mind. I felt completely thrown back on myself, which I knew was nothing, merely what seemed like a silly thing, this minuscule personal history immersed—this much I knew about poetry—in an art that was immense and arduous.

I now understand that I was looking for handholds, for any sort of anchoring as I slid into the confusion of self, of self-doubt, and was available for some sort of transmission. It was then that I took down the Oppen book. I probably reached for it because, although I had not really studied his work, I remembered that the lines of his poetry were fairly clean, unadorned, without metaphorical clutter. I didn't need to think about how I was going to decode it, but, rather, to be in contact with something graspable to my state of mind. I turned to the back of the book, to the last poem in it, "Leviathan"—this is a habit I have always had when casually browsing—and read the first line of the poem: "Truth also is the pursuit of it." I read the line over and over, like a chant, feeling a raw ache in my chest. What did the words mean to me? I had only the vaguest idea, but also a sense of wanting to weep. I calmed myself down and began to decipher my response. I took the "it" of the line as art, hunger, the clarification of the very confusion I was experiencing. Later, I would read that this word was, of course, one of Oppen's substantives, an order of nouns like "sun" or "rock," a "taxonomy," as he referred to them, which hinted or pointed at the real. In my own receptive state, the line, with its functionally medial "also" bridged a chasm between a pure skepticism of language induced by my uneasiness and some obdurate sense of the otherness of the world. "Truth" as I saw it in the line was not some abstract category of universal knowledge and fact but the more humble sense of what was going on around me. In other words, the facts before me, the room, my vertiginous almost nauseous falling into an abyss were also "truth." I could begin where I was— indeed, was there any other place?

A bit further down in the poem, there were these lines which vaguely reconciled me to my state of mind and fueled my desire to write:

We must talk now. I am no longer sure of the words,
The clockwork of the world. What is inexplicable

Is the 'preponderance of objects.' The sky lights
Daily with that predominance

And we have become the present.

We must talk now. Fear
Is fear. But we abandon one another.

(NCP 89)

I was looking at these lines, not only or necessarily as a poet; rather, I was reading them as one might read a theological tract or guide to the perplexed, as a form of wisdom. I was, in this reading, unaware of the 'art' of these lines, the way Oppen distributed cadence or language, or used parallel structures to link the "inexplicable" with the "preponderance of objects", with "talk" and "fear." There was, in the most profound sense that I can imagine concerning my response, no admiration present. One does not admire the spar to which one is clinging.

Instead, a certain kind of transparency was taking place, decidedly unliterary. (I did not understand then how the style of the work contributed to this effect.) I sensed only that the words were entering into me, inscribing themselves in a place where moments before fear was regnant. In retrospect, I believe I was inoculating myself into a way of apprehending poetry, not as a literary product at all. For even now, I still strip down my response to a poem to the, for me, essential question of its use- or meaning-value in my life. Oppen's poem had stung me, but also, like the invasive barb of a possibly poisonous insect, it left me irritated and anxious rather than satisfied. Later, after studying Oppen's poetry for months on end, this ground bass of uncertainty (which came only with the utmost precision and clarity of language) became for me the central function of the poem.

∾

Looking back, I also see how my Spanish experience had been very fruitful. While there, I had my first poems accepted for publication and had lived something of the writer's life I imagined for myself, looking every morning at a white page, attempting to mark it with words in some way meaningful to myself. Oppen's poetry had been the strait gate to that 'perponderance of objects' which both surrounded me and were part of my physical environment, and which impinged on that lost or somewhat alienated consciousness of a New York Jew loose in the stark and near mystical culture of Andalusian Spain.

A curious thing had occurred in Spain, a certain sense of intimate relationship in which, through the agencies of Oppen's work, I felt allied with the bleak purpled beauty of the Sierra Morenos, the slopes of which were covered as though in a new vocabulary of plants and trees.

Even the dramatic plunge of those mountains into the Mediterranean evoked the closures of poems, as though the physical escarpments of that coastline were moral landscapes, teacherly perspectives of poetic being. The poetry did not so much give me the sanctions of description or representation nor did it suggest a mode or style. Rather, its value as statement gave me a kind of confidence in the act of poetry, in a feeling of being aswarm *in media res* as a philosopher might put it, in a world of poetic availabilities.

At the same time, other ideas about poetry possessed me as well, the combined avant-gardisms of my youthfulness as a latecomer to poetry, which perhaps led me down a curious path in the stylistics of writing. Among the "influences" (and I would now say of this period that these came at the wrong time, requiring me to unlearn them in order to learn them again for myself) I would cite such figures as Mallarmé (particularly his *Un coup de dés*), the pointillist painters and, most importantly, the music of Anton Webern which I listened to over and over each morning as a preliminary to writing. I had found in these, I thought, the projection of the future lineage of poetries, the formally disjunctive and aleatory, which I heartily embraced.

I mention these influences because when, after a year and a half in Europe, I returned to the States, I had in hand a considerable body of poetry, of a kind which, despite my late start as a writer, had been well-received, published and even anthologized. And yet, as I looked again at this work, as I reread it daily, I felt no feedback from it. Rather, it struck me as clever and programmed, but down deep meaningless. Possibly, I was only experiencing what any poet feels about prior work—a desire to be elsewhere. And yet the feeling came as no ordinary case of merely wanting to move on to newer things. I suddenly and violently questioned the value of anything I had written.

So I began over again. I went back to the simplest, clearest writing that I could remember, the writing which had initially led me toward the act of making poems: the translations of the Japanese and Chinese poets, Williams, Montale's poetry and, once again, Oppen's work. I read philosophy, history, anything but that kind of writing, including much poetry, behind which lay some sort of dictatorial theory of readership or composition. Now, in an effort at 'purity,' I was excluding a lot, from the traditionalists to the surrealists to the contemporary avant-gardes. Without being aware of it, I was forswearing a large portion of the extant cultural apparatus. I was now thirty years old and, strangely, as though revisiting myself, feeling as I had in Spain, alone, disoriented, bereft of the poetic toolkit I had built for myself. I was at sea again, on the Atlantic Ocean of the *zeitgeist* which stretched before me and showed no hint of a landfall for my poetic making.

I think the truth is that I was again ripe, in a state similar to that when I first encountered Oppen's work. And it was in this climate, in 1967, that I met Oppen the man.

He and his wife Mary spent part of each year in New York City, in a small apartment on Henry Street in Brooklyn Heights. They were good friends of the poet Harvey Shapiro who lived only a short distance from them and at whose house at a small gathering of poets and writers I came face to face with the poet whose work had crucially affected me.

My experience of meeting him reminds me that there are situations where physiology has rhetorical (hence moral) force. I am speaking of the way we are drawn to certain faces in photographs, how they fascinate or move us. The self, Martin Buber suggests, is not a substance but a relationship, the knowledge of which comes out of an encounter. Already, as I was shaking Oppen's hand and mumbling a few words to him, the lines and leathery creases of his face, the slightly stiff posture, that of a workingman (which I believe he had cultivated when he worked as a radical populist in the Thirties and Forties) was prompting a response, some knot of emotion and language seeking a form. Not that I was moved to comment on his appearance but that that appearance was a conditioning aspect of what I might later say. Oppen's presence, and my heightened experience of his work were a kind of witness to the expression I sought, not then, but in the work I wanted to write. Buber's 'law' of intersubjectivity, as you can see, was already at play. I cannot remember the pleasantry which I uttered on that occasion, but I do sense that as I looked across the space between us, there was a shift in the way words were being created. There was something ceremonial about the occasion, much as if I'd been introduced to and then mesmerized by a wizened old medicine man in the jungles of the Amazon. As I reflect now, the encounter demonstrated to me Oppen's sense of what he meant by calling himself a "realist" poet, someone concerned with a fact outside of himself which he did not entirely create. Oppen, in that moment, had been the "fact" for me. Ultimately, such a concern became a central part of my own poetics.

In the time the Oppens spent that year in New York, I had much contact with them, eating dinner at their small apartment on Henry Street, taking long walks with George around the streets of Brooklyn or meeting them at readings and lectures. Soon after, however, George and

Mary went back to California, and I carried on my conversations with him through the mail. My correspondence with George was unlike any I've had with another writer. It was not merely the case that I was finding my way as a poet, for I had blundered into writing poetry the way I have blundered into many things in my life. Rather, the letters between us were pitched at a strange, existential level. I was trying to articulate to him my estrangement and feeling of lostness, my sense of disillusionment wih the activity of writing which filled every day with a blank anguish. And so these exchanges with George were not about specific poems or the business of poetry but about what poetry and life had to do with each other. George's response to these outpourings of mine were always kind, never dismissive but thoughtful and patient. The words from him seemed to go to the ground I was seeking:

> The type of mind necessary to the artist—or simply the mind   of interest—is touched always by experience, by   particulars;   cannot remain within dogma, no dogma   but this
>   which is not dogma but another and overwhelming force
> which we speak of or   speak of nothing
>   something like that, maybe in order not to speak of   any kind of
>   *correctness* other than awe—

(LETTER TO MH, late 1971)

I believe to this day that I stand under the shadow of these words, that they both harbor me and cast me in a darkness from which I seek to be free. Reading them, word by word, it was as though they were building in me not only an outlook on poetry writing but also a conscience, a code which was simultaneously liberating and confining. It was almost, as in Plato's parable of the cave, that I was seeing the world, certainly the world of making art, through the webbings of these phrases.

I remember, as an example of this simultaneous effect, how together, we worried the word "dogma," its meaning and use in our correspondence. For Oppen, the word had enormous philosophical and ethical weight. He meant it in some unspecified and hence all-encompassing way, not so much a terminological marker as a weight, a burden, which by that peculiar operation of the mind (and by the relationship I had established with Oppen) became, for me, a description of the mental environment in which we lived. Dogma, in Oppen's usage, delimited the totality of the philosophical, cultural and aesthetic views which we lived under. The first duty of the poet was to make himself aware of this fundamental condition, then to find a means of overcoming or subverting it through art.

As I reflect now on that correspondence, I wonder if I was turning Oppen's words into another dogma? If so, it felt like a dogma of openness, of receptivity to the world about me, and so came with that curious admixture of total freedom and total responsibility for what I was up to as a poet.

Oppen's letter had, in this instance, been partially in response to a question I put to him: "Is it a poetry that one writes?" and his answer in that letter framed the paradox I was living in:

> my refusal of the word 'dogma' above is questionable: this is, of course the question one MUST not attempt to answer or think of answering, this is what is wrong with all the 'courses' is it not? The question: 'is it a poetry that one writes?' is the question not to answer
>   Is it a poetry that one writes? Don't answer
>   Is it a poetry that one *writes*? alright: one's typewriter and one's desk could answer this.
>   and this can sustain discussion: the act of writing

Possibly these words led to nowhere and everywhere, but in them I felt deeply, for good and surely for possible ill, the absence of prescription, the refusal to impose a stylistics or mode upon one. They placed the act of the poem back, nakedly, with its maker.

～

What made Oppen's letters so powerful for me was the generality I hint at above. How to explain the effect of this generality? After all, poetry (to paraphrase Robert Frost) is at war with generality. Yet, as I read Oppen's work in the late sixties and came to know something of his personal history, the universality and even abstractness of his correspondence came to seem a kind of framing device, an arena which bracketed his poetic activity, heightened its gravity and disclosed the limit, for Oppen, of what could possibly be articulated by the poem.

Moreover, the poetry itself enacted, through its unique mixtures of poetic imagery and rhetoric, the boundary conditions of its own making, that dance between the known and the unknown which has been Oppen's singular contribution to twentieth century poetry. Oppen, from the first, struck me as a very different kind of poet from those of his generation, including his 'objectivist' peers, who came out of the Pound-Williams lineage and who were influenced in one way or another by Imagist theory and doctrine. In his practice, he departed radically not only from those poets but also from those who, coming after, would call him an influence. For me, this difference lies in how he used the poetic image, the building block of modern poetry, in an entirely different way from these other poets. For Oppen, the image, as I've written elsewhere, is neither descriptive not decorative but investigatory. It registers instead an impingement of a world upon him, and in following out in a phenomenological manner the dictates of this new knowledge, the element of vision becomes a kind of thinking. The concretions of the visible world and language which constitute the main element of his poetry rather than showing or putting the world on display led the reader unerringly to the brink of the unknown, to the sense of something incalculable, as, for example, in this excerpt from "Of Being Numerous:"

> The power of the mind, the
> Power and weight
> Of the mind which
> Is not enough, it is nothing
> And does nothing
>
> Against the natural world,
> Behemoth, white whale, beast
> They will say, and less than beast,
> The fatal rock
>
> Which is the world—
>
> O if the streets
> Seem bright enough
> Fold within fold
> Of residence . . .
>
> Or see clearly thru water
> Clearly the pebbles
> Of the beach
> Thru the water, flowing
> From the ripple, clear
> As ever they have been

(*NCP* 179)

---

* See "A Mimetics Of Humanity: Oppen's 'Of Being Numerous'" in *Pequod* 1990.

This powerful passage, one of my favorites, as it moves from philosophical statement to an uncannily ordinary and precise perceptual moment,
both consoles and takes away its consolations in the same poetic breath.
Technically, the strategically place "O if" of the fourth stanza and the
"Or" of the fifth stanza (which has no clear antecedent) undermine the
closures of imagist poetry that are usually invoked by a visual datum.
Here, these ingenuities but also the propelled dynamics of the language,
produce an entirely different effect. One feels—and this was one of
Oppen's most powerful teachings to me—that the poet is groping
within his own uncertainty, trying to resolve his own state of being as he
reaches for that which can not be articulated in language.

In a number of other letters to me, Oppen spoke directly of his own
poetry as such a linguistic and phenomenological quest, an attempt to
bring word and world, or reality into charged consonance, as in this
excerpt:

> suppose, instead of an 'instant archeology' that imagines   a
> personification of   things already known, one   imagines   the   first
> objects to become *object* to living   consciousness—their force in
> that among sensations they   emerged as   *objects*——can   we
> suppose, in the history of   the Sacred, a greater moment ?
>   this is the ground the poems mean to stand on. And   to   speak
> from.

> (LETTER TO MH, late 1972)

In his way, Oppen was reversing the contemporary ordering of our
thought, making the poem carry the reader from the known to the
unknown, rather than the other way around. He wanted to be precise,
but also to preserve the mystery of substance and otherness which he
felt was at the root of our creative lives. His poetry, looked at carefully, is
thus at odds not only with the gelid wastes of official literary culture
but also with the programmed experimentalisms of much of the avant-
garde. This was his strength, his radicality, and also the reason, I think,
for which critics and the poetry establishment have found it difficult to
come to terms with his work.

≈

"We wanted to know if we were any good out there," Oppen wrote in
"Disasters," one of his later poems. The phrase was not meant to exam-

ine a career in poetry in any competitive way; rather, it invoked, in its almost primal simplicity, the whole range of ethical questioning which had precipitated, in the Thirties, Oppen's poetic silence, a silence that lasted twenty-five years.

I remember reading those words and the sudden effect they had on me. In particular those two words "out there." They provided the fulcrum by which I was both able to feel deeply in Oppen's debt and yet also feel that I was a poet separate and responsible for my own work. I suppose, in saying this, I am mainly rejecting the idea that poetry is not a force in the world, and instead affirming my belief that both good and bad come of it.

~

George Oppen died in 1984, in a California nursing home. Still, increasingly, I find my state of mind ever ready to invite the dead poet to reenter the household of my psychic and artistic economy.

I did not see much of George in his last days, but I do recall his final visit to NY when Verna Gillis and I made a tape for Windmill of him reading from his work. This event, as though closing a certain kind of circle, took place in Harvey Shapiro's house where I had first met him. At the time, George was very frail and Mary hovered protectively over our taping sessions. George had lost not only his energy but also the power of intense concentration which had made his poetry so compact and powerful. He could read no more than a dozen lines at a time, and we had to stop frequently, sometimes even to remind George where he was in the poem. Verna and I had set up a makeshift taping studio in one of the bedrooms. Across the hall, there was another room with a day bed where George sat or lay down to rest between the short bouts of reading, eyes open, with a copy of his *Collected Poems* folded on his chest. There was a touch of fear in his eyes, and already one sensed he was peering into the very incalculable which his poetry had so assiduously courted.

Later, Verna effected a miracle by splicing the minute bits of poems into an almost seamless recital. When, recently, Oppen's literary archive became available to scholars, I was amazed to discover that George's method of composition in the poems had, all along, involved the splicing and pasting down of little slips of paper on which he might earlier have written anything from a word to single lines or passages. What had held that collage of language together, what had given an impressive coherence to his work, had been the ethical and philosophical depth he spoke from, a depth which anchored the most disparate language and tonalities. Oppen had spent his entire time as a poet searching for and recreating in these structures the uneasy meeting place of uncertainty and existence. When Verna and I had finished with the production of the tape, we had assumed we had put the poet back together. In fact, we had merely complied with the inmost dictates of Oppen's own poetry.

(1994)

Part IV

Avant-garde Propellants of the Machine Made of Words

> to get from inside to outside, man must
> cross through the narrow passage whose name
> is anguish
> — BATAILLE

"Tradition," Robert Creeley writes, "is an aspect of what anyone is NOW thinking, not what someone once thought" (23). Creeley's remark would seem to be self-explanatory, and, indeed, unimpeachable, for is it not so that "tradition" is already a figuration for the present, that is, a present ponderable. If we did not have tradition to think of we might have nothing about which to think. Eliot insists on much the same sense of tradition when, in "Tradition and the Individual Talent," he reminds us that the poet must be sensitive to "the present moment of the past . . . not of what is already dead, but what is living." (59) Both Creeley and Eliot express useful and much honored sentiments. But I would like to urge that even as we consider the "presentness" of tradition, we ought to keep in mind that tradition is also an aspect of what anyone is now forgetting and/or suppressing. For to transform is to forget, to suppress, to lower, even as one heightens, and always it is certainly to do more than baldly appropriate. What I want to track here is the appropriation and transformation of a number of avant-garde "tendencies" as they appear in contemporary work, in poetry written after Black Mountain, in writing programs, in the new formalism and in "language-centered" writing, and to comment on certain ironies which are engendered. I want to examine and touch upon such aspects of modernist poetry as imagism, discontinuity and the continuing elevation of "language" into an impersonal and over-arching entity which rules poetry and the poet at the expense of individual vision, historical circumstance and voice.

The central question to be raised is: What do these modernist techniques portend in their postmodern (I use the word loosely to cover the 1960s on) reincarnation. Do the exaggerations and suppressions within the bodies of the new poetries constitute a recognition of actual loss or are they the exclusionary gestures of careerist market forces? Do some of the new techniques and methodologies suggest an ultimate divorce of poetry from epistemological concerns (i.e. representations of world, self)? What is the relationship of the new poetries to history and memory? Does the reader need an *a priori* theoretical understanding of the rules of the game to "get" the new poetry? Does the term "theory" now significantly replace what used to be termed "tradition," and does it play such an excessive part in the understanding of certain contemporary poetry that a poem's audience is mostly the coterie or school that presided over its birth?

It was Rimbaud who remarked that "It is necessary to be absolutely modern," and so (perhaps unwittingly) launched poetry on a career of specialization and planned obsolescence, obsolescence in the Marxist sense as an instance of capitalism's "dynamic of perpetual change." Jean Francois Lyotard in *The Postmodern Condition* (a book best read as an ironic tone poem) specifies, quite accurately I believe, that the artist or writer has shifted focus, that in abandoning the idea of depth or interior in favor of the idea of surface, he or she now prefers to deal in "innovation" as opposed to "agonistics." The artist no longer works on the edge of being but at the margins of form where novelizing the object and specialization of skills take precedence over feeling or thought or sentiment. That a specialization of the poet has occurred, as in scientific professions and careers, can be inferred not only from the way we use terms like modernism or postmodernism, but from the increasing recourse to schools and movements by both poets and critics. To say one is a modern poet, however, is not nearly the same as saying one is a modern scientist. Science, for all the talk of its "being like poetry," still posits a world as its object whereas poetry is increasingly reluctant to make any such claim. Poetry's contemporary avant gardes, often critical of such notions as memory, representation and self, align themselves with Nietzsche's utopian claim that "no artist tolerates reality." We might put this alignment as one of our questions: how from 1910 to the present did the world get lost?

One answer may lie in an examination of one my propellants, a cluster of terms: image, Imagism, vortex, etc. which may indeed be the by-the-barrel crude from which have been cracked all our troubling distil-lates. Imagism is "old hat," and yet the play with and of the image is the central poetic activity of the twentieth century. In our critical texts, the image manifests as substance, as technique, as confirmation in the entire range of contemporary poetry.

Now our literary histories suggest that theories underlying imagist techniques as espoused by Hulme and Pound were meant to make poems more attentive to "reality." As A. C. Graham writes in his intro-duction to *Poems of the Late T'ang*, "the sacrifice of strict form for the sake of content was at first made possible by the doctrine that the essence of poetry is the Image, the exact presentation of which imposes an absolute rhythm out of accord with regular verse forms" (15). Graham, as with Pound, suggests that regular verse forms, the as yet unheaved pentameters against which Imagism rose, required the poet to forego the shape of reality for the shape of the poem. With imagism, the shape of reality would dictate the form of the poem. The image, it would seem was a step toward right representation.

Imagist practice was also a move away from the sort of artistic "ideal-ism" which characterized the late 19th century. "Poetry," T. E. Hulme insisted, "is not a counter language, but a visual concrete one . . . It always endeavours to arrest you, and to make you continuously see a physical thing, to prevent you gliding through an abstract process" (10).

Certainly, it was this sense of Imagism which appealed to Pound, but, if we examine Pound's writings on the image, we see that he proposed two somewhat contradictory theories of the image. There is one attitude expressed in Pound's remark that "the point of Imagisme is that it does not use images *as ornaments*. The image is itself speech" (*Vorticism* 469). In the context of these words, he relates the image to symbolism, claiming that it is "symbolism with a profounder sense," something closer to what he calls "permanent metaphor." The "image," is here relatable to the ideogram, "a vivid shorthand picture of nature." This formulation, even though it lacks neo-platonic underpinnings, suggests ideality ("picture") and mimesis ("operations of nature"). This is Pound the Confucianist.

In contrast to the above, we have Pound the Vorticist who promul-gates another view of the image as "luminous detail" as "that which presents an intellectual and emotional complex in an instant of time" (*Literary Essays* 4). Here the image does not depict "permanent metaphor" nor the "operations of nature" because these would be atemporal and acultural. Instead, the image as vortex is an historically deter-mined entity, a nodule of lived time caught as it were on the wing and transposed into language.

These two views are mutually exclusive, particularly if we consider them in relation to time: on the one hand there is the quickly perishing "complex in an instant of time," while on the other we have the eter-nally enduring "permanent metaphor." In one case, the image gathers in the flux of life which is ever construing itself in new configurations; in the other, the image accesses or points beyond the contingencies of reality to a timeless realm of forms. Thus, as Joseph Riddel has commented, "the image is irreducible to a singular notion of language" (218). There is what seems an inseparable breach between these two Poundian concepts. And yet, this breach (a creative tension, if you will) is effective only if we look at the image as it relates to our questions about reality. Historically, this argument was central in Anglo-American poetry until the early 60s.

Once, however, we abjure speaking in terms of representation or mimesis, under what I think is a mistaken reading of deconstructionist pressures, we reduce discussion of the image to a limited range of prob-lems. These problems focus narrowly on the question of poetic language. To a very great extent, this is precisely what we have done and are doing. The "postmodern" image is no longer a means by which we address representation of the world but a means to address the nature of the fictive worlds and constructs which language creates. We are, Riddel claims, "disallowed" a poetry which depicts truth or being. Somewhere, a link gets skipped in the chain of discourse—or, perhaps, we have made the elision consciously. Through the gap reality has evap-orated, gone up in metaphysical smoke, become hearsay.

For the student of imagism, this is a supreme irony. For along with all the other breaking down of conventions which the practice of the image performed, it was imagism that first decoupled language from what was once called poetry in order to deliver language to reality. But now, freed from the burden of interrogating the real, insulated from the impinge-ments of a world, the image has been recaptured for poetry (or more precisely a conception of poetry). Under this new *modus vivendi*, the image seems to have becomes a registration of our solipsism, one which both ends of the poetry production spectrum, the MFA schools as well as the experimental avant-gardes, freely uses. On the one hand, in the program-generated poetries of the academy, we find the image deployed in a totally unconscious manner as a hokey extension of naturalism and sincerity. The figurative mode of mainstream poetry draws on imagism's stock conventions, the "personal pastorals" (as Charles Altieri once called them), as though accessing the memory chip of a 19th century symbol bank.

On the other hand, and of concern in the argument I am raising here, in certain avant-garde modes, often where poetry attempts to approach the condition of the plastic arts such as music or painting or at the least to invoke their tactility, the image is equally freed from its engagement with the real to become, as Clausewitz might say, an extension of theory by other means. This latter path has lead, as Alan Robinson notes in *Symbol to Vortex*, to the ever-increasing sterility of aleatory post-modernism and minimal art (238). Freed from the need to trade coarsely in representation, freed from time and place, the poem can be handed over to method.

Now this triumph over the real has led, in imitation of the auto industry, to a certain planned obsolescence of poetic form. Poetic form no longer has what Louis Zukofsky once described as a "job" to do; it has become an end in itself, a *reductio* of poetic tradition.

I want to examine this diminution from the angle of tradition itself.

~

Some years ago, I came across this provocative item in *The New York Times*, 25 November 1987, datelined Baghdad, Iraq: "Hundreds of poets attending a poetry festival in Iraq were taken to the Persian Gulf war front and some read verse to Iraqis shelling Iranian positions, witnesses said today." The report is illustrative of a certain power of poetry which is no longer found in our postmodernist culture. Echoes and remembrances still exist, in the awe which the word poetry still inspires among general readers, in the preponderance of academic literary study devoted to poetry, even in the way major publishing houses continue guiltily to publish poetry at the expense of their bottom line. Auden claimed that "poetry makes nothing happen," but as the above points would indicate, there continues to be something special, even mythic about poetry in the consciousness of many. Let us label this collective interest the tradition of authority. Through it, the poet and poetry partake of some moral or divine force and perhaps impart it to readers and listeners. Godhead or goddesshead at the lips.

There is also the tradition of method, a tradition which, while perhaps of some importance for the audience of poetry, is of supreme importance for the makers of the poem. This tradition not only nests and is sheltered inside the tradition of authority, but is, by rupture or by overcoming of that authority, capable of standing outside it and, ultimately, of forcing that tradition to rise up and well around it, to re-enclose it within authority, so to speak. In this line of development, a technique or style has sanction based on the past, or is sanctioned by its rebellion against the past, enabling a poet to use, deploy or forego a technique in the process of making. The literary critic or interpreter looks not only for instances of these two lines of tradition but for the manner in which they interact (or fail to interact), how they animate each other as occasions of hypostasis, first the sacred function driving technique, then technical change enabling the sacred. Poet and critic look for these crossovers, these irruptions and tearings, for they represent, as Renato Poggioli suggests, the point where an avant-garde system is "transmuted in turn to a cause . . . where it becomes a dogma and a mystique transforming avant-garde praxis into principle and doctrine" (146).

"Principle" and "doctrine" suggest stasis, a mechanical application of practice, a movement of a technique out of the tradition of method embedded within the tradition of authority until it re-emerges as the whole of the tradition of authority. When the late Joseph Brodsky, in a time of the re-emergence of traditionalist forms, writes, for instance, of "holy metres," a rather old-fashioned absolutism seems to be rearing its head. One can understand this movement: in a time of crushing uncertainty, a little relief from the responsibility of form is the least the culture can grant the bewildered poet, the bewildered critic and the even more bewildered reader. "Meter" is "holy" even if, for some, it is merely what makes the car go, a propellant of the machine, if not an avant-garde one. (Recently we have had a spate of articles which insist that a new avant-garde was being created by poets "daring" to return to traditional forms.)

I use a word like "machine" above and in my title because it is part of a vocabulary of metaterms or paradigms for poetic practice as found in the work of traditionalists, new formalists and in the avant-garde. As an enabling notion, it is writ large across American poetic practice.

In the American avant-garde, to which nearly all contemporary poets, consciously or unconsciously, belong, we probably owe much of our machine/poem thinking to that of Williams who, in his preface to *The Wedge*, characterized the poem as "a machine made of words." Williams, when he coined the phrase, was arguing against sentimentality in poetry. Sentimentality was emotional overkill, redundancy, and Williams saw the machine as something without redundant parts (this was before space-age backup systems). Williams was for paring away superfluities, for taking words, as he wrote in the same place, "as (one) finds them interrelated about him and composes them—without distortion which would mar their exact significances—into an intense expression of his perceptions and ardors that they may constitute a revelation in the speech that he uses" (257). The machine-quality of the poem is of very little moment in Williams's mind; the statement is meant to enforce a distinction, to drive home a quality of good verse practice. It is not meant to name or define the poem.

Yet no one will deny that, along with Williams's line "Say it: no ideas but in things," this phrase has assumed canonical status in contemporary poetics. It points at a poetic self- sufficiency. One spins the poetry top and off the machine goes by itself. The phrase is inscribed in the neo-New Critical book of poetic rubrics and in the post-Black Mountain songbook, and it is hung over the door of many MFA departmental offices. The "machine"-ness of the poem has become a powerful propellant of contemporary poetry.

Now propellants, as in the case of "machine"-ness, like petrochemical compounds, remain essentially the same over time; however, their octane number can be boosted up or watered down by critical additives. Recently "machine"-ness has been upgraded and refined through an infusion of unleaded rehashes of Russian Formalism which have seeped into the poetics of such avant-gardes as the the sound poets, the concrete poets and the language poets. I will focus here on the language-centered poets because they constitute a contemporary version of the classical well-organized avant-garde, publishing and reviewing each other and issuing prescriptive manifestos. That they have now been taken up by a number of academic critics and gained positions within the academy may well signal that their moment as a significant force has passed; nevertheless, unlike any group in the last twenty years or so, they have raised the ante and forced the issues on the rest of the poetic community, poets and critics alike.

It is with these poets in mind that I have taken up the questions I have raised above. The "machine"-ness of the poem has become a pediment, the very word an archimedian lever of poetic principle. In *Total Syntax*, Barrett Watten, in a series of passages about the machine and avant-garde art, discusses Bruce Andrews' poetry as follows: "Where Williams's machine made of words is a self-contained entity, a whole consisting of interacting parts, each of which is necessary for the functioning of the other, in Bruce Andrews there is no limit to the whole, and the machine consists of the placing in motion of a sequence of unrelated parts found in the world at large. The machine imagined by Andrews is not a metaphor—its limits are those of the entire culture, in which dispersed objects are enmeshed" (160). Williams's spinning jenny has here grown into Andrews's strip mining consortium.

Williams's machine was lodged within the emotive-psychological horizons of sentiment and sentimentality. Its virtue as "metaphor" was precisely that it was not a "thing" in itself but an element for contrast; one ought to order the poem, says Williams, to reduce the sentimental redundant. Andrews' machine, on the other hand, simply scoops up and ejects linguistic material. We may be fascinated by what it ejects but that will likely be because we have syntax and the machine doesn't. This is to fall in with the formalist theory of defamiliarization or "perceptibility" which says that our awareness of the literary work is created by its structural difference from preceding work. In his *The Formal Method of Literary Scholarship* (in particular, Chapter 8, "The Work of Art as Datum External to Consciousness"), Bakhtin found this notion of perceptibility ideologically empty and meaningless (145–158). It is worth a moment of time to linger over his reasons.

Bakhtin maintains that the stuff of poetic conventions becomes "automatized" not for psychological reasons but because the conventions have ceased to be important in the "ideological" horizon. Against every technical novelizing of the poetic object, there is a cultural backdrop. In this sense, technique lives in two arenas at once. On the one hand, it is an art-historical vector, the message of which might go "you thought that *was* art, but *this* is art too." Here, the word "art" or words like "poem" or "novel", are less nouns than framing devices, ways of declaring certain territorial privileges for what is framed.

But at the same time, technique is, at least potentially, an arrow aimed at the culture, cutting into its notions of propriety and the sacred. Its "backdrop" is thought or feeling in a conventionalized form. Here, technique, in this latter activity, is a way of "reading" culture, bringing a new articulation into being and thereby displacing something else. And what gets displaced isn't simply an art form in the neutral sense, since an art form is always bound up with other cultural values. When the dadaists introduced aleatory works, the public threw chairs at them. When Cunningham or Cage present chance-based forms, they are funded by government agencies.

Again, our question is how to take machine-ness. What we look for in
the Watten-Andrews nexus of the word is the cutting edge, its relation
to culture. Williams introduced the term as contrastive and value-form-
ing whereas Watten employs it as a methodological designation meant
to draw our attention to the novel object. Formal rather than ideological
values are engaged. The work is in sync, rather than out of sync, with a
whole range of cultural productions, with Ortegean "dehumanization"
of the art form, with media generated information. Indeed, in his analysis, Watten makes constant identification of Andrews' work with the
Zeitgeist: "The structure of the poem is literally that of signs in social
space, which is identified with the formally coded subject" (160), or
"What at first seems to be a simple theory of a work of art [machineness]
is extended into a fantastic program for mass-psychology . . . the sense
that the form of the machine can be extended in cultural space" (162).
Here, Watten seems caught in a strange contradiction, valorizing the
replication of the given sign system of the culture he is criticizing.
Further, as the work and culture merge, as in Borges's prescient story of
the Babylonian lottery, one realizes that it takes a school or movement
using manifestos couched in Ciceronian rhetoric with its regular syntax
and belief in substansives (i.e. the very language-usage it presumes to
deplore) to invoke the occasions in which classical "deautomatization"
will take place.

Andrews' machine begins to look like the very capitalist-bourgeois
instrument it was aimed against. It is already part of what Guy Debord
calls the "society of spectacle," fetishizing not reality but language, as
though language were now suddenly capable of becoming an object
where all else had failed. Machine reads machine as the work becomes
a stimulus for purely private and subjective states. Bakhtin, we might
note, had already predicted that such works would reduce the reader to
the role of a psychophysical apparatus. For here, a reader's psyche no
longer encounters a meaning to embrace or resist but the sensation of
words to indulge or project upon. The "laying bare of the device" proves
to be little more than a *frisson*. Gaps and discontinuities are not so much
opportunities for creative co-participation as a kind of letting off the
hook, equivalent to the processes of manipulative political and cultural
media productions, the "feel good" ads, the 30 second campaign spots,
non-sequiturs to thought. This is the irony of an avant-garde practice
transmogrified into an art-historical squiggle.

A yet more mystical, hence unexamined, notion of political possibility seems to lie curiously buried in this same program of poetry, the very

aim of which is to demystify. This program claims for itself the creation of a poetry so suspicious of existing structures of meaning that by a nearly purified manipulation of language—what else could it use?—it builds replacements, new confabulations of language for inscription. The principle behind such replacements is a belief about how indeterminacy and discontinuity function for a reader. Watten, discussing Steve Benson's work in *Total Syntax*, hints at the role of such a poetry: "Benson's work pushes the ordering mind away from the particulars into a perception of the formal means of the work . . . The politics of the work are directed toward the capacity for and resistance to disorder in the spectator—how much indeterminacy can be allowed" (139). Watten concludes that "Benson presents multiple possibilities for identity, none of which are strictly determined" (139). "Indeterminacy," "multiple possibilities" and "disorder" suggest the fictious nature of the self, and the "political" nature of Benson's work seems, for Watten, to lie not only in such a discovery by the reader but in the consequent abolishment of that self-hood (a presumed good, because, in its attempt to maintain its self-ness, the self lends itself to the rhetorical constructs of political ideologies). In *The L=A=N=G=U=A=G=E Book*, Michael Davidson, in discussing the virtues of Stein's *Tender Buttons*, parallels Watten's thought: "What makes *Tender Buttons* so vital is not the strategies by which meaning is avoided or encoded but how *each piece points at possibilities for meaning*" (197). As with Watten, the operative word for Davidson is "possibilities." It suggests that a reader presented with language encoded into any meaning or meanings—in this case the 'meaning' is the "possibilities for meaning"—will grasp these with some retentive force simply because they are presented. Watten values Benson's work for its attack on the self-personality of the reader; Davidson values Stein because of the range of possibilities any one self is offered and hence may align it-self with.

Now such replacements can have no epistemological status, *per se*. Rather, we see here a form of reading which is aligned with Saussaurean linguistics, a flight from content—or, at least, an inscribing of a Saussaurean bar between sign and signified. If mimetics were not the point of the activity, it would be presumptuous to infer reality behind the words; the words would have to stand by themselves. There might be exceptions, as when some particular formulation is in a minor consonance with or shadows an already existing structure of meaning (in which case, minimalist parodistic or ironic overtones might occur). A reader of such work might be bemused and even inspired by the *project* of replacement, by its methodological indictment of "bourgeois reality", by its playful way with words. Still, as long as such works were the product of manipulations or dictated by *a priori* theories, they would have little ideological weight. For they would lack the conversing or dialogical element, the entangling whereby one meaning engages or competes with another. Rather, seen as minor aspects of polymorphous play (as opposed to competing or alternative versions of constructed reality) they are more likely to leave the world of ideas and concepts untouched, to flee, as it were, on the narcotic of *passage*. This narcotic effect is always the danger of work which has as its intention to move far from the normative. The poem of language here achieves a purity so absurd as to free it of any contingency whatsoever. Bakhtin sees such a reduction as moving a reader away from the articulations of historical contingency, transforming him or her, as I mentioned above, into a mere "pyschophysiological apparatus." Such an "apparatus" comes into being, according to Bakhtin, when the semiotic nature of language is forgotten, when we let go the chains of desire which link the instrumental uses of language with the poetic uses.

Maurice Blanchot, in *The Writing of the Disaster*, notes that "the healthy mistrust of language which Nietzsche teaches us . . . concerns the excessive uncontrolled importance granted to isolated words: Wherever men placed words, they believed they had made a discovery. . . . They had grazed a problem. When he [Nietzsche] berates "petrified, eternalized words," it is because he wants to come back to language as dialectic or to a tearing . . . " (106) Eternalized words are those we have shrunk from, words we no longer encounter, not in our thoughts, nor in the thoughts of others. The power of poetry, as I read the Blanchot-Nietzsche formulations, is that it puts a word back into the voice of an Other, that it is a power for him or her and so confronts my particular empowerment of it. The word again becomes an object of thought. Conversely, if I encounter this word outside of the realm of another, if I encounter it as a counter in a game of syntax or in an arbitrary setting rather than as another's voicing of it to and for my presence, I am left only with its eternal nature, a mystical and fundamentalist meaning of the word, couched within the protective confines of *my* psychology and *my* social circumstances.

Formalist and "language-centered" theory would deny the argument above. According to this denial, language is either in the service of poetry or is instrumental and/or representational. Lyn Hejinian, in the "SECOND FRONT" section of Ron Silliman's anthology *In The American*

Tree, discusses Silliman's work in a way which suggests that the emphasis is on just such a reduction. She writes:

> [In Silliman's work], the unit is what's contained between the initial capi-
> tal and the period, that is, the sentence. It is a sentence which lacks a verb
> yet remains active, even restless and in the present tense. "Along the
> coasts, on cots, in coats. A warm new storm. Blue ink on a white page
> between red lines." This is not a diarist's record of observed detail; no eye
> ("I") could be this ubiquitous. It is the realism of language under pres-
> sure, fully present. In work such as those collected here, content is not
> imposed from without, rather it emerges from independent initial points
> in the language itself. This method of composition, for that's what it
> really is, guarantees the possibility of a proliferation of works whose writ-
> ers insist on their independence from any fixing program or orthodoxy
> (487).

We have, in the above, all the obvious and unexamined sentiments of
the formalist agenda, the primary ones being the identification of art
with method and the focus on the physicality of the medium, as
suggested in Hejinian's phrase "the realism of language under pressure,
fully present." Now I'm not quite sure of Hejinian's emphasis, except
that Silliman's work, as with all works made of language, puts us in the
presence of, well, language. And perhaps further, that Silliman's
"sentences" do contain some playful effects, "coasts, on cots, in coats,"
for example. But the fact is that as soon as one moves into a feel or
awareness of these effects or begins to move off the physicality of the
language— i.e. begins making "contents" out of words at whatever level,
macro or micro—then the "realism" (but why "realism" and not reality?)
no longer seems to count for much. I suspect that Hejinian is trying to
claim Silliman's writing as a refusal of "representation" or "presencing," those bugaboos of post-Derridian critical thought. But this is to
envision a reader without history or memory, a reader who won't resist
the presence of the text. As Denis Donogue has written, in reviewing the
writings of Paul de Man: "I don't feel threatened by Deconstruction. I
oppose it because I think it is a scare-story. It sets up a straw reader and
then claims that he is deluded by a 'metaphysics of presence' into thinking that language can make something present. But who has ever
thought it could, or lost sleep over its failure?" (44)

Hejinian would have us pay attention to language "not as the instrument of expression, but the substance:" i.e. to the graphemic elements,
the "blue ink" of Silliman on the page. In short, she would like us to see
the literary work transformed into a visual and tactile one. That is, what

is actual to the work is the feel of it, the thingy weight of its being. But this limitation, so placed, is impossibly restrictive. No matter how one theorizes, the otherness of words is beyond our control, an otherness not found in script or text, but in the driftings of readers as words are encountered, the drifts into fantasies and reveries. Indeed, the source of these driftings might be in yet another text, but then what? The discovery of origins, like hermenuetical activity in general, leads only to more driftings, to more errancy in determining our fates. Ortega y Gasset, in his *Meditations on Quixote*, writes: "It is not enough for me to have the material body of a thing; I need besides, its 'meaning', that is to say, the mystic shadow which the rest of the universe casts upon it" (89).

Of the language-centered writers one wants to ask: why use words and phrases at all? And then, too, one must ask: from what orthodoxies and fixities are we freed? Once we try to claim for a work that it is non-expressive or non-referential, that its resonances as language no longer matter (a claim which by any test must fail), we have trivialized it out of existence. For what happens in some "language-centered" writing is not so much that we are freed but that we are *severed* from even considering the social meaning of freedom by being delivered into the polymorphic pleasures of the non-referential—*plaisirs du texte* indeed, but privatized and unavailable for the social agenda which many of the language poets claim, lies at the base of their work.

There is, however, a discernible "pressure" at work in "language-centered" writing, the art-historical pressure to "make it new." With modernists such as Pound or Williams, with the dadaists and futurists, the need to make it new lay in the social and expressive realms. It was never merely the pressure of innovation which motivated their works; rather, innovation was a means for exploring or debunking an entire range of social or culture expression *and* inarticulatenesses. Can similar claims be made for "language-centered" writing? I have some doubts..

In the first place, as students of twentieth century writing are likely to feel, there is a sense of *deja vu* when encountering much of the work found in *In The American Tree*. Many of the techniques on display in its pages are recapitulations of early formalist methods, of dadaesque dislocations, albeit with new, ingenious theoretical justification. The notion of a movement with all its submerged, often subconscious, motifs of coercion and manipulation, dividing up the literary sphere into saints and sinners, smells like a waft of stale air from the Twenties.

Indeed, one can find in any number of European anthologies of twentieth century poetry or in Jerome Rothenberg's and George Quasha's anthology, *America: A Prophecy*, earlier examples of virtually every modality which surfaces in Silliman's anthology. The differences in social agendas between the writers of these two periods may even be rather small. What we must judge is the value (strange word?) of the method of attack, of the wedge into consciousness by which the "language centered" writers wish to alter the socio-literary realms.

∾

In the *First Surrealist Manifesto*, Andre Breton remarked that: "Under the pretext of progress, we have managed to exclude everything which, rightly or wrongly, could be charged with being a superstition or a chimera, and to outlaw any means of seeking after truth which does not conform with established custom." (10) I take this as a cautionary note in considering the claims of any particular literary movement, its laws of exclusion, its desires to become itself an "established custom." This is not to say that one should disregard or minimalize the importance of such movements but rather to see in their discoveries further mechanisms for understanding language practice, which even as it adds to the "scepticism concerning language" vastly enriches our ability to read it. What we must ask ourselves about "language centered" writing is whether or not, in its urge to demystify the processes of writing, it has too easily invented a pretext of progress which would impoverish or abolish the very "superstitions" and "chimeras" necessary to seek after truth.

Perhaps the aesthetic/social theory of discontinuities ought to be replaced by a theory of what I would call *countercontinuities*, examining those works which, even as they construe new networks, necessarily deconstruct the old "mind forged manacles" of formerly held continuities. Reading such work would require us to dismember whole theories and reading strategies and pick up certain parts, building flimsy wattles rather than castles or fortresses.

∾

Countercontinuities? Walter Benjamin writes that "man's inner concerns do not have their issueless private character by nature. They do so only when he is increasingly unable to assimilate the data of the world around him by way of experience" (158). The key words of this passage, "inner concerns," "assimilate" and "experience," in fact the main thrust of the passage, is socio-political and cultural. Benjamin is less concerned about a "self" attempting to express its interiority than about an individual attempting to articulate needs which cannot be isolated as either public or private. Articulating needs is what modern culture works best at silencing. Benjamin, mourning the loss of the storyteller, observes: "It is as if something inalienable to us, the securest among our possessions were taken from us: the ability to exchange experiences" (83).

The difficulty of establishing both connections and limits to the notions of self and world would seem to lie in the nature of our terminology, in the antinomy of our categories such as "public" and "private." These words are less actual entities than the vectors of gestures, institutionalized gambits, ways to aim an emotional arc. As categories, as mythologies, they begin to collapse once we trace their arcs from beginnings to endings or vice-a-versa. In this way, we discover that the word "soul" in the political sphere, internal and otherworldly, is really in the service of our national timocracy; conversely, God's or the nation's work is the labor of the ego.

Benjamin's thought seeks to plumb the social mythology in order to reach for something simpler: how individuals can give meaningful shape to their experiences, and how they will be able to enact their desires, to sense what obstructs or limits desire and what can then be undertaken.

Put crudely, Benjamin's formulation suggests that if political action and literary works have a meeting ground, it lies in the work's or poem's capacity for a kind of local revelation. What culture has silenced, literature will articulate, not because words represent realities but because they offer us the sites of negotiation. The "data of the world" is incorporated by the poet into meaning-structures through the agency of the poem. The poem does not replicate the value- structure of the data but wrenches it from the utilitarian/socialized matrix in which it occurred. On the other side of the disjunctive act, the wrenching of words from their contexts in the structures of power is not silence but new conjugation.

In 1926, at the height of Russian Formalist experimentation, V. N. Volosinov (since there is still some dispute as to whether or not Volosinov and Bakhtin are one and the same person, I shall refer to the author of the work by Volosinov as Volosinov/Bakhtin), offered in the essay under his name, "Discourse in Life and Discourse in Art," a brief but thoroughgoing sociological poetics critical of both formalist and psychologistic literary approaches. Volosinov/Bakhtin reminds the reader that "a poet uses metaphor to regroup values and not for the sake of linguistic exercise" (116). The poem becomes a kind of "as-if" or "not-as-if" depending upon the poet's particularizing of the data, on the values the poet desires (even unconsciously) to instantiate. Thus the "political" meaning of a writer, Volosinov/Bakhtin tells us, lies in the two-sided nature of tone or intonation. "Intonation," he claims, "can be throughly understood only when it is in touch with the assumed value judgments of a given group, whatever the scope of that group may be. *Intonation always lies on the border of the verbal and the nonverbal, the said and the unsaid.* In intonation, discourse comes directly into contact with life. And it is by intonation above all that the speaker comes into contact with the listener . . . " (102). One question to be put to current literary culture is: what is the nature of a literary work when this quality of into-nation is consciously and ruthlessly removed, when the literary work attempts to free itself from historical time and historical beings who make utterances in speaking and writing?

We have lived now for nearly seventy years with the cry of "make it new." Some historian will undoubtedly reflect that at the beginning of the twentieth century, the work of art became the victim of the same ideology which infects the auto industry, consumerism, the arms race. The ideology is now noticeably incarnated in the world of poetry where one reads discussions of the poet as involved in the "production of texts." This Marxist note, a good beginning place from which to analyze the social consequences of a career of poetry, is, however, drowned under the louder industrial musics of obsolescence, of an institionalized avant-garde with its formalist scrap-heaps and commodity-culture. A text is no longer distinguished by what it has to say (the referential or mimetic text) nor by the indices of its form-content struggles. What is important is its formal difference from other texts. Saussure (our bad reading of him anyway) wins out over Blackmur or Brooks and Warren. The new text triumphantly announces its "technical ingenuity," as Jacques Derrida formulates it in a wonderfully ironic passage from *Writing And Difference*:

> Form fascinates when one no longer has the force to understand force from within itself . . . Criticism . . . henceforth knows itself separated from force, occasionally avenging itself on force by gravely and profoundly proving that separation is the condition of the work, and not only of the discourse of the work. Thus is explained the low note, the melancholy

pathos that can be perceived behind the triumphant cries of technical ingenuity or mathematical subtlety .... (4, 5)

Such pathos today seems to be singing a superficial victory over history, proving the ahistorical status of the work (at least until the next "production" comes along). But Derrida, with an almost buddhist insight, reminds us of the self's investment in forms even as it is disowning forms by claiming for them historical inevitableness. "Ingenuity," "victory," "melancholy," these words allude to the artistic manipulator, the producer of "possibilities" of the work.

~

To return to our argument: How does the "producer of texts" stand in relation to the imaginary "possibilities" which he or she creates, possibilities which are not entangled in lives and in versions of reality, which have no other status but that of language? Are not these possibilities the ultimate form of social repression, vitiating possibility itself by giving no one possibility an anchor or locus from which to act? One thinks again of Orwell's insight in 1984 that Big Brother's genius is in producing a social situation where there is no law, where since any version of the self is potentially illegal, all are. The climate is one of total, all consuming and numbing anxiety. Here Newspeak can be implemented because the great wealth of meanings in history and personal memory are called into question. Reference points are reduced to the vocabulary of Newspeak, to food and to hate. Winston's 'lesson' from O'Brien is not that there is a "wrong" self which has strayed from the right path, but that the "self," stripped by the State of any personal definition, is a fiction subject to the state's desires. The Orwellian underside of "possibilities" is that, far from engendering freedom, they weaken the very structures of resistance to the state's dominance of psychic life. When description and referentiality are consciously rejected by the maker of the text, the language field in which "reality" is constructed is left open to the play of socio-political forces which trade not on referentiality but on the decontextualized imagery of the media, the inflections of sentimentality in advertising, the easy symbology of patriotism. In 1984, we find Orwell talking, not only about the dangers of the "totalitarian left" but also of the capitalist nightmare of commodity culture where eveything is a "possiblity" because nothing is lived out.

≈

It is necessary to contrast the idea of an autonomous self (a phantas-magorical ideal) with the idea of some sort of psychological middle ground which is not synonomous with the self, but with that more central locus of linguistic activity by which the truth and falseness of the self (and thus history or social-mythology) can be perceived. Part of the perception will be the knowledge that one has been "inscribed" like the victim in Kafka's prescient story, *The Penal Colony*, with the culture's conceptions of self, against which only the self can testify. The poet as participant in this condition must also find, often in the incarnate, historical body, the place of the person as the inscribed victim. Otherwise, one is in danger of giving over to the thralls of "language," or to a carefree disjunctiveness of words at the risk of losing all force of words. Freed, supposedly, from contextualized reference, from the carnality of voice, do words write or inscribe? Inscription, Volosinov/Bakhtin maintains, occurs only via intoned sentences. The locus or middle, the site of negotiation then, is also an edge, a horizon, a boundary condition which might be characterized by asking the ques-tion: what if tonality were absent from what the poet said? Or better, what is on the other side of an intonation? What would it take to lift the pen, the blade of the penal colony machine and stop this particular writ-ing? It is always, as we know, another writing, the one which puts itself against the blade though it come out only as a scream.

As Julia Kristeva writes (working off of Bakhtin and Lacan): "In order to describe the dialogism inherent in the denotative or historical world, we would have to turn to the psychic aspect of writing as trace of a dialogue with oneself (with another), as a writer's distance from himself, as a splitting of the writer into subject of enunciation and subject of utterance" (74). Kristeva's formulation here is powerfully suggestive, opening the possibility that the dualism of the writer is not so much a separation of our old antagonists, spirit and matter, mind and flesh, eros and reason, but the dynamic point where, led by the semantic polyvalence of words, the writer can enact a break with the self. There, codified in language, is the momentary place of the middle, in love or affability with its own enlargement, regretful and remorseful of the self which was its starting block so to speak, but which has, momentarily at least, been deconstructed.

The idea of language as some ultimate reality becomes a flawed doctrine as soon as we enter into the social causation of any particular piece of language. Or, as Don Byrd, in a recent issue of *Sulfur*, in his critque of language poetry writes: "Language turns out to be the content of the world, not its structure . . . The whole awful thing must be taken up again: what it is to be a person, the pain and joy of history, the cosmos . . . " Admittedly, in the beginning there was the Word. God had uttered the frame of the world, but in the 19th century when He died, language was left to be taken up by the human subject. Now we breathe air and make words, but we are in danger of suffocating in the burn-off of our own propellants.

(1992)

Aspects of Poetics[*]

Proust sets the tone for these meditations with his comment that "a work in which there are theories is like an object which still has its price tag on it." To the extent that a poetics is a theory and that the poetry it generates shows forth theory or method through key tropes such as foregrounding the device or by making strange or via programmatic and formalistic procedures, including so-called traditionalist ones— choose your implement—then price tags are pretty ubiquitous. They tell poetry consumers, before the fact, what it is they are about to read and poetry writers what it is they are about to write.

Admittedly, poetics is a beclouded field. Responding to an earlier version of this paper, the poet Devin Johnston asked about the "slippage of the term 'poetics' between a statement or reflection on the generating principles of one's poetry" and "something like ideology." Johnston says "plenty of poets do not write a poetics, but only write poems." About the slippage, I'd say my emphasis here is more on poetics as ideology. As to Johnston's referring to poets who "only write poems," my response is that underlying his phrase is the difficulty, even pain, and uncertainty of poetic composition. I don't believe we can say with any surety that poets "only write poems," for such a notion of innocent composition flies in the face of what we do know: that each of us are products of traditions, of wars with traditions, impulses and hopes, and that we are informed, inhabited, guided, even unconsciously, by such traditions and psychologies.

But I am not arguing determinism here. I'm only saying that if we

---

[*] By "poetics," I'm thinking of one of the basic ways we take this word when applied to poetry, a proposal, a manifesto, a theory . . . .

look back we will see that there is a place or places we come from, and that by this looking back, seeing the traditions that inform us rather than being unconsciously driven by them, we will have achieved the first act of poetic freedom.

~

Walter Benjamin, in his *Charles Baudelaire*, makes a severe attack on the doctrine of *l'art pour l'art*. "This doctrine and its corresponding practice," he maintains, "for the first time gives taste a dominant position in poetry.... In *l'art pour l'art* the poet for the first time faces language the way the buyer faces the commodity on the open market." Such poets, he maintains, "have nothing to formulate with such urgency that it could determine the *coining* of their words. Rather they have to choose their words ... the poet's taste guides him in his choice of words. But the choice is made only among words which have not already been coined by the *object* itself—that is, which have not been included in the process of production." (105–106)

Benjamin's thought here is close to Coleridge's distinction between "imagination" and "fancy." Coleridge's "imagination" embodies notions of "immediate presence" or recognition, something which, because it is not totally self-willed, is close to Benjamin's "urgency" and the act of "coining." Coleridge's "fancy" resembles Benjamin's "commodity" and "taste." Benjamin is playing off the idea of the lost sacred bond between word and object. His "urgency" fuses that bond, a bond he contrasts with the more modern tendency, in the poetics of *l'art pour l'art*, to accept the divorce of word and referent and treat language from the side of its manipulable surface effect.

Another unintended aspect of poetics is that it sets up a hidden opposition between dogma and craft. As a rule-driven guide to composition, poetics may in fact dilute the poetic impulse even as it strives to maintain poetry's timeliness (sometimes fashionable timeliness). Alice Notley, for example, complains: "I want to stand face to face with whatever reality there is and I feel that all the friendly theoreticians in my neighborhood are keeping me from doing this by proclaiming that there is no such reality as is made evident in the works of so and so philosopher or poet." Notley, with some humor, is echoing Derrida's call for "the freedom to schematize without concept." To the extent that a poetics is primarily dictatorial by invoking rules and strictures on what constitutes a poem, it modifies or even attenuates the powers of the imagination, at least in its Coleridgian formulation of "intuitive knowl-edge" or "immediate presence." Poetics in this fashion is occult: the poet buys the lotto ticket of occulted dogma with its promise of poetic riches and potential for recognition by the clerisy (academe).

To embrace a poetics is to embrace a future-looking dynamic. I am referring here to the *a priori* nature of most poetics. As with the mystical blank page of the writing workshop, a theory about how to construct a poem beckons to the poet like an unappeased hunger demanding satis-faction, demanding that its conception of poetic activity be filled or demonstrated with words and images.

In this sense, a poetics has the power to stop the flow of time, to draw the individual into a new mode of contemplation or even action. It momentarily cuts off day-to-day life and delivers the poet into another kind of space-time continuum, subject to a different set of laws and considerations. Poetics, in effect, pre-figures or sets up reality.

Poetics has created a gap, one in which forces and vectors are occluded. Yet unlike Pound's image or vortex, that "emotional and intel-lectual complex in a moment of time," the as-yet-to-be-written-out page of a new poetics has already read the time and space before it, has already coined it. Pound's images read the past and present "reality," and, in many instances, have a pedagogic relationship to the future. By contrast, the future is still undifferentiated open time and space wait-ing to be filled, and so any poetics of or for the future may only be the 'reading' of an illusion.

In literary history, the future appears to generate at least two types of images of the poet. One is of the poet peering into the future, discerning the possibilities of the race. Shelley, in a somewhat hopeful vein, is exemplary, seeing the poet of time to come as a hierophant, a priest, of "an unapprehended inspiration, the mirrors of the gigantic shadow which futurity casts upon the present." (*A Defense of Poetry*, 508) There is a joy and daring, and wishful thinking, to this image, especially in the key word "inspiration." The poet is breathing in the future and will utter out its promise. And, indeed, such a possibility defines a poetic constant across time: the activity of poetry and of the arts as inspiriting the future. If the ends of poetic tradition are auguries of humankind's progress, of life constantly enriched and illuminated, this Shelleyan mode is part of the road map.

In stark contrast to the implicit optimism of a Shelley, we might ponder the peculiar nexus invoked by Walter Benjamin's Angel of History, as he derived it from Paul Klee's painting, *Angelus Novus*.

Benjamin's angel is a well-known, almost clichéd construct in contemporary critical thinking, but like all well-known and familiar constructs, it has many powerful contemplative uses. Here, I'm thinking of its role as a harbinger. The angel, an image created in a critico-poetic mode of thinking, is intended to show forth Benjamin's sense of historical process. As Benjamin imagines it, the angel of history does not face forward toward the future but is always gazing backwards into time past. Meanwhile, a storm "emanating from Paradise," as Benjamin constructs it, propels the angel toward the future. The angel, gazing back, transfixed, sees history not as a series of events, but as a catastrophe, a pile-up of man-made wreckage, political failures, wars, oppressions and famines. This storm, pushing the angel into the future, Benjamin ironically calls "progress." Dark pessimism and futility burden this image, for if "progress" means only an unfolding trail of further ruinations—consider Benjamin's experience of the twentieth century—what hope is there? It is difficult to imagine the angel having the wish or courage to face forward, to turn around and cast its gaze on the disaster-filled landscape looming ahead.

Here, now, is the rather anxious poetic angel of our present, functioning like some dark muse, uncertain, more than mildly depressed, aware of time not as fulfillment but as ominous inevitability. The Benjaminian poet, in the throes of composition, sometimes unaware of where he or she or the poem under hand will go, is riding on this angel's back. (And, yes, even that Shelley-like poet of promise who insists on facing forward might sit astride this angel as long as he or she wears thick rose-tinted glasses to ward off the bleak light of oncoming catastrophes.)

Which brings up another image or, at least, a sense of the future, one briefly alluded to by the late philosopher, Gillian Rose, in her book, *Mourning Becomes the Law*. The future, as she puts it, is the "supreme anachronism." Since we are thinking the future now, in the present, and since what will be cannot include us, all predictive thought generates only anachronistic material. While we are dreaming, time or death overtakes us and denies us the power to see our dreams or fears realized. Literary activity with respect to the future embodies the dynamics found in Rose's thought.

Let us throw in a bit of crude Freudianism: some traditionalist-minded writers fixated on the past, with tradition, repress uncertainty about the future. They go about reconstructing pre-existing artifacts, trying to make the present and the future conform to the past or to at least allay their fears of the future by emulating the tradition into which they have been inscribed. The repetition compulsion? On the other side, there are avant-gardist or experimental writers imbued with certainty about the future, who try to make the future happen by replacing the traditionalist's manufactured anachronisms with the production of objects that can only be understood at a later time. The work of these avant-gardists is directed toward being appreciated in, and to being completed by the future. Yet this work too is already a gamble —how the future turns out is yet to be seen.

We generally think of anachronisms pejoratively, as artistic embarrassments or failures. The writer of the historical novel has his medieval heroine take a shower. Or the playwright puts a twentieth-century street-wise word in the mouth of a nineteenth century character. But what is cast into the future, out of time, out of time's place, can be viewed, from a futurist's perspective, more positively. By a curious logic, the anachronisms of both the traditionalist and the avant-gardist writer provide us with unique interpretative material: an image of a defamiliarized future. Art, we know, defamiliarizes by plucking something out of its utilitarian mode of existence—Duchamp's wine racks and urinals, for example—not merely to emplace it in a category called art (whatever that means) but to refresh it for our senses. We see it again, but out of context and in a strange new light. The object embedded in the thought of the future, does not necessarily make itself strange in this way—it is already too familiar.

But what it can do potentially is make strange the space of the future around it, complicating this "supreme anachronism" and thereby breaking the mental chains of inevitability which possess both the Shelley-like poets and the ones somberly hooked on Benjamin's angel of history. The anachronism, normally an ungainly part of a temporal pastiche, when projected into the future transmits ungainliness to a time and a space yet to be predicated. We normally ask of an anachronism, "what are you doing here?" But the anachronistic object lodged in the future makes us ask a different question: "what future could possibly contain this?" You may remember Robert Heinlein's science fiction story of the butterfly that the time-traveler, eons in the past, accidentally crushes and so alters all of the future. The anachronism posted ahead is like that butterfly given a new life and thus is quite capable of revising the future. Of course, everything we write about the future continues to be, following Rose, an anachronism.

While there is thought, nothing is inevitable. If a new poetics signals closures, and thereby new openings, we might meditate on Ernst Bloch's words in *The Spirit of Utopia*. There Bloch maintains that "the sign of an authentic end opens into emptiness." If we posit a poetics as an "authentic end," that is, if we desire that it be significant and create the opportunity to remake human time, we are required, according to Bloch, to address it toward emptiness, without overlaying it with preconceptions. Against our usual psychologizing, we would have to think of a new poetics without the kind of Golden Ageism that we normally apply both forward and backward to our historical thinking. In this regard, Rose's notion of the future as anachronism is helpful. For if the future which we carry in our minds is bound already to be an anachronism, beyond our power to control, then it stands to reason that only by freeing ourselves from a heavy-handed premising of that future can we be led into what Bloch calls "the *unfated*, or at least into a fate that can be modified." (*Critical Inquiry*, Sp.93, 420).

"The unfated" is in itself a remarkable idea, worthy of further contemplation from both the literary and philosophic-historical perspective. As a potential for poetics, the idea is already prefigured in Keats' poet of "negative capability," or, closer to Bloch's time, in Robert Musil's comments in *Precision and Soul* on the poet Rilke. "Rilke," he says, "leads us into the future;" he gives us, not prophecy, but an "anticipatory scent." For we are not, Musil insists, "to be called again to this or that ideological fixity, but to the unfolding of the creation and possibilities of the spirit."

$\backsim$

Bloch's "the unfated," Musil's "anticipatory scent," these are suggestive rather than prescriptive terms. How might they help in thinking through a new poetics? As David Kellogg reminds us in his essay, "Perloff's Wittgenstein: W(h)ither Poetic Theory?," the poet is often inscribed in a "contemporary circle of belief," (in his discussion, especially the belief system fostered by postmodern theory). Such "belief" systems, patrolled by critics and poetic cliques, are not benign. They produce an anxiety of acceptability, of correctness and righteousness which dictates to practicing poets forms, groupings, restrictions on the self, on subject matter. At any moment, a poetics, one of our many "circles of belief," can exist as a kind of malevolent sclerosis. Gillian Rose, in many regards a student of Benjamin, talks about the "trauma in reason," its quest for certainty by severing what she calls "existential eros" from "philosophical logos." Philosophical "certainty," she claims, "does not empower, it subjugates—for only thinking which has the ability to tolerate uncertainty is powerful, that is, non-violent." Rose's "uncertainty," seems to me sympathically aligned with Deleuze's and Guattari's call for a "minor literature," one that does not seek out, to use their words, "a major function in language," or try to become a "state" or "official language."

In the past, there have been methods that work against the hegemonic reductive logic of a missionary poetics, indeed, against a whole project of a rational utilitarian world-view. These methods, in the service of an imaginative or speculative view of poetry, put literary versions of reality up for grabs. I'm thinking of the constant re-imagining, discursive breakdown and personal wanderings of impressionist and surrealist gambits. A new anti-reductive poetics might simply propound a litany of advisories something like this: phantom world of the future, phantom native land, phantom North America, phantom this, phantom that, most importantly, our phantom self! A bit of a mantra to be sure, but from the poet's perspective, this string of invocations is perhaps more reflective of our fluxual state of mind and is in a sense less *fantastic* than the more hardened methodologies of poetic predications and codifications.

That is, for the poet, this "phantoming," this making a phantasmagoria of reality can be what really amounts to a new poetic *real*, perhaps closer to the essayistic assay or try-out than putative distance or objectivity or reading the *zeitgeist*. Otherwise, the poet is in danger of being reduced to the role of voice-box for the status-quo or becoming one of the cheering squad for the way things are in which the poet might as well be a government official, speaking unironically in the dulcet, often hegemonic, poesy of bureaucracy.

So let's say that my sense of a possible poetics is based on a proto-science of or at least a receptivity to what we might call "phantomology." A poetics which, to borrow Gershom Scholem's words "descends into the abyss in which the freedom of living things is born." A receptivity which recognizes that behind word-facts and thing-facts, phantoms are loose, or as George Oppen put it in "The Language of New York," words are "ghosts which have run mad/In the subways/And of course the institutions/And the banks" (*CP* 96).

In poetics, in the mode of phantomology that I envision here, then, two terms, slightly modified, become important: "precision" and "uncertainty." Precision is operant here not only to register or document fact and object but, by a technique of intense concentration on and investigation of appearance, on what is, to release the phantoms behind things. I am thinking, of course, of an unarmed phenomenology, or at least—in terms of a poet's self-work—the hope of one. Freud speaks of an "evenly-suspended attention" without which one is "in danger of never finding anything but what one already knows." That is, precision can have a style of interrogation in seeing what is and in rendering accurately.

Its discipline might be construed as the mixing of experience with patience. Precision in this sense becomes a pressure on the object-world, something like a phenomenological reduction or even an electron microscope uncovering the seed-syllable of poetry in thing and event. It may reveal how much interpretation (substitute the word mind-phantoms) comprises our so-called objectivities. In this interrogative mode, through its powers of representation and figuration, through its capacity to isolate and disjoin and to suggest recombination, precision becomes correlative with the possibilities of the poetic medium, a medium which I would maintain is only partially language, even on the page. (Intention and longing constitute at least two other elements of the poetic act.)

Uncertainty produced by such precision, far from consuming one in doubt, becomes a registration, even an acceptance of one's phantom-like existence. I'm not referring here to the indeterminancy or undecideability induced in some contemporary practice by chance operations or by the prepared effects of textual manipulations. Rather, I'm thinking of a condition induced by knowledge of our unreliability, our deference if you will, before the limitations and understanding of language and of otherness. Uncertainty, in effect, is already an aspect of an utterance, of saying and affirming. It advocates a kind of lightening up about our purported certainties and the hopes and fears in which most of those certainties are lodged.

Clearly, in this mode, value-labels such as "natural" and "authentic" (among the more highly politicized words in discussions of contemporary poetry) will also be rethought, not because, as Hugh Kenner suggests, they are "inventions," but because they are sites of desiring. In other words, lying between the categories of the natural or authentic and the invented, is another realm, that of unsaying or, to use a term from C. S. Peirce, abduction. As I understand it, abduction is language in its refusal to play the game of systematic power. Unwilling too to go along with conventionalized format or 'commonsensical' meaningfulness. It is, poetically speaking, lyrical anti-logic which obtrudes against the repressiveness of a state-speech or discourse. And its method is not necessarily to rely on the disjunctive or fragmentary but to place the imaginative or "*as if*" object in juxtaposition or apposition with norms and logic. As I wrote in "Avant Garde Propellants of the Machine Made of Words," "perhaps the aesthetic/social theory of discontinuities ought to be replaced by a theory of counter-continuities . . . producing writings which, even as they construe new networks, brush up against and deconstruct the old mind-forged manacles of formerly held continuities." Here, a phantomology would exist to register the alternative reality of the unsaid, to highlight the ghost-like functioning of language as it uncontrollably expands our notions of idea, limit and time.

The western model of the poet committed to such use of language would be someone (again) along the lines of Keats's poet of "negative capability," aching after neither fact nor reason but rather for a virtual construction of desire in words. Buddhist notions such as *shunyata*, of a life-world wrapped in human projections and concepts, or of the Hindu *Maya* where appearance is perceived as dream-screen or illusion, allude to the perspective I am seeking here.

An ethics of otherness belongs to this perspective. Clearly, poets are already Other to themselves; they have an anthropology and a structure that is opaque, and which becomes available to articulation only by the trial and error of composition. For poetry, like other disciplines, is almost always looking two ways at once. It is always reading its own graphemes and seeing, in the handwriting of its gestures, the potential of consequences arising out of antecedents (tradition) and the reverse, seeing antecedents in consequences (ghostings, hauntings, voices of the dead, that is, phantomology).

Let me briefly sketch out a provisional, open-ended architecture of an "unfated" poetics, one in which I try to apply the two terms of precision and uncertainty, not to create another battery of techniques but to suggest an attitude toward the components of this architecture. By architecture, I'm thinking of relatively simple guidelines, codes of behavior or thought, a set of boundary markers that arouse socio-spatial responses such as "here's a wall; don't walk into it" and as well "here's a wall; what would it be like if it wasn't here?"

One component of the architecture consists of the congeries of imaginable existences in any one so-called individual. Whitman's "I am multitudes" or Robert Duncan's participatory mythopoesis are models of a self embodying or dancing with other selves, with texts and masks of selves and the attendant cosmological machinery of those dances. Such multitudes are embedded in the sympathetic magic of language, in the sense that the employment of a signifier creates or arouses the specter of the signified, thus always producing an environment of interpretation. An interrogative cliché-destroying precision is needed to map the psychic traceries of a situation, of a human encounter, and thus rescue it from sentimentality or false identifications. Such a poetics seeks to free a culture from its entrapments rather than propel them, in the secret biases of language, into a pre-conceived future.

A corresponding component would be the imagining of the Other as neither a monolith nor a collective. The other, like the self, is a slate of potentials, representations, evasions, disguises and as yet unlabeled complexities. These complexities, too, though the perceiver often sees some bits of the data as more objective than others, are also given as occultations of language which have been mediated by one's provisional self.

Before the complexity, the psychic and physical distance of the other, uncertainty, induced by the potentials for these fictions and distortions, becomes a form of humility. Or, as Bakhtin instructed, carrying this discussion beyond the poetic sphere and into our own backyards, we are to regard no other person as finished, as fully understood. This way, admittedly, lies open to the contingency of being foolish or wrong, but isn't such risk-taking the real task of poetry in an over-mediated and discourse-ridden culture?

The poet lives best in the land of as-if, in the space of that "storm of *paradise*" where neither certainty nor uncertainty rule. Instead of fixity, there is "anticipatory scent." Everything then becomes a matter of accepting the weightlessness of situations, perhaps becoming something like the buddhist adept who lives, as the sages referred to it, in the 'fourth moment' beyond past, present and future.

If culture and self are now understood as variables, co-existing in fluxual and recombinant phases, if the millennial is acknowledged as all emptiness, then the repeatability of either the experimental set-up (theory) or the recorded result (imagism, testimony, etc.) are best seen as poetic will-of-the-wisps, as merely other branches of phantomology. A new poetics would have as its primary goal the unsettling of conceptualization and of identity, the constant transforming and renewing of our image of the world.

(1999)

Notes on Lyric Poetry or at the Muse's Tomb

Translating the language of things into that of humans entails not only translating silence into audibility; it means translating the nameless into the name.

— WALTER BENJAMIN

One of my close friends, also a worker in the mine fields of the poetic, says to me "the lyric is dead." I cannot but agree, if by lyric we mean that private self-regarding effusion of language, that romantic *mea culpa* by which a world is nostalgically recalled, privileged and measured against *what is*. Likewise, I would emphatically add, poetry is dead or at least dying out of a swoon of novelty if it subscribes too closely to those collocations of contemporary thought we call theory or cultural studies, studies which invoke other nostalgias for certainty, for 'rightness,' for order.

Another way of putting this might be: the lyric is dead primarily as it re-inforces a masked ideology, including the myth about the "myth of the personal." But, as well, the typical critique that the lyric is "subjective" ought to be juxtaposed against the *sub-rosa* reality, more difficult to enunciate in the face of avant-garde tribalism (do we know of anything more tribal, more nationalistic than the poetic clique?), which reminds us that poetic bandwagons are never merely matters of aesthetics, indeed, may involve many more 'subjective' dimensions than we'd care to explicate.

What can be stated concerning the theory- or philosophically-driven work is that it is clearly a product of statism and would-be statism, what Deleuze and Guattari point out in *Towards a Minor Literature* as those "styles or genres or literary movements, even very small ones, [which] have only one single dream: to assume a major function in language, to offer themselves as a sort of state language, [an] official language." On the grounds Deleuze and Guattari are making, the lyric as judged by a post-modern mentality, can never be sufficiently political; it is not doing a man's job, lifting the weight off the masses, creating utopias, etc.

But a case can be made that, in this century, this is *precisely* the lyric's strength, that strictly speaking, the lyric is neither a product of thought nor of intention but rather comes as a recognition of a gap or rupture in one's thought and intention. (My use of the impersonal singular pronoun is meant to suggest that the lyric *qua* lyric has no hope of ever becoming a kind of group-think.)

Casting the lyric against other poetic forms, one finds something that is more than merely interesting. The narrative mode, the rhetorical mode and the gnomic mode, even the purely private or expressive mode of the lyric (with its hidden ideological baggage) as well, have a kind of self-sufficiency. The reader participates by wandering around the entities created by such forms. Indeed, a form is erected that in some way does not depend on a reader—as in the case of story, a form which, even as it wants hearers, is ultimately enclosed and folded in on itself. Not so much interactive as presentational. The self-containment of such forms, the polished-egg quality of either story or poetico-logical structure may already seem anachronistic when set against the polyvalent and even fuzzy operations of the mind. And the old romantic lyric, especially that poetic trace of delicate impressions caught on the wing, now strikes the reader as orotund and even unsympathetic to contemporary awareness and consciousness.

So we must admit that if we are to talk positively of a lyric moment, of a moment for the lyric, we must acknowledge that while presenting itself as something gathered out of the flux of existence itself, it is no more free of the contingent, the historical or philosophical than any other form of life or thought. And yet, the function of lyric, and by implication poetry's first principle, is that it exceeds or modifies the very conditions it arises from. Even in the minims of speech or figure, it is always the unplanned, unaccountable supplement. And like a pebble dropped from eternity, it offers itself, in a limited and privileged way, to our curiosity, our inspection. That is why, in speaking of the lyric, the guiding principle for the poet is recognition as opposed to production. I am thinking here of the linguistic philosopher Emile Benveniste's thought that "language is so organized that it permits each speaker to appropriate to himself an entire language by designating himself as *I*."

The poet trains in attentive recognition of such an appropriation, in one sense, because what he or she finds represents the actual objectivities of language, its history and inheritances. But language is also an otherness and does not immediately give us, in its traditions and collective knowledge, an account of our experience. It is this otherness which produces lyric activity with its previously unaccountable tries and assays.

On this basis, I would maintain, there is a place for the lyric, not so much in self-presentation but in a recognition of what, in language, is peculiar to the lyric. The initial moment of lyric production is also, in its refusal of language's history and in its embrace of its otherness, the point of radical undoing, the unaccountable (let us admit, the most personal) trope by which the creative and the resistant impulses are expressed. Because the lyric has no adherence to *a priori* doctrine, because it is not a pre-thought out technique or modality, no one, least of all the poet caught in its activity, can predict the form of a lyric utterance. It remains 'original' even while subject to the hidden mythos of lyric production and the subterranean mysticisms by which ideologies infuse thought and practice.

Let us go further. If lyric's peculiarity is held in view, wouldn't it be the case that all attempts at keeping the lyric mode alive, or of restoring it, are attempts at recognizing and communicating a particular kind of intersubjectivity? Lyric, as I am thinking of it here, is undoing, opening, un-finishing (un-completing) the overt or stated concept, logic or discourse which had been deemed finished. It is undoing openly and in print; it is exposure of what is not received idea, not theory, *i.e.* of what may even just be foolishness and embarrassment. It is radically anti-agenda driven in that any project which the lyric might undertake can never be something proven or confirmed. It can only be attempted, and that attempt must be made with as full a knowledge of the poetic environment of one's times as is possible. The "intersubjective" lyric must be based on the fullest foundation.

One aspect of 'intersubjectivity' revolves around the notion of representation, a term now used almost pejoratively in post-modern discourse. But one could argue (as does Gillian Rose in *Mourning Becomes the Law: Philosophy and Representation*) that the mode we call representation—the mode perceived as the enemy by post-modern thought—is that mode which creates the conditions not for recognition but for misrecognition. A representation in this sense, since it is always a reduction of all possible elements that are contained in what is being represented, can only be misread. And in this sense, representation can be the central engine by which social and political values and their mystifications might be perceived and acted upon. On the plane of artistic production and tradition, every work of art expresses a hunger for completion by that which has been left out. Or, as Guy Davenport puts it in his beautiful essay, "The Artist as Critic: 'A work of art wants to know what it is.'" Playing on Matthew Arnold's well-known remark, poetry is criticism of life, but we might also read this backwards: the lyric which is necessarily a fractionated composition provides life, inversely, with a criticism of poetry. Certainly these two acts of criticism are a good part of the artist's life.

Representation in the sense I'm using it here requires closure to operate. Closure not as the cutting off of thought but as its starting point. Which means that the poet risks making a statement, presenting a version of a state of affairs, so that the poetic object, or as Zukofsky might say, the object's "rested totality" can be contemplated. And *found wanting*, the basis of further production. A composition must end in order to be a composition. On the other hand, the perpetual *frisson* of postmodern poetics, its anti-closural bias, which attempts to deliver its reader into a freedom of linguistic signification relies on an old idea— an old 60s leftist idea one wants to say—of *jouissance* by which the reader is delivered from the State, but, alas, the State remains after the trailing off, the letdown into the prosaic, the non-closure closure from the free-floating signifiers. And often there is no connecting analytical thread between the pleasure of language and the oppressions of modern life. One's high derived from a kind of *soma*-language holds one even further out of touch than the excrescences of the self-absorbed lyric poet.

Another kind of lyricism is in order. Baudelaire had a formula for poetry which he described as "poetry within history." The phrase is suggestive to me of a rhythm to things, to time and event, to which poetry is receptive, a rhythm—and this is the key point—which lies outside or athwart the rhythm of historical description, discourse or logic. A rhythm which lies outside of the precincts of 'theory' as well. By this I mean a poetics, a lyric poetics, which can not be mastered by rationality.

Baudelaire often tried to find this poetry by means of the proscribed; hence his satanism, dandyism and the like. But we are too knowing today to invest in any of these anti-bourgeois demonstrations. An effective rhythm of "poetry within history," if it were to be more than sound or triviality, would require a continual practice of uncertainty and resistance. The expectations for such a poetry would be its ability to resist or treat ironically not only the conventionalized linguistic constructs of contemporary thought and culture but perhaps as importantly, the constructs of literary making as suggested by any theory-community of poets, scholars and critics.

The British poet Geoffrey Hill, in *The Enemy's Country*, his absorbing study of the pressures placed on the poet, includes criticism and by extension 'theory' among those forces against which the poet must write. Looking at criticism as part of the poet's contexture, the environment of composition, he writes: "Criticism which is, on many occasions, the faculty and instrument of judgment is on other occasions, possibly more numerous, part of the body of circumstance out of which and against which the single voice of creative intelligence must be made articulate. Modern criticism in this guise is one of the shapes of protean Opinion, one of the petty 'lords of the temporal world . . . '" Hill's terminologies, "the single voice of creative intelligence" contrasted with the "petty 'lords of the temporal,'" suggest a somewhat past poetry-time, but the fact is, for the most part, the production of poetry is the work of an individual organizing consciousness writing within and often in ambivalent relationship to a pervasive critical and cultural zeitgeist.

∾

The poem is not timeless. To be sure, it does lay claim to being infinite, it attempts to reach through time—through it, not over and beyond it.
                                                              – PAUL CELAN

Any writing on the current state of poetry would be a controlling projection over its past and, however subtle or 'objective', an attempt to control its future. Therefore, it might now be useful to think of the activity and production of poetry as a kind of occultism. By occultism, I mean something close to what Merleau-Ponty formulated when he said that occult objects, and he was talking from the viewpoint of anthropology, are those, like charms or fetishes, which we believe put us immediately in touch with supernatural or extraordinary powers. He was contrasting this occultism with the more usual spiritual work, work, such as becoming a member of a religious order, usually requiring initiation, spiritual discipline, knowledge and lengthy preparation.

The potential for occultism is present in all areas of culture and social life, from beliefs in names, in statistics, in dress codes, in status and street address. So too in poetry. In the workings of poetics, in the practice of poets, an analogous situation obtains: all technique, stylistics, theories, movements, naturalisms and non-naturalisms are objects for occultation. Especially in poetry, it would seem that that which is authoritatively asserted is already occult.

In the virtual or *as if* world of poetry, an occult object can become a spiritual one. Occultism and lyricism have this in common: they create intelligible nodes of language around which all sorts of powers and investitures, human and nonhuman, are gathered. Yet, as figurations of words, they can be interrogated as well as capitulated to. In the meeting place of an individual and a self-created or self-existing sign, one writes not only to express but also to live through the teachings or insights of that writing.

These nodes and figures of language focus our attention. They create different kinds of fascination with a poet's work which often can only be found in its lyricism, of character, struggle, etc., elements which have been underplayed or dropped in our more experimental poetries, but which, strike me as needing more exploration than ever.

For the appropriate response to poetry *is* fascination, a certain glimpse of mathematics, of symmetries, some supplied by the reader alone, of an incandescent nature. Even if the poet speaks only within his own borderlines, he or she at the least represents a site where inner echoings and outer world are woven into knots. The social, exterior world is always larger than the poet. And so the poet always finds oneself in one's writing as another 'other,' a dynamic always threatening to tip the poet's well-being. Always off balance itself, always expressing a kind of madness found only in and through poetry, lyric language is the additive which evens the scales.

At the Muse's Tomb

AFTER READING

The long eerie sentences were fates as the savannahs of Georgia and the Carolinas were endless stanzas in pine and swamp water.

Searches were made among the word-habitats that mattered, consonances of landscapes and self, half-geographies contoured from remembrances, shadowed and opaque.

The rest, the unexplained, the transparency, the mirrors and the dust, were to be talked away as dreaming.

The investigation missed horror.

Yet no one complained, preferring to imagine a pale language, paler than a linen tablecloth or the desert's unlit night.

Poe's white Baltimore stoop mounting to a door.

FORM

Nothing to ennoble the passion for measure and number, for the hard precincts of form, that uncanny love, surely as indictable as any great crime or gratuitious enormity.

Yet, with one's attention span, the mind wandered out, a weighted thing to be pushed forth on a cloud of moistened breath, to soar and curl itself about a street or a city.

Hungerings occurred amid the silted isobars of hope, in love's calms and tempests, sloughs of logic gone astray which had left us open to chance and to a desiring to persist.

The self's tellings were another moon haunting its own sublunary. It sought itself as a name high over soil it had made, rocks, cities, isolate worded beings.

MNEMOSYNE

O Mother memory, yes!

I had visited in Spain, did my Goya-walk to the *n*th, but it barely got me to Lorca.

The *duende*, mysterious visitor, came and went.

The dead war ravaged among villagers.

And suddenly the muse was no longer a headstone stippled with *palabras*.

THE LOCAL

Actually, by accident of birth, I was born to homelessness and nothingness.

Later I opted for the local, for the 63rd A. D. election district and its bands of refugees who vanguard at the doors to ATMs.

Also to what the city advertises, gunk or hair-gel, the stickiness of lost meanings, of signs secured by ripped awnings, foreclosures on the dark, dry pavings of a night skittish with deaths.

Beyond words' portals, I was always turned back, a bewildered Orpheus, city gentleman to Eurydice, an Amphion who gathered up stones into another hell-heap.

And now I feel a bit sickness-haunted, peering at the ineffable from an alley.

OUR TIME

Media voices overwash all, blurring the inevitable: Psyche's credit-card sorting of the selves into collectives.

From the great engarblement, words are lifted out, and, in the current lexicon, crowd aside columns of pictures, taking one past new literals for contemplation among metonyms of blank.

GHOST

I was thinking about memory again, writing its letter home.

Before she died, her face, her favorite objects, etc.

Breakfasts were sweet, even . . .

On the table, the plunged gold plate of the bell on a silver creamer.

Someone left a world in it, a layer of puddled whiteness resembling a page, viscous, absorbent, richer than the *néant* Mallarmé inscribed on.

NEVER ONE

Because it is almost sound, it was meant for sharing.

We watched together the sun pour in the window, motes of light on glass and wood.

Who was home to this homeless light?

Together we dreamt of transports, of residences as glints off mica-ed rocks, centerless sheens bouncing from the frozen lake.

One felt the very slightness of being, almost validity's dusting up.

Yet also love, which hid us from the fiction's glare.

Pointless to ask for the addressee of desire.

Or that the mind misspoke its sonic phantoms and conjured the self which erred and brought us to this place.

APHASIA

And now, the demiurge possesses a lightness, a wet nuzzling of hope blind to the part played by the geometer's art.

Bleached one, O muse, I think of you, your silences where the throat catches on emptiness, *that free flight into the wordless.*

O teacher, the sky's light is fading, and I have sought that one place, speechless to the moon, an omen blossoming at its own edge, a bizarre portraiture in the rush of things portentous.

Bleached one, what was strategy?

What was truth?

The plangent lucidity, the glass through which the light flowed.

(*EF* 135)

(1997)

Works Cited

Ackroyd, Peter. *T. S. Eliot: A Life*. New York: Simon & Schuster, 1984.

Bakhtin, M. M. *The Formal Method In Literary Scholarship*. Trans. Albert J. Wehrle. Cambridge: Harvard University Press, 1985.

———. *Speech Genres & Other Late Essays*, trans. by Vern W. McGee, edited by Caryl Emerson and Michael Holquist. Austin: University of Texas Press, 1986.

Benjamin, Walter. *Illuminations*. Trans. Harry Zohn. New York: Schocken Books, 1969

Bernstein, Charles. "Pounding Fascism," *Sulfur* #13, 1985.

Blanchot, Maurice. *The Writing of the Disaster*. Trans. Ann Smock. Lincoln: University of Nebraska Press, 1986.

Breton, Andre. *Manifestoes of Surrealism*. Trans. Richard Seaver and Helen Lane. Ann Arbor: University of Michigan Press, 1972.

Bronk, William. *Life Supports: New and Collected Poems*. San Francisco: North Point Press, 1981

———.*Manifest and Furthermore*. San Francisco: North Point Press, 1987

———.*The Brothers in Elysium*, essays by William Bronk. Jersey City, NJ: Talisman House, 1998.

Byrd, Don. "Language Poetry, 1971–1986." *Sulfur* 20 (Fall 1987): 149–157.

Creeley, Robert. *A Quick Graph: Collected Notes & Essays*. Berkeley: Four Seasons, 1970.

Dante Alighieri. *Cantos From Dante's Inferno*. Trans. by Armand Schwerner. Talisman House. Jersey City, 2000.

Debord, Guy. *Society of the Spectacle*. Detroit: Black and Red, 1977.

Derrida, Jacques. *Writing and Difference*. Trans. Alan Bass. Chicago: University of Chicago Press, 1978.

Donoghue, Denis. "The Limits of Language" in *The New Republic*, Vol 195, No. 1. 7 July, 1986.

Duncan, Robert. *The Opening of the Field*. New York: Grove Press, 1960.

———. *The Truth and Life of Myth*. Fremont, Michigan: Sumac Press, 1968.

Eliot, T. S. *The Sacred Wood*. London: Methuen, 1920.

Felstiner, John. "Mother Tongue/Holy Tongue." *The Tel Aviv Review*. Volume No. 3, Winter 1991. pp. 148–164.

Florsheim, Stewart J. Ed. *Ghosts Of The Holocaust: An Anthology of Poetry by the Second Generation*. Introduction by Gerald Stern. Dayton: Wayne State University Press, 1989.

Friedlander, Saul. *Reflections of Nazism: An Essay on Kitsch and Death*. New York: Harper & Row, 1984.

Froula, Christine. *To Write Paradise: Style and Error in Pound's Cantos*. New Haven: Yale University Press, 1984.

Gadamer, Hans-Georg. *Truth and Method*. New York: The Crossroads PublishinCompany, 1982.

Garcia Lorca, Frederico. *Deep Song and Other Prose*. Trans. Christopher Maurer. New York: New Direction, 1980.

Graham, A. C., editor and trans. *Poems of the Late T'ang*. Harmondsworth: Penguin Books, 1965.

Grossman, Allen. "Summa Lyrica," *Western Humanities Review*. Vol. XLIV, No. 1, Spring 1990. pp. 5–138.

Heller, Michael. *Conviction's Net Of Branches: Essays On The Objectivist Poets And Poetry*. Carbondale: Southern Illinois University Press, 1985.

———. *Exigent Futures: New and Selected Poems*. Cambridge: Salt Publishing, 2003.

Hulme, T. E. *Further Speculations*. Ed. Samuel Hynes. Minneapolis: University of Michigan Press, 1955.

Ignatow, David. *Figures of the Human*. Middletown, Conneticut: Wesleyan University Press, 1964.

———. *Leaving the Door Open*. New York: Sheep Meadow Press, 1984.

———. *Tread the Dark*. Middletown, Connecticut: Wesleyan University Press, 1978.

———. *Whisper to the Earth: New Poems*. Boston: Little, Brown, 1978.

Johnson, W. R. *The Idea of the Lyric*. Berkeley: The University of California Press, 1982.

Kenner, Hugh. *Motive and Method in the Cantos of Ezra Pound*. New York: Columbia University Press, 1954.

Kristeva, Julia. *Desire in Language*. New York: Columbia University Press, 1980.

Levi, Primo. *Collected Poems*. Trans. by Ruth Feldman and Brian Swann. Boston: Faber and Faber, 1988. (Earlier edition, Menard Press, 1976.)

———. *The Drowned And The Saved*. Trans. by Raymond Rosenthal. New York: Summit Books, 1988.

Levinas, Emmanuel. *Proper Names*. Stanford: Stanford University Press, 1997.

Lyotard, Jean Francois. *The Postmodern Condition*. Minneapolis: University of Minnesota Press, 1984.

Malcolm, Norman. *Ludwig Wittgenstein: A Memoir*. London: Oxford University Press, 1962.

Mallarmé, Stéphene. *Mallarmé: The Poems*, Translated and Introduced by Keith Bosley. Harmondsworth: Penguin Books, 1977.

———. *Mallarmé*. Edited with an Introduction and Prose Translations by Anthony Hartley. Harmondsworth: Penguin Books, 1965.

———. *Stéphane Mallarmé: Collected Poems*, Translated and with a Commentary by Henry Weinfield. Berkeley: University of California Press, 1995.

———. *Selected Letters of Stéphane Mallarmé*, Edited and Translated by Rosemary Lloyd. Chicago: The University of Chicago Press, 1988.

Merleau-Ponty, Maurice. *Sense and Nonsense*. Evanston: Northwestern University Press, 1964.

Monk, Ray. *Ludwig Wittgenstein: The Duty of Genius*. New York: Penguin Books, 1990.

Moore, Marianne. *The Complete Poems Of Marianne Moore*. New York: Macmillan/Viking, 1967. (CMP)

Morse, Jonathan. *Word By Word: The Language Of Memory*. Ithaca: Cornell University Press, 1990.

———. "Words Devoted To The Unspeakable" by Jonathan Morse, forthcoming in *American Literary History*.

Morson, Gary Saul. "Prosaic Bakhtin: Landmarks, Anti-Intelligentsialism, and the Russian Counter-Tradition." *Common Knowledge*, Vol. 2, No. 1., Spring 1993. pp. 35–74.

Niedecker, Lorine. *Collected Works*. Edited by Jenny Penberthy. Berkelely: University of California Press, 2002 (CW)

———. *The Granite Pail*. San Francisco: The North Point Press, 1985. (TGP)

Oppen, George. *New Collected Poems*. New York: New Directions, 2002. (NCP)

———. "The Philosophy of the Astonished." *Sulfur*, Fall 1990. pp. 202–220.

———. *Primitive*. Los Angeles: Black Sparrow, 1978.

———. *The Selected Letters of George Oppen*, edited by Rachel Blau DuPlessis. Durham and London: Duke University Press, 1990.

Ortega Y Gasset, Jose. *Meditations on Don Quixote*. Trans. Evelyn Rugg and Diego Marin. New York: W. W. Norton and Co. 1961.

Perloff, Marjorie. "Toward an Avant-Garde Tractatus: Russell and Wiggenstein on War." *Common Knowledge*, Vol. 2, No. 1., Spring 1993. pp. 15–34.

Poe, Edgar Allan. *The Fall of the House of Usher and Other Tales*. New York: New American Library, 1960.

Poggioli, Renato. *The Theory of the Avant-Garde*. Cambridge: Belknap/Harvard University Press, 1968.

Pound, Ezra. *The Cantos of Ezra Pound*. New York: New Directions, 1970.

———. *Gaudier-Brzeska*. New York: New Directions, 1970.

———. *Guide to Kulchur*. New York: New Direction, 1971.

———. *The Letters of Ezra Pound*. Edited by D. D. Page with a Preface by Mark Van Doren. New York: Harcourt, Brace & World, Inc 1950.

———. *Literary Essays of Ezra Pound*. New York: New Directions, 1968.

———. *Persona*. New York: New Directions, 1971.

———. *Selected Prose*. New York: New Directions, 1973.

Rakosi, Carl. *The Collected Poems of Carl Rakosi*. Orono, Maine: 1986

Ricoeur, Paul. *Hermeneutics and the Human Sciences*. . . .

———. *The Rule of Metaphor*, trans. by Robert Czerny with Kathleen McLaughlin and John Costello, SJ. Toronto: University of Toronto Press, 1977.

Riddel, Joseph. "'Neo-Nietzschean Clatter'—Speculation and the Modernist Poetic Image" in *Boundary 2*. Spring/Fall 1981.

Rilke, Rainer Marie. *Duino Elegies*. Trans. J. B. Leishman and Stephen Spender. New York: Norton, 1939.

———. *Letters on Cezanne*. Introduction by Heinrich Weigand Petzet, trans. by Joel Agee. New York: Fromm International Publishing Corporation, 1985.

———. *Translation from the Poetry of Rainer Marie Rilke*. Trans. M. D. Herter Norton. New York: Norton, 1938.

———. *Where Silence Reigns: Selected Prose*. Translated by G. Craig Houston, and with a Foreword by Denise Levertov. New York: New Directions, 1978

Robinson, Alan. *From Symbol to Vortex*. New York: St Martin's Press, 1985.

Schwerner, Armand. *Selected Shorter Poems*. San Diego: Junction Press, , 1999

———. *sounds of the river Naranjana & The Tablets 1–XXIV*. Barrytown, NY: Station Hill, 1983.

———. *The Tablets*. National Poetry Foundation, Orono, Maine 1999.

———. *the work, the joy & the triumph of the will*. New York: New Rivers Press, 1977.

Seiburth, Richard. "In Pound We Trust: The Economy of Poetry/The Poetry of Economics. *Critical Inquiry*. Vol. 14, No. 1, Autumn 1987.

Scott, Bonnie Kime, ed. *The Gender Of Modernism*. Bloomington: Indiana University Press, 1990. (GOM)

Silliman, Ron. *In The American Tree*. Me: National Poetry Foundation, 1986.

Stevens, Wallace. *The Necessary Angel*. New York: Vintage Books, 1965.

———. *Opus Posthumous*. New York: Alfred A. Knopf, 1989.

———. *Stevens*, edited by Helen Vendler. New York: Alfred A. Knopf, 1993.

Volosinov, V. N. "Discourse in Art: Discourse in Life" in *Freudianism: A Marxist Critque*. New York: Academic Press, 1976 (pp 93–116).

Watten, Barrett. *Total Syntax*. Carbondale: Southern Illinois University Press, 1985.

Williams, William Carlos. *Selected Essays*. New York: New Directions, 1969.

Willis, Patricia C, ed. *Marianne Moore: Woman And Poet*. Orono, Maine: National Poetry Foundation, 1990.

Printed in the United States
42768LVS00005B/22-24

9 781844 710577